THE SKULL

THE SKULL

INFORMERS, HIT MEN AND AUSTRALIA'S TOUGHEST COP

Adam Shand

Black Inc.

Published by Black Inc.,
an imprint of Schwartz Media Pty Ltd
Level 5, 289 Flinders Lane
Melbourne Victoria 3000 Australia
email: enquiries@blackincbooks.com
http://www.blackincbooks.com

The National Library of Australia Cataloguing-in-Publication entry:

Shand, Adam.

The skull : informers, hit men and Australia's toughest cop /
Adam Shand.

ISBN: 9781863954389 (pbk.)

Murphy, Brian (Brian Francis)
Detectives--Victoria--Biography.
Crime--Victoria--Melbourne.

363.25092

Book design by Thomas Deverall
Printed in Australia by Trojan Press

CONTENTS

For Jack and Noliwe Shand

PROLOGUE

"This is a tape-recorded interview between Constable Paul McGregor and Brian Murphy of 66 Walsh Street, Middle Park," the young officer intoned. "Do you agree the time is exactly 8 p.m.?"

"Correct."

"What is your name?"

"Brian Francis Murphy."

The old man spoke quietly, answering the policeman politely, but there was no doubt who was in command. Through the gloom of the small, dun-coloured interview room, Murphy gazed straight at his interrogator with cold, piercing blue eyes. Even at rest, the irises were round and full, as big as pennies, mesmerising and terrifying at the same time. The shaven head completed an almost idol-like appearance: a burnished skull with sapphire eyes. Even at sixty-two, there were few who dared to hold his stare.

Murphy knew the etiquette, the protocol of a police interview. He had conducted thousands of them in a 33-year career with Victoria Police. Too often, he had found himself on this side of the table, answering the questions. And he knew this interview was going nowhere.

Murphy sighed as he watched the young copper work through his questions: detached and efficient, but utterly without purpose. It was a performance for the cameras and the tape recorders. A report would be filed, the complainant would be advised of the bureaucratic process at regular intervals, but nothing would happen. Nobody really wanted anything to happen.

Constable McGregor was investigating an allegation of indecent language and threatening words. The complainant was an old woman who claimed that Murphy had threatened to shoot her dog. She suspected Murphy also had something to do with the dead rat she had found half decapitated by her back fence.

The only witness, Billy Longley, was unlikely to assist the investigation. Otherwise known as "The Texan", Longley was one of Australia's most celebrated villains: a gunman and convicted murderer, a legend of the waterfront in his days as secretary of the Painters and Dockers Union. These days, Longley and Murphy were partners in a mediation business, operating under the slogan *Everything is negotiable*. And Longley knew that reality was the most negotiable and contestable commodity of all. It didn't matter what the truth was – what mattered was what the young constable could prove.

To underline the dilemma, Murphy revealed that the complainant had a well-known penchant for making up stories: she spent her nights on the telephone masquerading as a sexy young vixen on a fantasy phone line. There was no reaction from the earnest investigator, but it's fair to say the case evaporated at that precise moment. Perhaps an image of taking it to court flashed across his mind. In that moment, he might have pictured Murphy entertaining the magistrate with details of the complainant's story-telling skills, the tittering of the court reporter, the roars of derision from his colleagues back at the station, and the hot shame of realising that the power of a policeman was nothing more than the good judgment he possessed.

It's okay, son, Murphy thought to himself. You have learned a valuable lesson today. What you have to realise is that you are always alone as a police officer. Though each of us wears the same uniform, every decision you make is yours forever more. A decision taken in a split-second can be analysed for two years in the highest court in the land. If you come up trumps, the bosses will say well, of course, he's one of ours, that's how we trained him. But get it wrong and no-one will stick to you. They will be saying: I hope you don't own your house.

You didn't have to make a fool of yourself for this old crow.

*

Constable Brian Francis Murphy, badge number 11885, knew early on that he was always alone. He was part of a brave cohort of officers that fought a battle for the streets while Australia slumbered in a post-war dream of peace and prosperity. He may have looked like the other young officers as they marched on the parade ground at Russell Street in 1954, but there was a different drum hammering away in his head. It wasn't long before he realised that some of his most dangerous foes were marching alongside him or watching from the parade stand.

By the end of his career, there would be a thousand stories told about The Skull: the forty men he had shot, the hundreds he had beaten in hand-to-hand combat, the handful of enemies that had mysteriously died, the fear he had struck in the hearts of villains. And he would regret nothing. Once he had worked out his course of action, it was right for him. Let the Privy Council decide for the benefit of society – Murphy lived and died in the seconds between cause and effect. And in those moments, there is no-one but yourself to rely on.

In telling this story, I went to Murphy's service record to see if all the stories of dash and disobedience told of him could possibly be true. Turning to the disciplinary record, I found it was completely blank. Reality was indeed contestable, and in this life Murphy had won the argument.

Yet every day the same sights and sounds played over and over in his head: the face of a man he was alleged to have killed, the sound of a woman screaming in the dark, to name just two. Some of these things he shared with me, others remain locked away. Blessed or cursed with a vivid, almost perfect recall, Murphy would take them to his grave to face the only judgment that mattered to him.

And even in the face of the Divine Host, he would not be sorry. Not a bit.

PART 1

BLUE CENTURION

CHAPTER 1   A COPPER IN THE FAMILY

As the tram rolled down Swanston Street through Melbourne's city centre, Reg Murphy could reflect with some satisfaction that he had achieved everything he had ever dreamed of in life.

In his youth, with a shock of white-blond hair, "Snowy" Murphy had been a street fighter and a knockabout around South Melbourne, a wharfie with an abiding dislike of police. Now his hair had darkened. With his Brylcreemed centre-parting and horn-rimmed spectacles, Reg looked like an entirely different person. His had been a life of transformations. He had entered the world as Reginald Frederick McGlynn, the product of a short, passionate union between his mother, Maude McGlynn, and a Swede named Andersson in Sydney. Later Maude took up with a new man, Willy Horsenail, and relocated to Melbourne, leaving young Reg with a distant relative named Murphy in Sydney. However, when he was six, they decided the boy should be with his mother and packed him off on a boat to Melbourne with a cardboard sign slung around his neck that said *My name is Reg Murphy.* He waited like that on Station Pier for eighteen hours as the ships rolled in and out all day. He slept on a wool bale among the cargo as families came back and forth all day to meet their loved ones. His mother had mistakenly believed the boat was arriving on the following day. That pretty much summed up her attitude to her son. She had given birth to another boy with Willy Horsenail and Reg was surplus to requirements. He grew up on the streets; at ten he supported himself by selling race books at the pony track in Richmond, and at nineteen he signed up for work at the wharves.

But now he had a loving family – his wife Maggie and six children – and a modest weatherboard home in South Melbourne. He had attained a degree of social respectability that he had never thought possible.

Reg Murphy was a man of few words, but strong opinions. Whenever the kids would bring a new friend home, Reg would sum them up in an instant. He could tell the quality of a boy just by the firmness of his handshake or capacity to look him in the eye. And he seemed to have special knowledge of family background: whose father was a blackguard, a hoon or a bludger.

Despite a lifelong wariness of the police, Reg became a probation officer for troubled kids in his area and he served for forty years as a member of the St Vincent de Paul Society. His obituary would eventually read *Mr Reg Murphy Was a Great Worker for the Poor.* And that was achievement enough for Reg.

It was just after seven o'clock in the morning. In a few minutes, the tram Reg was sitting on would rattle up to the Carlton and United Breweries in Bouverie Street, Carlton, where he would supervise the kegs rolling out of the loading dock for another day. As the tram passed Bourke Street, Reg looked at all the fine suits in the windows of the Leviathan Clothing Company. He recalled the big police strike in 1923, when rioters had smashed all Leviathan's windows and looted the store, throwing the shop dummies out into the street. Reg and Maggie had rushed into town to join the throng that gathered to watch the extraordinary outbreak of lawlessness. In the absence of manpower, the police chiefs turned an army of hoons and louts from Richmond into special constables, and they made mounted baton charges against the looters. Maggie, in her fearless way, got too close and, as the mob withdrew under a hail of baton strikes, she was pitched straight through a plate-glass window. Reg fished her out of the debris, unharmed save for a twisted ankle, and they both ran for their lives.

Today it appeared that someone had dressed a shop dummy in police uniform and left it slumped in a doorway. Reg yanked on the cord and the tram came to a shuddering halt outside Leviathan's. He approached the slim figure standing, fast asleep, in a voluminous overcoat and observed him a moment. Imagine that, he thought: a son of mine as a copper.

"Wake up, boy. Time to get the tram home, I'd say," he said, giving his son a gentle shake.

Probationary Constable Brian Francis Murphy woke up with a start, rubbed his pale blue eyes and adjusted his uniform.

*

Three months earlier, Brian had come home and banged his new police baton and handcuffs down on the table, defiantly telling his father he had joined the Victorian police force that afternoon. He was twenty-two and the year was 1954. His siblings waited anxiously for their father's reaction.

"Well then, if you're going to be a copper, just mind you're a good one," said Reg, going back to his newspaper.

Reg had good reason to dislike coppers. During the wharfies' strike of 1929, he had been coshed half to death by police at Station Pier. He had lain unconscious under the pier with a fractured skull and nearly drowned when the tide came in. Reg was a moral man but he had always answered to God before the

King's law. During the Great Depression, when food was scarce, he had broken into a grocery store in South Melbourne and filled his two-wheel cart with bread, butter and flour. He distributed the booty among his mates and their families, but a week later was racked with guilt. That Saturday in the confessional, Reg related his sin to the old Irish Catholic priest, who reassured him that God would not punish him, even if the police might. "God's not interested in such things," said the priest. "He's not interested in crimes of necessity." Nor, it seems, was God averse to working men having a flutter with the illegal starting-price bookies that operated in pubs and back lanes all over South Melbourne. Every Saturday for years, Reg sent young Brian out to the SPs to lay two threepenny bets. Brian's elder brother, Patrick, had even planned on joining the bookies in the back lanes, but his mother put a stop to that.

In contrast to Reg, Maggie was overjoyed that her Brian was becoming a policeman. It confirmed the progress the Murphy family was making and it would help to set them off from the riff-raff of South Melbourne. Maggie had passed on her fierce blue eyes and quicksilver temper to her third son. She was the enforcer of the household; she set the standards and the routines, and Reg, happy just to belong, simply followed her edicts. Every weekend, the house at 4 Morris Street, South Melbourne, was cleaned from top to bottom. The unsealed boards of the front verandah were scrubbed with soap and water until they shone white. Maggie believed in hard work, discipline and the Catholic faith. Her father had walked to Sydney to earn the money to start a construction business and he had built many of the homes and pubs in the neighbourhood. However, late in life he had gone into business with a scoundrel and lost his fortune. He had never recovered from this loss and Maggie was determined that her family would retain its respectability, regardless of its modest means.

If Reg's life had been turned upside down at six, then it was Maggie's turn at eight. She and her elder sister were walking back from Saturday-night confession at Saints Peter and Paul's Church. It was a ritual; they didn't have a big load of sin to tip, so they would be in and out of the box as quick as a fiddler's elbow, as their mother used to say. When they arrived home, their beautiful regal mother with her long, flowing brown hair would have the bath ready, and when they were clean the meal would be served before they all gathered around the fire to say the rosary.

But as they turned from Coventry Street into Morris Street, they could see the old horse-drawn fire-truck parked outside their house. Smoke billowed from their front door. A neighbour stopped them from getting any closer. There had been an accident, she told them, and their mother was gone. She had been lying on her bed, reading a newspaper, when she fell asleep – the candle had caught the newspaper, sending the whole room up in flames.

From that time on, Maggie and her sister looked after the men of the house. They cooked, cleaned and tended to every need. One night when Maggie was twelve, her brother Bill, a builder's labourer, stomped in and demanded his dinner, slamming his fist on the table. He was going to a union meeting, important men's business, so why wasn't his dinner ready and on the table?

Maggie felt the burning loss of her mother rising in her. The injustice of a man taking a woman's labour for granted made her blood boil. No man, not even her brother, was ever going to stand over Maggie. She dug her ladle into the rice she was cooking on the stove, scooped up a full steaming load and flung it straight into Bill's face and chest. He chased her through the streets, swearing he was going to kill her, but she outran him and hid in a neighbour's garden. From that time on, Bill never raised a hand against her and Maggie's reputation as a fierce, proud woman spread through the neighbourhood.

She raised her six children in the house where her mother had died and she set them strict geographical boundaries: they were allowed on the south side of City Road – the main drag into town – but not the north. Maggie called that side of the street "Salt Lake City" or just "The Pits". If they were caught there, they would cop a sound hiding. So Brian and his brothers, safe on their side of the block, would watch the mysterious goings-on at Nelsons, a notorious Painters and Dockers pub, the Hoyts theatre and the little burger shop, which was the extent of social life in the area. On most Friday and Saturday nights, as the liquor took hold, there would be rolling brawls in the street. And they were good fights too; no knives or guns, just fists, elbows, boots and headbutts. They never ended until someone got carted away or the local police decided to wander down on their pushbikes and lock a few up.

South Melbourne was divided into Catholic and Protestant precincts back then. It was an incidental distinction – they were all poor – but Maggie instilled in the kids the unswerving certainty that they enjoyed a moral superiority through their faith. Many of the Protestants lived nearby in Tin Pot Alley, in rows of prefabricated iron bungalows where British immigrants had settled before World War I. The Murphy children were convinced all the kids in Tin Pot Alley were bastards because they weren't Catholic. And if you were a bastard, you were beyond the reach of God's redemption.

Like his brothers, Brian had been an altar boy at the local church – although he was unlikely to ascend to heaven on this service. He had been a ringleader in a pillow fight one night that had sent a coffin, with body inside, crashing to the floor of the church. The final straw came when a fellow altar boy took Brian's hymn book during Mass one Sunday and refused to return it. Brian knocked the kid out cold in front of the whole congregation. During communion, when the priest placed the Host on the tongue of the parishioners, Brian was ordered to hold a silver plate below each chin. Mother Maggie came forward, scowling. The priest placed the wafer in her mouth and she swallowed, her eyes blazing at her son. "I'm going to kill you!" she mouthed noiselessly. Seeing he was already in for it, Brian pushed the plate a little harder against Maggie's windpipe, choking off any further threats.

At home that night, Maggie was in the middle of flogging Brian when the priest came by to say her boy would no longer be required for service.

*

After a brief stint at police headquarters in Russell Street, Brian Murphy was stationed at North Melbourne for three months, mostly on night shift. It was easier than working in his home area where so many people knew the family. But soon he was transferred to South Melbourne, where he met his first police hero, Sergeant Jack Meehan, stationed in neighbouring Prahran. Meehan was a tough, wiry little bloke who had played league football for St Kilda as a rover. He is pictured getting smacked in the jaw by Richmond player Jack Dyer on the cover of Dyer's autobiography, *Captain Blood*. It was a cowardly king hit but Meehan could take a punch and return the investment.

Meehan was an amazing thief catcher. He was also a scruffy dresser, often leaving the station with scuffed shoes and one collar turned up. But more often than not, he would duck into the first laneway he saw and come upon some villain hauling away a safe or whacking up some stolen property.

There were many in the force who said that Meehan was mad and bad and that he would get everyone he worked with into trouble. Yet Murphy and the other probationary constables loved him and fought stand-up battles for the right to work with him on night shift. Meehan taught Murphy that in each station there was only a handful of blokes who had the dash and commitment to go out and catch crooks. They were the heart and soul of the station, they kept the place going. The rest ranged from time-servers to hopeless bludgers who saw their badge as a means to squeeze free meals and drinks from hoteliers or graft from brothel keepers. Meehan embodied the idea of the independent police constable with the gumption to arrest even the chief commissioner if he had a case. In particular, he loathed officers who used their uniform to stand over SP bookies or sly groggers. It was a classic case of bad laws making bad policemen. The legislators had decreed that consumption of alcohol in hotels should cease at 6 p.m., which led to the infamous "six o'clock swill" when drinkers would put away as much grog as they could before closing, spill out into the streets to fight and vomit, then go home to belt their wives. Of course the lawmakers could freely enjoy their grog all night at gentlemen's clubs like the Athenaeum or the Melbourne Club. This hypocrisy was bad enough, but to stand over those who provided working men with a drink, or a chance to bet, was more wicked still. There were no shades of grey in Meehan's world: either it was right or wrong. You enforced the law without fear or favour, or you were corrupt – simple as that.

One day, it came to Meehan's attention that an officer had been extorting £5 a week from the SP bookies in South Melbourne. He rang the officer and told him: "Jack Meehan here. You better pack a change of clothes and a toothbrush, 'cos I'm going to lock you up." Despite the pleading of various higher-ups, Meehan was not to be dissuaded and the officer preferred to quit the job hastily than face the music.

Either it was good or bad, right or wrong – that's what Murphy learned from Jack Meehan. The cadets at the training depot were taught precious little about the ethics of the job. They were issued with the "Brown Bomber", a manual setting out police procedures, but in thirty-three years Murphy never opened it. Many years later, a senior officer sent back a report Murphy had written, haughtily suggesting he refer to his Brown Bomber. Murphy responded by taking a mouthful of cigarette smoke and blowing it through the paper before scrunching it up and sending it back to the officer. The outraged superior sent the paper off for forensic testing to see if Murphy had wiped his arse on it.

Murphy's book learning had stopped with *A Tale of Two Cities* by Charles Dickens, *For the Term of His Natural Life* by Marcus Clarke and *They're a Weird Mob* by Nino Culotta. He had also read a brochure spelling out "Peel's Principles", the foundation of the modern police force as outlined by British Home Secretary Sir Robert Peel in 1829. Much of that was forgotten, save one line: "Police, at all times, should maintain a relationship with the public that gives reality to the historic tradition that the police are the public and the public are the police; the police being only members of the public who are paid to give full-time attention to duties which are incumbent on every citizen in the interests of community welfare and existence."

In Meehan's mind, this translated into a more down-to-earth message: "If they aren't doing anything wrong, leave them alone." And if you did decide to pick up a sly grogger or an SP man on the street, use a little psychology, Meehan would tell Murphy. If you were seeking a cove who frequented a sly-grog establishment, you were better to suggest to the proprietor that he give you information or risk having his place raided and closed down, forever. You might also suggest that *all* the sly groggers would be closed down if they didn't cooperate.

But when a policeman threw his weight around, he did not always get his way. This was brought home graphically to Murphy one morning in 1955, while he was on traffic duty. He had been standing in the middle of the intersection feeling very pleased with himself in his blue uniform and white pith helmet. Just one flick of his hand would stop the cars in an instant; he felt like the conductor of an orchestra. Let's see how fast this one can stop, he thought, as a fully laden cattle truck approached. Even as he held up his hand, he knew it was a mistake. The truck was going too fast and began to skitter over the rough surface under brakes. Murphy jumped out of its path to avoid being run down, but that wasn't the end of it. The sudden deceleration of the vehicle had slammed the cattle together, kicking up the mud and manure under their feet. When the truck had passed, Murphy was covered from head to toe in a fine spray of fresh, green compost. It was all over his lovely white pith helmet and uniform, on his face and in his mouth. He stood there spitting, cursing and spluttering while the onlookers completed the misery with taunts and laughter.

He never got his pith helmet clean. It was a constant reminder that every day on the beat there were lessons to be learned – lessons that did not come from the police manual but which would guide Murphy throughout his career. First and foremost: if you make a mess, clean it up yourself and never put yourself in if there's another way.

On the night shift, Murphy would patrol the entire North Melbourne area on foot. He felt a great sense of freedom as he walked the quiet streets, trying doors, looking in windows where a light was on late. He might stop in a doorway and watch the night traffic, looking for anything out of the ordinary. Murphy recalls it as being a far cry from today, where Victoria Police drive around in their vehicles like they are on a Cook's tour. From inside a vehicle, you can choose what to see and what to ignore by simply opening or closing the window. On the street – on foot – you had no choice. You were in the middle of things before you had time to think. And that's where Murphy wanted to be, whenever he could.

One night, as he walked up a back lane, he heard some movement in a factory yard. He drew his .32 revolver, cocked it and proceeded to investigate. It was one of the first times he had drawn his gun on the job and he was yet to fire it. Back then, a police officer would fire about ten shots a year on the firing range at the training depot, and that was about it – the rest was on-the-job training. He felt the blood pounding in his ears as he crept between the stacked containers. Just as he got to where he thought the sound had come from, the motor in a refrigerated container started up with a crash, like two pieces of steel being clapped together. A startled cat leapt off the fence and onto Murphy, who fell on his backside, pistol pointing skyward. *BANG! BANG! BANG! BANG!* He let four shots go in the air. The first may have been accidental, but if someone was lurking to bushwhack him, this fusillade would deter him. He trudged back to the station in shame and anxiety. He told the senior sergeant he would not be requiring his gun again that night. He went into the locked gun cupboard, found another .32 and exchanged the magazines. He had collected the shell casings before leaving the factory yard. Now if there was a call over the mysterious burst of gunfire, there would be no evidence linking him to it.

Murphy learned to cast a sceptical eye over everything he saw. It was odds-on that a man driving a truck loaded with oxy-acetylene bottles and a boilermaking kit in the middle of the night was not a tradesman and it certainly didn't hurt to ask. Days after his gunfight with the cat, Murphy had seen an oxy bottle fall off a truck. He rushed over to give the man a hand re-loading it. The man was so grateful that he wanted to give him a £10 note, which Murphy refused. Just doing my job, sir, he told the grateful truckie.

Three days later, Murphy discovered the man was a safecutter and had busted a safe over in Kensington, grabbing £10,000. He didn't tell anyone about that either.

CHAPTER 2 SUGAR BAGS

LIFE IN THE ANONYMITY OF NORTH MELBOURNE had been easy for Brian Murphy, but that all changed with his next posting. Upon being transferred back home to South Melbourne, he was instructed to break a network of illegal SP bookies and to report on the corrupt officers taking a quid to turn a blind eye.

That Saturday afternoon, Murphy and another officer were doing the rounds of South Melbourne, paying visits on a dozen thriving operations. They weren't hard to find, being set up in cobbled bluestone lanes near hotels. Some would draw a mob of 1000 people, crowding round the day's prices on a chalk board slung over a corrugated iron fence. At either end of the lane, nitkeepers – lookouts – would warn if the law was approaching and punters, bookies and helpers would scarper when the signal was given. Until then, raids had been rare. A policeman was more likely to stop by just before the last race to place a £5 bet that would invariably come home a winner. It caused great resentment among the punters. Five pounds was a week's wages, and here were coppers taking it for wearing the uniform. They called them "sugar bags" and the bookies had to keep them sweet.

First stop for Murphy was a bluestone lane off Normanby Street, where Jack O'Hanlon plied his trade. O'Hanlon had been at school with one of Murphy's sisters and was probably expecting the young copper to lay a bet or perhaps cop a quid or two. Murphy had other ideas.

"John, I'm here to tell you that next week we'll be coming back and locking you up," announced Murphy, puffing out his chest to hide his fear.

"Is that right, Brian?" said O'Hanlon, smirking as he glanced at the rows of tough, raw-boned working men around him. One word from the bookie and the cops would never get out of this lane.

"Yes it is, as a matter of fact," said Murphy, glaring at the biggest bloke he could see.

"Well, you're going to have to catch us first," said O'Hanlon, motioning for the crowd to let Murphy and the other cop leave the laneway. And so it went. He visited another dozen SP operations, some of whom had taken Reg's threepenny bets all those years ago. What the bookies didn't know was that Murphy's mother knew the owners of the homes that backed onto these lanes. She had recruited these God-fearing residents as informants for her son, who could now obtain all he needed to know without fronting up. As promised, Murphy, disguised in a railway conductor's uniform, came back the following weekend and collared ten of the bookies. He handcuffed them to his bicycle and walked them back to the station one after another. One refused to give his real name so Murphy threatened to use the electoral rolls to find out his identity. The bookie gave in immediately, telling Murphy, "Please don't put me on the electric rolls, I'm gettin' married next week." The sugar bags were horrified that their rort had abruptly ended.

One morning after this, Murphy was coming out of a hardware shop when he ran into an old wharfie, well known to his family.

"Young Murphy, you're doing a good job, they tell me. A little bit too good as a matter of fact – you're making enemies," he said.

"I couldn't care less," replied Murphy contemptuously. "They're all dirty sugar bags who need locking up."

"Well, I've been told someone's going to fix you up, good and proper, that's what I've heard," said the wharfie.

This grabbed Murphy's attention. "How's it going to happen?" he asked.

"They're going to load you up with a gun and get you kicked out of South Melbourne," he said. "You would do well to read a certain case, *R v. Devenish and Donnelly*, from 1926. The case revolves around stolen property found in a waterside worker's locker, see. The whole thing turned on whether the bloke could be said to have dominion over the goods if he didn't have a key to the locker and always left it open," said the old wharfie. "Just something to bear in mind."

From that day on, Murphy never had a key to his locker. That way, no matter what was found in there, according to *R v. Devenish and Donnelly* he could not be held responsible.

Soon after, the top brass from Russell Street called a snap inspection of the South Melbourne station. The men were asked to line up next to their lockers. When the superintendent came to Murphy's, he bent down and, as if he knew it would be there, fished out a shotgun that had been dismantled and wrapped in cloth.

"Murphy, do you know anything about this gun?"

"No," said Murphy, lying. He did recognise it, but he had no idea how it got there. It was one of several that the South Melbourne cops had confiscated from the publican of a nearby hotel. Several of the senior constables were sleeping with the publican's wife. Each time the publican discovered this, he got drunk, acquired a gun, and promised to march on the station and kill the cops concerned. And each time the cops got to him first and disarmed him.

"Do you know how it came to be in your locker, Constable?"

"No sir, I don't use the locker. I don't even have a key," Murphy replied.

The boss looked at Murphy and realised he had been blind-sided. He retired to another office to work out what to do next. The men stood silently in their ranks for a minute or two. Then one of the bent coppers leaned over to Murphy and said in a triumphant voice, "Murphy, you're in deep shit, son. You're stuffed."

Big Jock Cameron, a 25-stone Scottish first constable, knew better. A man of few words, he threw a look of contempt at Murphy's tormentor. He then turned to Murphy and chuckled. "You're a cunning little bugger, aren't you?"

*

But the sugar bags weren't going to stop there.

The telephone at 4 Morris Street began ringing at odd hours of the night. Maggie would answer and threatening voices would tell her that her son was a dog and a rat. He would soon get his for what he was doing. The police were informed of the calls and Inspector Jack Matthews, who would later be jailed for corruption, was despatched to investigate. When he arrived, Maggie was sweeping the front verandah. Matthews put one foot on the top step and leaned on his knee, pushing his hat back on his head. He asked a few desultory questions, clearly going through the motions.

"Now just for some particulars, madam," he said, as he

prepared to leave. "Are you legally married?" he asked with a lop-sided grin.

This was no question for a mother of six, a church-goer and pillar of her community. The implication was that a bastard like Brian Murphy could only be the fruit of an adulterous relationship.

Maggie Murphy was not a big woman, only about five foot four, but she possessed a towering hatred. She could reduce men like Matthews to rubble with a withering stare from those pale blue eyes.

"How dare you, you drunken miserable cur," she said in a low, menacing tone, her face reddening with anger. "How dare you come here and make such filthy insinuations, you thieving dishonest blackguard!" She advanced on Matthews, brandishing her broom at head height. He beat a hasty retreat lest the furious matriarch knock the hat off his head.

A fortnight later, the telephone again rang in the night. Maggie rushed to the phone, ready to swear damnation at the mystery caller. But it was her neighbour.

"You better get out here, Maggie. Brian's car's on fire," she said.

Maggie and Reg rushed out into the street to see Brian's little convertible going up in flames. From the fumes, it appeared someone had poured petrol over the rag top and lit it up. Brian was on night shift and whoever did this probably knew it. It was a sign to back off. By taking on the SPs, Murphy was unpicking the fabric of the working class. Even the family of a copper should know that they are part of the weave and Murphy should know the limitations of his power, how things worked in South Melbourne.

Maggie watched the car hiss and bubble as the flames

consumed it. She resolved that her son would be strong and defiant, would never bow to the police curs that ran these tawdry, immoral rackets and their spineless bosses. She would make sure that no-one ever got over the top of him. She would drive him on and attack anyone who dared to criticise him. And if he ever showed weakness or mercy, he would answer to her.

CHAPTER 3 THE PSYCH

IT SEEMED TO BE THE SAME SCENE over and over that first year in South Melbourne. The woman would always be wearing the same floral apron, clean and ironed, a pair of new stockings held up by a gaiter or, in the poorer households, a rubber band. Her hair would be neatly washed and set and whatever make-up she could afford carefully applied. And there, in the middle of the spotless kitchen floor, she would be lying, sometimes already bloated and blue, the smell of gas thick in the air. A couple of kids might be bawling and sobbing or just numb with shock. And the husband would slope in later, smelling of alcohol and cigarettes, and glumly exclaim that Mabel had been a lost cause – he couldn't please her, much less save her.

"How am I going to look after the kids now?" he would wail, addressing the corpse of his wife, as if she had failed him yet again.

And Murphy would have to restrain himself from smashing the newly widowed father in the face, giving him the same treatment as he had doubtless given his wife, judging from the bruises often found on the body. He could not help thinking of his own mother at those moments, not that Reg would ever dream of raising his hand against Maggie. But what touched Murphy's heart was that even in poverty and chaos these women had maintained a quiet dignity, a sense of order and cheerfulness, the hope of better things in the future. They kept their houses clean and tidy, washed the kids daily, even if the bath water was soupy when the last one was done. And then one day, despair overwhelmed them, all the light just drained from them, and they knelt down as if in prayer before the gas stove, a domestic sacrifice to an unseeing god. And so on night shift, when he was called to domestic disputes, there would be no mercy if physical violence were involved. He would set out to inflict as much pain on the husband as the wife had suffered. He wanted to look in the eyes of these hapless cowards and see the same terror their wives and kids had experienced. There was no law protecting these women; they were little more than chattels, unpaid domestic slaves for cleaning the house and raising the children. These were the days when a woman could not yet bear witness against her husband. She took his name, vowing to honour and obey his every tyrannical, drunken whim. Short of killing his wife, the man had complete dominion over the affairs of his home. And so the battered wife took the only option she had left and turned on the gas.

Throughout his career, Murphy felt pure, unaffected scorn for officers who treated these moments as "just a domestic". On the night shift, they might say: "I'll just finish my fish and chips then I'll take a run down there." Murphy would stomp over and sweep the meal off the table into the bin and shout in the man's face: "What are you going to say when this domestic becomes a homicide, eh? Will you tell the court, 'Oh, I just had to finish my dinner before I answered the call'? I'm going to tell the court you stood by and let him murder his wife, okay?"

Murphy's job, as he saw it, was to dispense justice, even if it meant dispensing with the law. A bully might escape punishment in the court for standing over the weak, but Murphy would be waiting for them. It stirred a cold rage in him to see a man who had nearly kicked someone to death standing up there in court, clean shaven in a brand-new suit and tie. Once Murphy got hold of him, he would have a broken nose and a shirt full of broken ribs to remind him how his victim had felt. There was a risk, even back then, but he didn't think twice.

*

Murphy was beginning to get so revved up before a shift that his stomach would rumble. He was a coiled spring of nervous energy. If a small part of him was crazy, as people said, then at least that part had a purpose and a focus. His senior sergeant, Jimmy Ryan, had nicknamed him "The Psych" and it became common to hear over the police-radio channels: "Is The Psych in your car?" "Has anyone seen The Psych?" "Did you hear what The Psych did today?"

The night streets were Murphy's turf. He liked nothing better than operating on his own, patrolling darkened suburban streets, looking for the light that shouldn't be on, watching people, checking cars parked in side streets, noticing anything out of the ordinary. He began to develop a sense for when things weren't quite right. Two men unloading a truck at South Melbourne Markets was nothing unusual, but why would a merchant be driving a truck with no windscreen? So he'd go and ask the blokes a friendly question or two, one of the blokes would run, he'd catch them and find £2500 worth of stolen goods in the back. In his first eight months on the job, Murphy made ninety-six arrests. Each morning, he just couldn't wait to get out of bed and among the crooks.

And he always had his "best mate" with him – a Smith & Wesson .38 calibre. The double-action, swing-cylinder revolver was the most reliable colleague he'd ever had. Even if his .38 got wet or covered in sand and dirt, it would never let him down.

In those days, the community expected police to use their guns and didn't ask questions. There was barely a week in the mid-1950s when Murphy's gun stayed holstered. Of the forty-odd men he wounded during his career, most of the shooting injuries occurred in his first few years on the force. The .38 was not a high-performance target pistol but Murphy was extra-ordinarily accurate; his targets were invariably hit in the but-tocks, arms, legs or feet – it was a sign of marksmanship that no-one was killed or seriously wounded. Either that or they were just plain lucky. Some copped it at close range, a painful reminder that Murphy was handy with more than just his fists. As most of the serious villains carried guns, Murphy wanted them to know he too was prepared to use his firearm. Most of these shootings were never reported. Officers were supposed to enter such events in the police hospital book, but somehow most never got around to doing it.

Some of Murphy's most effective gunplay never wounded anybody. If an adversary was becoming arrogant, five or six "chirpers" through his front windows would quieten him down remarkably. And the power must have been intoxicating.

CHAPTER 4   MEETING THE SKULL

FIFTY YEARS LATER, I WAS ON MY WAY to meet Brian Murphy for the first time in a St Kilda café. I had not seen a recent picture of him. The most current shots were from the 1980s and they showed a fit, balding man with sandy-brown sideburns in early middle age.

His most distinctive features were, of course, his pale-blue eyes and lop-sided smile. The smile was the product of a thin upper lip that flared out on the left-hand side of his mouth – a mouth that seemed capable of animating great humour and warmth as well as pure, cold-blooded savagery. These emotions seem mutually exclusive, but my inquiries to date had shown that Murphy was capable of anything.

Mentioning his name to policemen above the age of forty-five elicited a knowing smile, a laugh and a shake of the head. Everyone knew a part of the story, but no-one was sure of the whole. Murphy's name had surpassed legend and taken on the murky qualities of myth.

One former assistant commissioner, Bob Falconer, declared, "Either Brian Murphy is the most corrupt and dangerous man ever to be a member of Victoria Police or the most maligned. I don't know which." Another former assistant commissioner, Paul Delianis, was no great admirer of Murphy but could not condemn him: "I did not agree with many things he did, in fact some of the methods he employed frankly appalled me, but I can confidently say that everything he did was in the service of the community."

Even then, in 2004, he was still at it – if the talk was right. He had a large and devoted following among serving members, mostly to the rank of sergeant and below. Some were old-school cops who, as young officers, had fallen under Murphy's spell before his retirement in 1987. To the bosses at the time, including Chief Commissioner Christine Nixon, Murphy was a dangerous, destabilising influence. Murphy, on the other hand, believed that Nixon and her deputies ran the force as though it were a business, with 13,000 employees and one key shareholder, the premier, who appointed her. Her management team was isolated from the rank and file; the *esprit de corps* of the old days had been replaced with a mission statement, corporate weasel words written to appease the civil libertarians and other "stakeholders".

But if Victoria Police was a corporation, then in 2004 its balance sheet was showing a deficit and its dividend was meagre indeed. A gangland war was raging; drug dealers and their thugs were being murdered in the streets. A group of corrupt officers were making fortunes in the amphetamine trade, pulling the strings of their puppet kings in the underworld. The Labor Government and the police leadership were resisting calls for a royal commission – it might topple the government.

In this politically charged atmosphere, honest cops felt abandoned. Their calls for extra resources and powers were ignored, and if they landed in trouble, they received little if any support from their bosses. Murphy was seen as a rallying point for officers steeped in the old, paramilitary values and force command hated him for it. He gave voice to a philosophy of policing that placed the office of constable at the very heart of law enforcement. Power did not emanate from the chief commissioner's office, nor did it reach him via the corporate hierarchy. Murphy's constable received his authority from God, with deference to the Crown when justice required the seal of the court. His constable ruled his turf and didn't wait for orders from above.

Nixon and her corporate acolytes wanted shot of Murphy and his ilk. They produced expensive reports with glossy covers dealing with the history of corruption in Victoria Police, with references to the shadowy influence of former officers. They never mentioned Murphy by name, yet he was implicitly there, sticking his nose in where it wasn't wanted, commenting on their plans, even thwarting them when he chose. He met regularly with some very senior police, although he would never make the contact or probe them for inside information; he would also embarrass the bosses by giving them information about crimes they should have gleaned themselves.

Even more dangerous to police were his friendships in the underworld. Long retired, Murphy still maintained his network of criminal informers. He was close to the Carlton Crew, a personal friend of its leader Domenic "Mick" Gatto and a confidant of many of the old crime families in town. It was said that he had mediated a number of disputes between such groups. There were even wilder rumours that he had been part of the gangland killings. One version claimed he had murdered enough people to field a cricket team.

Little wonder that I was nervous about meeting him. I had called him at home first and he had rejected the invitation to meet. He couldn't be bothered, too busy with other things, he said. In desperation, I wrote him a long, impassioned letter suggesting that, according to Peel's Principles, he had a public duty to assist me.

The public are the police; the police being only members of the public who are paid to give full-time attention to duties which are incumbent on every citizen in the interests of community welfare and existence.

If I had been honest, I would have written: "I need your help because I don't know what I'm doing. Without your help, I will be utterly lost." At that point I had little courage and fewer contacts. Perhaps he knew it, so he took pity on me and agreed to meet that summer afternoon.

*

The café was sprinkled with elderly, bald men, the sun glinting off their shiny pates and gold-rimmed glasses as they negotiated their coffee and pastries. On several occasions I approached the wrong person, until one possibility remained.

"Are you Brian Murphy?" I asked, already extending my hand.

"No," said the man, going back to his newspaper. I was crestfallen. "I'm his brother," he added, with a wink. "Come on, sit down then, have a coffee will you?"

What I witnessed for the next couple of hours is best described as pure entertainment. Murphy gave me his take on gangland wars stretching back to the 1950s. There was mimicry of Italian gangsters, Yugoslav hit men, Jewish fences and toffy magistrates. There were bird calls and dog whistles, and dazzling repartee with waitresses and passing customers. There were religious and social commentaries, raps on the sanctity of women and children mixed with forensic discussions of how best to dispose of a body and the virtues of killing with a .22 over a .38 calibre firearm. And there was anger. Some things stirred him so deeply that his anger was visceral and frightening. He would rage and grimace, bringing his face so close to mine I could feel his hot breath. It was like standing up against the lion's cage at the zoo and feeling the beast roar right in your face – safe only so long as the bars protect you. I had been warned that Murphy could well be someone to fear, and it seemed entirely credible when he raged and frothed. But seconds later, the terrifying blue light in his eyes would fade, as if on a dimmer, to a pleasant, humorous twinkle. And I was left wondering if the anger was a glimpse of the real Brian Murphy or if it was just an act.

In the years to come, I would often hear him introduce himself to people as Brian Murphy's brother. I wondered which brother he meant and I finally asked him in November 2008.

"Probably Pat," he conceded. "I always felt he was better than me. A better, more moral man you could never find."

Pat was a plumber and a man beloved by all in the South Melbourne district. If anyone was ever in trouble, they came to Paddy Murphy. If a man was in jail or done in by the drink, Pat would be there to put in a new copper or a hand basin for the wife and kids. He would say they could pay him when they could, but he never came back for the money. Growing up, Brian idolised Pat. Pat had never lifted a finger against anyone, it just wasn't in him. He was a moderate drinker and a happy man with a few ales inside him, full of laughter and philosophy. He was closer to his father, Reg, than to Brian because they could go off to the pub for a beer and talk politics and social issues. Meanwhile Brian, the teetotaller, would stay at home with Maggie and together they would sharpen their hatred for villains and blackguards within the police force and without.

Had he been a drinker, by his own admission Brian Murphy would have been a vicious, unpredictable bastard. Some say he was that and more, even without the drink. But by remaining sober, Murphy could keep his darkest impulses in check. He could never be Pat, but he could strive for the same goals as his brother through God and public service.

Murphy agreed to meet me because he *did* believe he had a duty. But our relationship was not to be straightforward. As we parted, he smiled warmly and encouraged me to believe that at seventy-two years of age he had mellowed into a benign, friendly figure. And then something else flashed: he imparted a piece of remarkable information that even today I cannot reveal. His lip curled and he levelled me with a ferocity that told me the lion in Murphy was still at home.

"Now mind, if you tell anybody about what I've told you, you will be walking on stumps," he said.

I thought he was joking. "Yeah sure, Brian," I said, laughing. "But one problem, mate."

"What's that, mate?"

"I'm a journalist. It's my job to tell people."

"Aah, yes. I see the problem. See ya," he said.

I was left with the impression the problem was all mine.

I wondered (and perhaps I still do) how things might play out if Murphy had to choose between me and someone closer to him. In a crisis, he would not hesitate for a second before killing me. And being close to him for a while now has taught me something civilised society likes to avoid. If the positions were reversed and I had to choose, I would kill him too. But damn, he would take some killing.

CHAPTER 5   JUSTICE IS BLIND (AND OFTEN DRUNK)

THE RUN-INS WITH THE SUGAR BAGS of South Melbourne and the burning of his car had hardened Murphy's resolve to do things his way. No matter how corrupt his colleagues and his bosses were, he had the power to run his own race. And he was also learning the limits of his power, or at least its proscribed uses, without the guidance of his Brown Bomber.

One night, Murphy had given a suspect a terrible coshing with a torch and it came out later in court. After sentencing the man, the magistrate, Bill Cuthill, asked to see the young constable in his office immediately.

"Listen, laddie," he said, taking off his robes. "Our newly crowned sovereign, Elizabeth Regina, in her infinite wisdom, being the law, being the *Crimes Act – Police Offences*, has issued policemen with batons." He looked over his half-moon glasses at Murphy. "Under regulations, if you kill someone with a baton you are covered, but if you kill them with a torch then you are not covered."

Murphy was smiling but the magistrate was not.

"You can bring them to me in any condition as long as the force hasn't been excessive, and I will convict them, but I will never convict them again if you belt them with a torch."

Cuthill went on to become Victoria's chief stipendiary magistrate and a fine, upstanding jurist. Most magistrates, however, did not care too much about methods as long as the evidence stacked up or their mates were well served. They were simply functionaries in the system. Most of them weren't lawyers by training, only justices of the peace, political appointments by the local area's bosses of the day.

Justice of the Peace Arnold Coppel was a Jewish baker who promised to give every policeman a gold watch if they treated "his" defendants nicely. He said Murphy was a gem of a police-man who racked up promises worth seventy watches for all the times he spoke up for Jewish defendants. Murphy never asked for the watches; he would have spoken up for them anyway.

If a Painter and Docker was in court, the JP would invariably be Tommy Buckingham, who owned a local haberdashery, or Jack Woodruff, a powerful, vicious man who ran a local dairy and later became Lord Mayor of Melbourne. If the magistrate sat with one JP, he could override him; but if there were two JPs, the magistrate could be outvoted. In such cases, a magis-trate would often say, "My goodness, gentlemen, we have got a busy day today," and promptly send the JPs to the back room to preside over the garbage cases (committal mentions and traffic cases). The magistrate himself could then deal with the politi-cal cases involving members of the Painters and Dockers, who would have paid the JPs to secure bail for them or have the charges dismissed.

Murphy quickly discovered that local justice was a game. If you booked twenty cars for double-parking outside the South Melbourne Market, the senior sergeant would go through the pile of tickets and remove about half of them. "This one's been a great supporter of the police for many years, and this one's a great law-and-order man, and of course this one's a local magis-trate," he would say.

The first time this happened, Murphy took all the tickets and threw them in the wastepaper basket. When asked what had happened, he replied, loud enough for everyone in the station to hear, "Gee boss, looks like they all knew policemen – imagine that!"

These were the "bad old days" of corruption, when it went right through the system. In fact, in some areas corruption *was* the system. Barristers would play golf with magistrates on Sunday and hand them money from clients. Murphy heard villains talk openly of bribing judges. One particular judge liked taking prostitutes out in his car and giving police a run for their money. After a full-scale car chase, complete with roadblocks, the judge would invariably get pinned. But when he appeared before the court, the charges would suddenly be pulled.

Court was where you learned the facts of life as a policeman. You could have a million mates around you when you did something and still be alone in the dock. In late 1955, Murphy gave evidence against a man who had been caught with a firearm. He hadn't been the first to see the gun, so his testimony that it belonged to the suspect was based on the advice of the other police on the scene. Only the gun didn't belong to the suspect: the police had loaded him with it. Defence counsel Ray Dunn carved Murphy up on the stand, making him look a complete fool, the fall guy in a plot to frame his client. No police gave evidence supporting Murphy and the defendant was acquitted. The judge thanked Murphy for his excellent evidence, but noted that his story had been inconveniently contradicted by the truth.

Murphy left the court in a blind rage. Fit to explode, he walked off in the wrong direction and had to turn back, passing the court again just as Dunn was leaving. The barrister sympathetically asked the young constable how he was feeling after his ordeal.

"Go and get fucked," said Murphy. The last thing he wanted was to have salt rubbed into his wounds.

"Oi! Don't you talk to me like that," said Dunn sternly. "Come, I'll give you a lift into town and acquaint you with a couple of important facts." Murphy reluctantly accepted – it was better than the tram – and once he'd cooled down he received an important piece of advice.

"You did a great job in there, but in the service of an unworthy cause. You've been let down by your mates, and it won't be the last time either. They thought only of themselves and they let you take a kicking in the witness box."

When Murphy got back to the station, he flew at the senior constable who had set him up for the fall in court. Why hadn't they told him they had loaded the suspect with the gun? The senior connie smiled and said, "Come on, Brian, you would never have fought as hard if you knew we'd loaded him." Murphy felt like smacking the copper right in the mouth, but he knew that this treacherous bastard had done him a big favour. He would never again rely on another copper in a situation like that.

It soon became obvious that quite a few of his colleagues were not working for Queen Elizabeth II, despite being on her payroll. One night he was on foot patrol in the Albert Park village, a few blocks from the bay. All was quiet, but as he passed by the post office, he saw the intermittent blue-and-white flash of an oxy-acetylene torch behind a window. He drew his gun, crept through the unlocked door of the post office and found a safe-breaker hard at work with his oxy torch. He later found out it was one of Melbourne's most notorious "tank men", Bertram Douglas Kidd. Murphy bailed Kidd up and was about to handcuff him when three other policemen from South Melbourne burst through the door. They claimed they had been staking the place out and that Murphy, by stumbling in, had nearly blown their plan. They would take over from here, they told Murphy, and sent him away on his foot patrol. He complied but he knew something was not right. The whole scene had a pantomime quality.

The next day it was the talk of the station. Three officers had nabbed a safe cutter at the Albert Park post office but before they had even had time to take his name, he had escaped and disappeared into the night. When one of the officers saw Murphy, he nervously asked whether he had established the villain's identity before they came on the scene. When Murphy replied that he hadn't, the other cop seemed very relieved. Murphy later learned that Kidd was working for these corrupt police, cutting safes and sharing the profits. They had been sitting in their police vehicle keeping watch while Kidd worked. Murphy knew better than to blow the whistle. It was that kind of devotion to duty that got a young policeman killed.

For the most part, the bosses left him alone. They had plenty of junior officers to do their dirty work. Blokes like Murphy couldn't be trusted. He was too independent and obstreperous. And he didn't drink, so he couldn't be leaned on during the Friday night piss-ups at the police club or compromised by some foolish act committed while on the booze.

Murphy liked to say that he had finished with drinking by the age of ten. Uncle Bill, his mother's brother, had lived next door in Morris Street. He was a local legend in the Australian Labor Party and a prodigious consumer of his home brew. Young Brian would sit for hours with his uncle listening to stories and sipping on jam jars of sweet, frothy beer. Uncle Bill was a hero to Murphy. He was shot during a union battle in Church Street,

Richmond, and pitched into the Yarra River for dead. But his mackintosh overcoat kept him afloat and he drifted all the way into town, where he was plucked from the water at Princes Bridge and saved. Uncle Bill's yarns were beguiling even without overproof liquor, but they were pure magic to a drunken ten-year-old. When Murphy's teachers began to complain to his parents that he was falling asleep in class, his visits to Uncle Bill's place abruptly ended.

At twenty-four years of age, Brian was fit and strong, still slight and boyish in appearance, five foot ten and eleven stone. His wavy, sandy hair was rapidly thinning. On his days off, he was swinging an axe at Huey Logan's woodyard, splitting logs, so his hands were rough and calloused. It was hard to believe, looking at him now, that he had once been an apprentice watch-maker, in training for the fine work of repairing and maintaining clockwork. That vocation ended when he threw a chiming clock at the boss. He didn't have the temperament for indoors work. He was too hyperactive and easily distracted. Policing was the perfect occupation for him.

Also, by this time, despite his smooth, baby-like face, he had gained a reputation as a savage street fighter. He was ruthless: if a headbutt and a kick to the balls could achieve in mere seconds what the Marquess of Queensberry rules could in minutes, why waste valuable time?

Murphy did everything with gusto and never took a back-ward step; but there were many who still underestimated this young man. Looks could be deceiving. Murphy liked to say he was a very fast healer. Yet inside there was scar tissue forming that would stay with him for life.

CHAPTER 6 HIS RIGHT WHACK

ONE SUMMER NIGHT IN EARLY 1955, Murphy was with another officer, Cliff Carroll, driving down St Kilda Road in the divisional van. It was a pleasant, balmy evening and people were out in the parks and gardens enjoying the moonlight. It was an easy night to get a few pinches, thought Murphy. If you tracked around the back streets, sooner or later you would catch a thief trying to pop a car or snatching a bag from some lovers sleeping on the grass. A chase and a fight was just the thing to get a good spirit going on a night shift. Cliff Carroll was one of the strongest men in the police force and he used to go round nursing homes and schools performing feats of strength. Maybe tonight Murphy would get the chance to test this bloke's dash. It was dash – a man's courage – that impressed Murphy, not the size of his muscles. But still, you had the feeling that, with a bloke like Cliff Carroll around, nothing bad was going to happen to you.

A few hundred metres away, a nursing sister from Ballarat was sitting under a big Moreton Bay fig tree. She had arrived on the evening train and caught the tram from Spencer Street Station to her friend's flat in South Yarra, as arranged. However, when she got there, she found a note from her friend saying she was at the opera and would be back soon. So the nurse crossed the road into the Domain Gardens and found a grassy spot under the fig tree to relax and wait. She wasn't afraid of dangers in the dark. She sat in full view of the passers-by.

It was after 11 p.m. when the radio in the blue police Dodge crackled to life. Residents had reported the sound of a woman screaming in the Domain Gardens. Nine times out of ten, these calls ended up being nothing: a loud, drunken argument that was resolved before the police arrived, or an over-enthusiastic coupling in the bushes. But when Murphy heard the sound, he knew this was something quite different. You never forget screaming like that – the mortal anguish of someone being consumed alive by a wild animal. He floored the Dodge and sped towards the sound. The streets had ten-inch gutters in those days and the old vans were big and cumbersome, but Murphy angled it across the footpath and into the park at high speed. As they bumped over tree roots and potholes, he could see flashes in the headlights of the ghastly scene unfolding: the outline of a man crouching over a woman, a pair of stockinged legs flailing in the air, the monstrous silhouette framed in the trunk of the fig tree.

Murphy stopped the van close. In the blaze of the high beam and the red and blue lights, he saw they were both covered in blood. The man had his hand deep inside the woman's vagina. He was pulling and wrenching at her innards with all his might, like he was trying to turn her inside out.

Murphy leapt from the van and made straight for the assailant, kicking him flush in the throat. Despite the crushing blow to his larynx, the man continued his horrifying attack. Murphy kicked him again and still nothing registered. All he could think was that he was going to kick this demonic bastard to death right there and then. The small, wiry man was determined to disembowel his victim before anyone could stop him. Finally he looked up at Murphy, his eyes sticking out of his head, not even trying to parry the kicks and blows, but just clinging to the thrashing body of the nurse. If ever a man needed murdering, Murphy thought, it was this crazy, bug-eyed sadist.

Officer Carroll was forced to protect the assailant as much as defend the nurse or they would both be fronting a homicide investigation. "Right-o son, you've done enough, you've done the right thing. Now let's pull up, okay?" he said, hauling Murphy off the rapist.

They got the man handcuffed and into the van. An ambulance took the nurse to hospital, where doctors fought all weekend to save her life. Even though she had lost a huge amount of blood, she survived – to the doctors' amazement. But recovering psychologically from the ordeal was another matter.

It was just on midnight when Murphy and Carroll took the prisoner into custody in Prahran. Under questioning he stared through Murphy uncomprehendingly, as if the policeman were not there. Eventually they identified him as Janas Tuingla, a Lithuanian immigrant who had worked as a powder monkey in the mines of Western Australia. He had no criminal history in Victoria, but there was no doubt in Murphy's mind that Tuingla had done this kind of thing before and that a careful scan of unsolved sexual assaults and murders would yield enough to lock this monster up for a long time. They were satisfied they had not only saved the nurse's life but also the lives of others in the future.

Tuingla was remanded from Saturday morning until Monday morning so he couldn't get bail. He was then handed over to Prahran detectives, who made a few desultory checks on the prisoner's background and left it at that. Tuingla served about six months in jail on remand and was soon back on the streets: despite the assault on the victim, there was no way of knowing whether she had initially consented to the sexual advances.

Murphy and Carroll's horrific, blood-soaked evidence wasn't enough to convict.

Only the nurse could say what had happened in the dark under the fig trees, but she was in a mental institution and wouldn't speak to police. She had blanked it all out. Eventually charges were withdrawn and Tuingla walked free, an evil wraith in a shabby overcoat.

*

"Here, I have a photograph of him somewhere," said Murphy, pulling out a cardboard box from the bottom of the cupboard in his sitting room. It was January 2008 and The Skull was opening his files for the first time, laying out the pieces of a mosaic from which we would tell his story. A box of mug shots served as a library of the notable villains he had come across in his career. There were several hundred photographs: sallow-faced coves in hats and overcoats, wild-looking thieves, assassins, SP operators and fully-fledged gangsters of the George Raft–Jimmy Cagney variety. A card file began flipping over in his mind as he looked at the photos, each with its own story to tell.

"Joseph Patrick Turner, alias Joseph Patrick Monash, a terrible bastard ... Sydney A. Stuckenschmidt, he threw a rotten orange right in my eye down the markets one day. I couldn't see so he gave me a flogging. The other blokes grabbed him and put him in a cell. They told me to come square up with him but I couldn't do it, so they made me watch as they gave him a fearful hiding ... Brian Raymond Kane, a ton of dash, do anything, this bastard – he wanted to be a copper when he was a kid. True story."

They peered out from the pictures, surly and uncooperative, holding their identity slates. Some of them he had never met, but he had memorised their faces in case he ever came across them. Some he kept as a reminder that one day he would encounter them again.

And then there were the creatures from his nightmares. Men like Janas Tuingla, who had crawled from the darkest recesses of the night. He looked at the photograph of Tuingla for a moment; even after more than fifty years, he felt a cold chill pass through him as the memory of that night came back in full, living colour.

"Some years later," he said, still looking at the picture, "a woman by the name of Elsie May Boyce was killed in the toilets at the corner of Dandenong Road and Chapel Street. There was a big murder investigation. Women back then used to wear corsets made out of canvas, and some lunatic had got in and torn her corset apart, raped and then murdered her, partially disembowelling her."

Murphy had rung the Homicide Squad to say the latest killing bore all the hallmarks of Janas Tuingla. They cut him off before he could continue – they were handling it, they said, and they didn't need any help from a uniform constable in South Melbourne.

"That was how Homicide treated you back then. They thought they were the cream of the cream. There were some good blokes, but the old guard were a bunch of drunken old bastards. People like Bluey Adams and pricks like that. Anyhow I'm spewing on them, the way I was treated."

Janas Tuingla finally appeared in an identity line-up. An elderly woman who had been with the victim had seen the assailant but would not identify him – she was terrified he would do the same to her.

Murphy was furious that Tuingla had gotten away with destroying another life; he had to be stopped or he would kill again.

Murphy told anyone who would listen but without a positive identification and supporting forensic evidence, no jury would convict.

A couple of weeks later, Murphy was at Russell Street headquarters and the murder came up in conversation with some detectives. With more than a little force, Murphy suggested that "someone should burn this bastard to death". Sure enough, within a month, the St Kilda bungalow where Tuingla lived was set ablaze and he was burnt beyond recognition.

Murphy was dragged into Russell Street and questioned over the death. He stoutly denied having anything to do with it – he had not been recruiting volunteers when he made his prescient comment about the fire. An inquiry concluded that the fire had been an accident, one of those things that happened from time to time. No-one would mourn Janas Tuingla; there would be no grieving family pressing for further investigations. Homicide had concluded his profile was right for the Boyce murder, so they didn't press this case too hard.

"He got his right fucking whack," said Murphy. "It wasn't a bad experience; it was a very enlightening experience. I was in a tight squeeze and I'm pleased with the way I came out of it, the way I handled it. You're in what you're in, and you do the best with what you've got. It's all in the way you were reared."

CHAPTER 7 THE GAMERS

Senior Constable Sinclair Imrie "Mick" Miller was a meticulous and moral leader of men. He was tall and ramrod straight, with a regal bearing that prompted junior officers to liken him to a young Duke of Edinburgh. Under Miller, Murphy graduated from general policing duties to a specialist unit, the No. 3 Special Duties Gaming Squad. Where Murphy had once terrorised the SP bookies of South Melbourne, Miller's squad covered the entire state. Murphy felt lucky to be working under his new boss. On the streets, he had learned the range of his powers, but under Miller he came to understand the limits of them.

On this particular morning in late 1957, he would learn from his mentor that the ends couldn't justify the means. To wit, he could not lie in ambush like a sniper, even if by shooting dead a pair of gangsters he might prevent a more heinous crime.

The previous night, as his colleague Fred Silvester clambered across the roof towards him, Murphy had been in position for the kill. Kneeling behind the parapet with just his head exposed, Murphy commanded the street. When John Eric Twist and Freddy "The Frog" Harrison arrived, he could pick them off at his leisure with the pump-action Browning .22-calibre rifle he had resting on the parapet. Or he could wait for them to drag their victim, Jack Dow, out of his house and then intervene. Either way, he was primed and ready for action.

Harrison and Twist were members of the Painters and Dockers Union. They were nominally waterside workers, but actually stand-over men who terrorised SP bookies like Jack Dow into handing over their takings. Dow was known as "The Rocking Horse Man": he had a business in coin-operated kiddie rides in shopping centres. But his real money came from a national SP bookmaking empire. With furs, baubles and restaurant meals, Dow bought the services of a team of women from the PMG telephone exchange. They would book interstate trunk calls for Dow and leave the lines open all Saturday afternoon. By the time he was finally collared, it was found that Dow had paid out nearly £150,000 to the PMG in cash.

Earlier Murphy had received a tip-off that Harrison and Twist were going to kidnap Dow. They planned to torture him into revealing where he hid his loot; as soon as he coughed it up, they were going to kill him and take over his empire. Miller's Gaming Squad had unwittingly helped men like Harrison and Twist ascend the criminal hierarchy. By driving the most powerful SP bookmakers out of town and breaking their corrupt connections with police officers, the Gamers had created a void which the Painters and Dockers were all too willing to fill. The remaining SP bookies were forced to work for the union or face the music from Harrison and Twist. The wharves had provided an opportunity to get involved in smuggling, drug distribution, extortion and loan sharking.

With the union on the rise, Harrison felt untouchable; but with one well-placed .22 slug, Murphy could change all that. Unfortunately, Murphy had confided his plan to Silvester while preparing to leave city headquarters. Silvester had in turn called Mick Miller at home; if Murphy was about to kill two of the state's top gangsters, the boss should know about it, he reasoned.

Silvester was despatched with a message for Murphy to cease and desist from his plan and return immediately to base.

The next morning, Murphy fronted up to the boss.

"Not a good idea, Murphy, not a good idea at all," said Miller, drawing thoughtfully on his pipe. "We'll go about this a different way – not with ideas like that. We don't go about this business by toting guns around town."

To Murphy and the other fourteen young cops on the Gaming Squad, Miller was not only a fine boss but possibly the most impressive man any of them had ever met. Miller was rebuilding the Gamers. Six months earlier, Chief Commissioner Selwyn Porter had disbanded the old squad after corruption allegations; he had ordered that they be marched to Russell Street headquarters, sacked and reassigned to uniform duties. Inspector Maurice "Mick" Healey, with Porter's blessing, then invited Miller to form a new squad by hand-picking the men he wanted from the suburban stations. At a 1958 royal commission into illegal gaming, Miller had suggested that four-fifths or more of the police who worked on illegal gambling were on the take. It was time to apply a new broom.

Murphy was one of the few officers in the squad whom Miller didn't know personally before recruiting him. He was recommended by a priest from South Melbourne, who suggested that Murphy, having broken the SP bookies in that area, might become a valuable asset. Although Miller didn't know Murphy, he found the Irish in him beguiling enough to take a chance. Yet there was also an impetuous side to Murphy that concerned him.

"If you get in trouble doing your job lawfully, Murphy, then you come straight to me and I'll go to the wall with you. But if you're breaking the law," he warned, "then you stay right out of my way, do you understand?"

It was imperative to Miller that all was done strictly according to the book. In his blue cardigan and immaculately pressed trousers, collar and tie, Miller more resembled a bank manager than the boss of one of Victoria Police's most dynamic and successful squads. But Miller had more dash than most of his troops, leading them in countless raids on illegal gaming houses and SP joints. Together, they broke the back of a racket worth £200 million a year. Personally, Miller could see little wrong with the SP bookies providing working men with a means to bet off-course, but his opinion was irrelevant. It was the law and no matter how poor the laws of the land were, you couldn't start making your own. If every officer did that, it would be a short trip to social anarchy. Or if a policeman abused his power, despite getting results, where would he stop? Would he ever be able to stop? Like Murphy, Miller had seen enough misery wrought by bad laws to last a lifetime, and it affected him deeply, but he would never allow himself to become a vigilante cop.

Instead, he pushed down any doubts he felt and became an objective collector of evidence, which he then fed into the system. The courts were for dispensing the law, not justice. A policeman should go about his work dispassionately and never play judge and jury. If a villain walked away a free man, then the policeman had failed to prove the case. There would be no fitting up of suspects or squaring up for the sake of morale. The squad just moved on; there would always be another opportunity.

He and his fellow ex-services colleagues had seen totalitarianism up close in Japan and Germany during World War II. The police were always the agents of oppression, stripping the liberty and dignity of the people they were supposed to be serving. Without restraint and fairness, a policeman risked falling into this moral void, even when he carried out his duties effectively.

On this point he liked to quote the Roman poet Juvenal from the first century: *Sed quis custodiet ipsos custodes?* But who shall guard the guardians?

After years of corruption and graft, Miller had a clear mandate to change things. Transparency would be the order of the day. And he would demand total loyalty from his men. He taught them that when faced with enforcing questionable laws, they would fall back on process and method, or risk being diminished and even debased.

At the end of each day, every desk in the office would be wiped down, the waste-paper baskets emptied and the chairs stacked neatly. Any dirty tea cup left on the table would be deposited straight in the bin. Miller liked to say that each man was responsible for himself and for every other man. In practice, this meant that if you weren't out on a job come five o'clock, you would clean up the entire office by yourself.

Soon after his team was installed, Miller was looking intently at an opaque window in the squad room that overlooked the courtyard. Everyone assumed it was frosted glass, but Miller ran a fingernail down it to discover the frosting was in fact a thick glaze of cigarette tar that had built up over years. Somewhere along the line, the window had stopped being cleaned and the pallid, yellow light that passed through it had become everyday reality. It was typical of how things were back then in Victoria Police. Few were prepared to take responsibility, so the bad habits were never addressed. In front of the men, Miller took a bucket and soap and cleaned the window to a sparkling, clear finish. The effect on the men was instantaneous. Here was a man who led by example.

To others, this rigid attitude made Miller a zealot and he had many critics in the force who hoped he would fail. So far, the squad hadn't put a foot wrong. They were driving some of the biggest SP bookmakers out of business, and in some cases out of the state. There were weekends when they would shut down five or six major players. With little or no cooperation from the post-master-general's office, Miller's squad detected and silenced more than 600 telephone lines used by the SP bookies. They found many of their targets by looking in the telephone book and monitoring the weekend activities of businesses that had multiple phone lines.

Miller had moulded his young team into one of the best and most courageous units in Victoria Police. They worked as a force within a force, never discussing their operations with other men in case word leaked out to their targets. Miller had drilled into them the importance of exercising personal judgment as well as spontaneous action. Murphy took to the task with relish. He and a number of other cops dressed up as bodgies to break up gambling rings operated by the owners of suburban milk bars, using their pinball machines as props.

However, Miller still needed to keep an eye on proceedings, as the events of the previous night with Harrison and Twist had demonstrated.

"You're only a young chap," said Miller, "and you're going to finish up in big trouble if you go around in that fashion. If we cannot defend you, then we cannot afford you. Just remember, there is one ship and I am the captain. There aren't two ways of doing things, there are four," he added, tapping his pipe. "There's the right way and the wrong way. There's the department's way. And there's my way. You follow my way, you'll never come unstuck."

That night, after Murphy had finished work, he went back to Miller's office.

"Thanks, boss," he said. "That was good advice."

A few months later, on 6 February 1958, Freddy "The Frog" Harrison pulled up on South Wharf in his Ford Customline to collect his wages and return a borrowed trailer. As he bent down to unhook the trailer, a man strode up with a shotgun and said: "This is yours, Fred," and blew half his head away. The gunman was Harrison's erstwhile partner in crime, John Eric Twist.

CHAPTER 8 EXPEDIENCY

THE CHIEF COMMISSIONER OF POLICE, Major General Selwyn Havelock Watson Porter DSO CBE ED, was a military man and understood well the mind of the soldier. And so he was dismayed by the antics of the No. 3 Special Duties Gaming Squad. If they, as soldiers, had engaged in a mutiny, he could have had them court-martialled. But in this instance, faced with the resignation of the entire squad along with its leader, Porter could do no more than try to talk them out of it.

Fifteen men had resigned from the squad the previous day over Porter's handling of the suspect games operating in newspapers and on television. The squad, with Mick Miller's approval, had deemed the *Herald* newspaper's popular feature Wealth Words a game of chance. A brief had been prepared and lodged with the Supreme Court, but somewhere along the line a hand was laid on the case and it failed to be processed before the statutory deadline. The men were furious – it looked like their boss had been sold out. They had been hand-picked to clean up illegal gaming and its associated corruption and now they were being nobbled by those very same forces. It didn't matter that there would be a storm of protest from *Herald* readers if Wealth Words was dropped: the law was the law and enforcing it was not a popularity contest.

The force was full of ex-servicemen in 1958, and Porter's constables looked just like soldiers as they marched up and down the parade ground at Russell Street. The police force, however, was not a standing army and its members swore no oath of fealty to the sovereign or its officers. The community spawned the copper and he remained a member of it at all times, despite the uniform. Unlike the soldier, for whom force was the solution to all negotiations, the copper could only do his job with the consent of the community. If he failed to obtain that, he would soon come unstuck.

The policeman would give loyalty to his superiors, of course, but it was a qualified, fragile thing that often did not extend any higher than the squad sergeant. Each policeman was running his agenda in his district. The priorities of the boss might intersect but not always. The chief commissioner could punish a cop by keeping him in uniform on the beat, but for the corrupt ones that was a bonus. With graft, a bent copper could make more than the chief commissioner while still locking up crooks and doing his job. A promotion to a desk job would entail a pay cut. Cops like Murphy were different again. While he was locking up crooks there was little his superiors could do about his insubordination, not to mention his bad language. This was a matter of concern to Porter, who had tried to instil a formality of conduct and language utterly foreign to the knockabout cops like Murphy.

Chief Commissioner Porter knew that addressing these men was a tricky proposition; they could just as soon tell you to piss off as listen to you, and the thin film of authority conferred by all the stripes and crowns on the uniform would dissolve in a flash.

"Who is the spokesman for this mutiny?" asked Porter. He had gathered the Gamers in a staff room and closed the door. He cut a resplendent figure in full uniform, but to Murphy the uniform meant little. For all he cared, Selwyn Porter could have been the Rt. Hon. Sir Joseph Porter, K.C.B., First Lord of the Admiralty, from Gilbert and Sullivan's *H.M.S. Pinafore*.

"I guess I am *a* spokesman, sir – for myself," said Murphy, standing up from his desk.

"And who would you be?"

"First Constable Brian Francis Murphy 11885."

"Well, First Constable Brian Francis Murphy 11885, what do you have to say for yourself?" asked Porter, haughtily.

"This might be the opinion of a lot of the blokes here, but it's my personal opinion. I haven't discussed it with anybody else," said Murphy, conscious that he could be charged with causing disaffection in the ranks. "But I spoke with a bloke from the *Herald* the other day and he said your boss is as weak as piss."

He paused, letting the defiance settle on the room.

"He reckons the *Herald* boss, Sir Frank Williams, has you over a barrel regarding Wealth Words and is sticking it up your coota."

Porter's face turned a bright crimson. Murphy wasn't sure whether the chief commissioner was going to shoot him or burst into tears.

"Well, First Constable Brian Francis Murphy, I'll tell you something ..." But his voice trailed off. He did not know what to say. By rights, he could have had Murphy charged for insubordination, but instead he began looking around the room for support among the others.

"Gentlemen, is this a collective opinion?" he asked quietly. "Is there anybody else? Nick, what about you?" Nick was a great guitar player and he used to perform at all the Masonic functions, where Porter was a regular attendee.

"Sir, I have no problems with you. I think you're doing a great job," said Nick, his eyes downcast. The room was silent; Murphy felt his heart sinking. And then Ernie Cartwright, a bloke for whom Murphy had little respect, jumped up.

"I listened to what Brian Murphy said and I agree with him wholeheartedly," he told Porter. Murphy looked round in amazement. The squad room was suddenly in uproar and Porter withdrew, the power and authority draining from his comic-opera uniform.

"Well, we won't be accepting anyone's resignation," said Porter, reaching for the door. "You chaps just carry on with what you were doing. This business will be sorted out at a higher level." He began to leave but instead bumped into Fred Silvester, who had been listening to proceedings through the door.

"You!" shouted Porter. "Silvester, it's you, isn't it? You've caused all this trouble, haven't you?"

Silvester shot back with full force. "Don't you bloody talk to me," he said, shaking an angry fist in the chief commissioner's face. He stepped towards Porter and those in the muster room held their collective breath, expecting Silvester to punch the chief commissioner. But a senior constable stepped between them and pushed Silvester back.

"Now steady on, Fred," he said. "Wake up to yourself." Porter looked fit to burst, but then just laughed, shook his head and walked away.

Murphy ran to the telephone boxes on Bourke Street to call Mick Miller. Whether by design or coincidence, Miller had been off that day. Through his absence, he had avoided the conflict with Porter. Murphy related the confrontation with the chief commissioner. Far from admonishing him, Miller laughed and simply said, "Well done, Murphy. Good job."

After a respectable interval, the *Herald* dropped Wealth Words from its pages despite its continuing popularity. It wasn't the kind of vindication the squad was after, but it was a win of sorts. As Murphy remarked, it was better than a kick in the arse with a sharp shoe.

*

After the Wealth Words debacle, Mick Miller was through with the No. 3 Special Duties Gaming Squad. He felt let down by his superiors. Enforcing Victoria's gambling laws had become a game and its players were prepared to use his men as pawns. He put in for a transfer. On the form, he summed up his reasons in one succinct word: *expediency*.

Murphy was becoming aware of the delicate balance between law and order that underpinned the power of his police badge. Miller had shown him that a policeman could enforce unpopular laws without falling to graft and corruption; he could carry out his duties ethically by following the law and placing his faith in the leader of his squad. Sadly, there were few leaders of the calibre of Mick Miller in Victoria Police back in 1959, and to Murphy most of the bosses would suffer terribly by comparison.

In 1959, the *Daily Mirror* ran a story on the demise of Miller's Gaming Squad under the headline: "NO Bullets, NO Glory for them". Hollywood would have seen it differently: Inspector Maurice "Mick" Healey, the veteran police officer and honest cop who masterminded the drive that wrecked a £200 million-a-year gambling racket, was cut down in a hail of machine-gun bullets; Senior Constable Sinclair Imrie "Mick" Miller, the fresh-faced zealot who spearheaded the drive and kicked in the doors, survived to win honour and glory and marry the girl next door.

But in Melbourne, the two Micks rated neither bullets nor glory. In Melbourne they were simply transferred. Indeed, among the fifteen members of the Special Gaming Squad that asked for transfers to other duties, Commissioner Porter declared there was no "dissension" and their simultaneous application for transfers was merely a "coincidence".

As the *Daily Mirror* noted: "It was a disappointing ending to an exciting story."

CHAPTER 9 DETECTIVE IN TRAINING

MURPHY SAW THAT THE GAMERS would soon disband and put in for the Criminal Investigation Branch. Twelve months later, on 15 July 1960, he passed the detective training course. He was set to trade his uniform for plainclothes, but first he had to get past the chief commissioner.

It was 4 p.m. when he was summoned to Porter's office; the sun was low and streaming in the window from the west. The venetian blinds were open and Murphy could hardly see Porter with the sun shining directly into his eyes. The chief commissioner motioned for him to take a seat in front of his desk. A chief inspector was standing, unsmiling, in the shadows. It seemed to Murphy that Porter wanted to make him squirm, to leave him there squinting and blinking in the bright light, and not say a word.

"Excuse me, sir," said Murphy. "Do you mind if I close the venetians, sir? I can't see your face."

Porter said nothing. After a few moments Murphy got up, walked behind the chief commissioner and closed the blinds. Now the room was dark, so he switched on the light. They sat suffused with an even, equal, fluorescent light. Finally, Porter spoke quietly and deliberately.

"Well, First Constable, maybe Detective, Brian Francis Murphy. Has your opinion of me changed in the last twelve months?"

Porter was showing the strain of managing these unruly, insubordinate cops. It occurred to Murphy that all he wanted was an affirmation of loyalty, perhaps even to be liked. It was sad, really, that the chief commissioner should need his approval. Murphy had been told that the chief commissioner had recently asked the garage attendant to bring his car to him. When the attendant readily agreed, Porter was moved to tears.

"You would do that for me?"

"Why, of course, sir. You're the chief commissioner."

"No-one seems to recognise that fact," Porter said through his tears. He had survived the mud and blood of the Kokoda Track, but the jungle that was Victoria Police was doing him in. Murphy tried to think of something neutral to say.

"Well, sir," he replied. "Nothing in the past twelve months has changed my mind about anything."

"And you want to be a detective?" asked Porter, icily.

"Yes, I do."

"Then get out of my office," said Porter.

*

A few days later, Murphy was walking down Little Bourke Street with another detective, not far from police headquarters. Murphy had been chosen for the CIB but the appointment was not yet gazetted. In theory, they could still bust him back to uniform; but nothing could daunt Murphy's sense of adventure now. As a detective, he had the freedom he never had as a member of the Gamers under the watchful eye of Mick Miller. His new boss, Superintendent Harry McMenamin, was a different character altogether – as Murphy was to discover. Far from simply following orders, Murphy would have to exercise his own judgment on a daily basis just to survive the politics and corruption of the CIB.

On this particular day, Murphy and his partner were watching the comings and goings from the Greek-run card clubs on Little Bourke Street when a well-known villain strutted towards them. The Greek was hard to miss in his cream suit, panama hat and two-tone shoes. It was outlandish clobber for a tank man, a caper that relied on keeping a low profile. But not this bloke: you could hear his gold chains clinking and rattling before he even got close.

"Sir, a minute of your time, if you please," said Murphy, but the man pushed straight past him.

"You can't pull me up, you're not authorised to do so," said the Greek, contemptuously.

"And why would that be?"

"Because Superintendent Harry McMenamin of the CIB – he'd be your boss, I believe – said so. I have his personal guarantee I won't be bothered by little shit-pots like you." The arrogance was breathtaking.

"Well, fuck you and fuck Mr McMenamin," Murphy growled, pushing his suspect against the wall and body-searching him vigorously. The Greek began shouting that Murphy would be sorry; he would make sure he lost his job. Such a challenge to Murphy's authority could not be tolerated. The Greek was charged with offensive behaviour and hauled into Russell Street, still yelling, "Mr McMenamin is going to hear about this."

The next day, Murphy found himself in McMenamin's office. Before he could close the door, the boss was into him.

"Don't you tell me to get fucked," roared McMenamin, a fair indication that the Greek had contacted his police minder.

"Well, who are you going to believe – me or a Greek criminal?" Murphy shouted back.

*

The answer to that question was abundantly clear, thought Murphy a few days later, as he sat on a train bound for Broadmeadows. For daring to lock up the Greek, Murphy had been banished from Russell Street to the wastelands of Broadmeadows CIB. In the years to come, "Broadie" would produce some of Victoria's best criminals, but for now Melbourne's outer north seemed to Murphy to lie beyond the edge of the civilised world. However, as he was walking from the train to the police station, Murphy was pleased to spot a familiar face in a telephone box, one he hadn't seen since his youthful days in South Melbourne.

"Brian Murphy! How are you, mate?" Time had evidently been good to this working-class kid, as he was dressed in an expensive suit. "Tell you what, Murph, you fancy a nice suit?"

"Do I what? Of course, whatcha got?"

"Well, me and some mates knocked over the Roger David store in town last night and we've got the lot over in a house. I could let you have one real cheap. You wanna come look?"

"Whacko, let's go!" said Murphy. Clearly this old acquaintance was unaware of Murphy's vocational choices in recent times.

They arrived at a house nearby, where an accomplice was sorting through racks of suits. "Hey, mate, I've brought an old chum from South Melbourne. He's going to take a suit, if you don't mind," said the South Melbournian. The accomplice, who had been around a bit longer than his mate, took one look at Murphy and changed colour.

"Whaddaya doing? This bloke's a cop, you imbecile!" he exclaimed.

"No way, he's not a copper … I've known him for … for years," the South Melbournian stammered.

"Well, how long since you've seen him, you idiot?"

"It's been a while, hasn't it, Brian – but you aren't really a copper, are you?"

"Yeah, your mate's right, I am a copper and you're both nicked," he said, pulling out his handcuffs. Murphy marched his prisoners back to the telephone box and called a divvy van for the trip to the Broadmeadows police station.

The senior sergeant on duty looked up from his newspaper as Murphy and his prisoners walked into the station.

"Where have you been? You're late!" Apparently the senior sergeant, a friend of McMenamin's, had called the superintendent looking for Murphy. "You left the DDI's office forty-five minutes ago. What's taken you so long?"

"Sarge, sorry for being late, but I was busy arresting these two offenders," replied Murphy.

The senior sergeant scoffed. "What are the charges? Drunkenness, I suppose, or maybe offensive behaviour?"

"Actually, a big break-in in the city," replied Murphy.

The sergeant couldn't call McMenamin quickly enough to claim credit for solving the break-in. He didn't mention Murphy. That set the tone for Murphy's time in Broadmeadows. There was plenty of crime to chase, but the senior sergeant made it clear he was to be kept like a dog on a chain. There would be no solo patrols and he was to be accompanied by a uniform officer on every arrest. Most of his time was spent sitting at a desk. This was McMenamin's way of bringing him into line. In time he might be a good detective, but he had to learn the system, how things worked in the CIB.

After a few months of this purgatory, he was transferred to Brunswick police station and then to Coburg. Then, after almost a year as a detective, he landed the plum posting: South

Melbourne. Murphy was coming home and every villain in the district would soon know his name.

CHAPTER 10 FAMILY MAN

MURPHY AND MARGARET BLANCHFIELD met at a dance at St Kilda Town Hall in 1957. He had recently broken up with a long-term girlfriend and his mother had warned him not to "fall in love with the first piece of skirt you meet". Among his mother's many deep, abiding hatreds was anyone with red hair, but when Murphy saw Margaret's strawberry-blonde locks, he forgot his mother's warnings. As they danced, when he held her hand for the first time, he felt a charge of electricity that never died, even after more than half a century of marriage. It was a 50/50 dance – an old-time song followed by a new one – so he booked every second dance with Margaret for the whole night. He was wearing a Young Christian Workers badge, a Catholic fellowship group.

"Are you a blood donor?" she asked.

"No, it's the YCW," he replied.

"Oh, my brother's a member of that," said Margaret, establishing the family's Catholic credentials. Murphy had gone to the dance with his younger brother, Kevin, who now had to find his own way home because the gallant young policeman had offered his dance partner a ride at the end of the evening. When Kevin arrived home, his mother was waiting.

"Where's the other one?" Maggie asked, sensing something was up.

"He's taking a girl home from the dance … and she's a red-head," replied Kevin.

66

Maggie was still up when Brian arrived home an hour later. "A redhead, eh? You know you're an imbecile, don't you?"

"Yes, Mum, I understand," said Brian.

"No, you don't! You have no idea," she growled.

"Mum, yes I *do* understand," he said, with enough force to end the conversation. Even Maggie knew when to back off.

The following day, after Mass, Murphy ducked a family outing and turned up unannounced at the Blanchfields' door in nearby Glenhuntly. Margaret came out from the kitchen, her hands covered in flour from baking. She impressed Brian immediately: the house had an orderly, settled feel to it, much like his own home under his mother's regime.

Margaret's mother had died when she was seventeen, and from that time she and her younger sister had run the household. She was a devout Catholic but loved to read dime novels about cowboys and Indians, cops and robbers. "Deadwood Dick" was a favourite character. The stories were set in the lawless West, where a struggle was taking place between good and evil to determine the fate of civilisation.

DEATH NOTCH! Did you ever hear of a more uninviting name for a place, dear reader? If so, you could not well find a harder role, where dwelt humanity than Death Notch, along the whole golden slope of the West.

It was said that nobody but rascals and rough could exist in that lone mining camp, which was confirmed by the fact that it was seldom the weekly stage brought anyone there who had come to settle. Even the government officials, cognizant of the lawlessness within the border of Death Notch, hesitated to interfere, because of the desperate character of the residents – hardest of the hard.

The town lay in a sort of mountain-surrounded basin, on the route from Pioche, Nevada, to Helena, Montana, and had formerly been an Indian camp, until a "well-heeled" but notorious young gamble named Piute Dave had come along and driven the reds away, as he was able to do, having backing of some forty ruffians of his own stamp.

Deadwood Dick was a masked and mysterious hero known for pursuing with his trusty six-shooter a masked villain known as "The Skull", the leader of a renegade band infamous for its violence against the Deadwood residents.

Margaret had dreamed of meeting a dashing man of action like Deadwood Dick, and her mother had always said she would marry either a detective or a cowboy. Little did she know that in her real-life adventure story, The Skull would be the hero driving the villains out of Dodge City, which South Melbourne in those days resembled. Margaret believed that good men, like those heroes, were decisive and heroic, providers and defenders. There was even a place for vigilante violence in the service of the moral imperative. A man did what he had to do to protect the community. And in return for her man's derring-do, Margaret would keep house to a high standard and raise their children in the Catholic tradition to be upstanding citizens.

They were married at St Anthony's Catholic Church, Glenhuntly. There were congratulations from the chaps at the South Melbourne station, several of whom had been involved in the plots to burn Murphy's car and load his locker with a shotgun. Some of the plotters had come to respect his dash; the rest had learned it was better to stay out of his way. Brian and Margaret Murphy had five children together: Reg, born in 1959, was soon joined by Bernardine (1960), Eileen (1961) Danny (1964) and Geraldine (1969).

Murphy liked to say that he and Margaret had a book on birth control but neither of them found time to read it. Usually the kids were born as a result of Father's Day or Christmas or Murphy's birthday because sex was the only present they could afford to give each other.

The joy of having a wife and family brought with it new responsibilities and concerns. His mother automatically sided with him and he could share any aspect of his work with her. But his wife, though bound by marriage to him, was not blood. He wondered how much a policeman should share with his wife, and when it would become a burden for her. His first senior sergeant at North Melbourne, Tom Nally, set him straight.

"Don't treat a wife like a moll. Don't tell her lies," Nally said. "Better to tell her nothing than lie to her, because if you do, one day she might give evidence in the Supreme Court and she'll tell the bloody truth about you!" So Murphy would share the minimum, generally responding to her concerns in a lighthearted and dismissive tone, even if he had spent the day in rage and fear.

"Everything okay, dear?" she would ask as they went to bed.

"Good as gold, love," he would reply, switching off the light. He would stare at the plaster wedding cake on the ceiling until he settled down enough to get to sleep.

Occasionally, though, his exploits would make the newspaper and Murphy would have to explain himself. One day in 1960, Murphy and his partner were driving down Chapel Street, South Yarra, when they noticed a man lurking by a car. When they slowed down to talk to him, the man ran into a shop. They gave chase and a mighty struggle ensued: punches were flying, elbows, knees and headbutts rained down. The shop was in ruins by the time they subdued him. Murphy's partner was hobbling, having badly turned his ankle in the melee. He needed crutches to walk for the next few days.

It turned out the man was a Hungarian immigrant who had fled the Soviet invasion of Hungary in 1956, having suffered at the hands of the Hungarian secret police, the AVO. During the struggle, members of the AVO had been lynched in the streets of Budapest and money stuffed down their throats. Well-versed in savagery and torture, the AVO's motto had been: *Whatever it takes to make them confess.*

When the man, a recent arrival, had seen Murphy and his partner get out of the unmarked car, put on their hats and point towards him, he assumed they were secret police. Before both parties realised they had been at cross-purposes, the cops had given the Hungarian a thorough going-over. Several weeks passed before the man's court hearing; Murphy's partner's ankle had well and truly healed, but he hung onto his crutches anyway. The case was heard in Prahran Court, and Margaret, having read of the case, wanted to attend to see her man give evidence. There was no doubt that the police had used excessive force, but the case turned when the magistrate saw Murphy's partner limp into the witness box. The "beak" assured the hapless Hungarian there were no secret police operating in Australia and warned him that assaulting and injuring a police officer was a serious matter indeed.

Margaret walked out with Murphy and his partner still on his crutches. Halfway down the thirty steps of Prahran Court, Murphy's partner began tap dancing, waving his crutches in the air. Margaret was outraged; this was simply not fair, she thought.

"Would you do the same thing?" she asked, looking at her husband.

"Well, I wouldn't have used the crutches, but I might have had a limp," he replied.

So it was better that Murphy not burden his wife with details of his exploits. Murphy wanted Margaret's scruples to hold sway in the home and in raising the family; but once he crossed the threshold and into the street, it was "the Fitzroy ways and means" that guided him.

Certainly, in South Melbourne, Murphy was living a life closer to Deadwood Dick's than Dick Tracy's. Barely a week went by when he wasn't involved in a blue; some weeks they went out every night looking for it. They wanted to instil the fear of the law into the Painters and Dockers and their associates who ran graft and crime operations out of pubs all over the district.

Sometimes Murphy would go into a pub hopelessly outnumbered, often with just one other officer. He could smell the danger; if he got into strife, he might go down and never get up again. The adrenalin made his mind race, but he was always clear and determined. No-one would get over the top of him. He would fill the room with the force of his personality. The theatre started even before he entered the pub. He might let off two or three backfires as he approached in his vehicle by turning off the ignition, letting the compression build up and then re-starting the engine. It risked blowing up the motor, but it threw the enemy into confusion. Often, by the time he entered the pub, the only ones left were the drunks, so he locked them up, kept them safe and avoided a conflict. A witness could get up in court and swear black and blue that he heard a volley of shots before Murphy stormed into the pub;

but of course he hadn't, and there was no evidence. So what else could this witness be mistaken about, a prosecutor might ask.

If it came to a confrontation, Murphy would walk in with his hat on straight and clean as a new pin in his suit, exuding an air of quiet authority. You could never command respect if you looked like a dirt bag, he would say.

"Have a look at this bastard," one of the lags might say, feeling proud and safe with numbers around him. Murphy would fire back something like: "Hello, have you been reading my fan mail?" or "I might have been your father, only a rat beat me to it." Everyone would laugh, and while the lag was stuck for words, Murphy would follow up with another verbal salvo: "How's your mother going? Jesus, she was a good root!" Then he would grab him by the collar and drag him out. If there was a chance of being on the wrong end of a kicking, Murphy would single out the biggest bloke in the pub for a headbutt. The element of surprise was crucial; Murphy would stand there with his thumbs tucked into his lapels, and while the target was looking at Murphy's hands, his forehead would suddenly crash down on the bridge of his nose. Murphy usually found that the biggest guys in the joint had the smallest balls; they had plenty of tongue but not much intestinal fortitude. Sometimes he might tactically withdraw if the odds were too heavily stacked against him. He could always catch up with the head on the street a few days later when he wasn't surrounded by his team.

Indeed, it became a well-known routine around South Melbourne and St Kilda. Murphy would pull up at the curb and say: "Listen you, we're going to have a talk. Get in!" And he would drive to the end of Williamstown Road, a lonely strip of rubbish land between the docks and the bayside. At the end of the road was a drainage culvert: a big V-shaped grave with five or six feet of muck and gunk at the bottom. Immediately on arrival, the suspect knew he was in for more than just a talk. Murphy would suggest they take a stroll and when they got to the edge of the drain, he would push him in. There was a thick crust over the ooze which, for a brief moment, gave the illusion of solid ground; but soon the bloke would be floundering and sinking in the crap. Once the crust was broken, a pungent acidic stench would be released. The sloping concrete sides made it almost impossible to climb out, especially with Murphy towering above, threatening to kick him back in. When the man was finally let out, he would stand shivering and stinking, begging to be taken back to civilisation. To add insult to injury, Murphy would make him walk back to town, covered in slime and grunge, a once flash suit all but ruined. It was a humiliating experience that few were keen to repeat. In Murphy's opinion, a trip down Williamstown Road was better than a trip to the magistrate. Most who made that dismal journey never gave him trouble again.

Murphy's reputation as "The Psych" was officially translated into comments on his service record such as "Well-conducted, reliable and efficient". Unofficially, Murphy was terrifying when his blood was up and stories of his quicksilver temper during a short stint on the Wireless Patrol were already circulating. The Wireless Patrol was one of the first mobile squads with a brief to go wherever they were needed, at 100 miles per hour, much to Murphy's delight. He loved the adrenalin rush of pursuits and he could get completely carried away. On one occasion, they chased a hood in a stolen car all over Prahran and South Yarra. Murphy thought the villain was getting away so he leaned out the window and, without warning his colleague, let three shots go, smashing the stolen car's back window. There was uproar inside the police vehicle – the other copper had no interest in turning a stolen-car docket into a homicide investigation. "What are you doing, you lunatic? Put that gun away!" he screamed. But the gunfire had frightened the villain into ditching the car and running for his life through the back streets. The constables gave chase and saw the man leap a fence into the backyard of a house in South Yarra. There the trail went cold. They searched the entire premises but found no-one. Just as they were about to leave, Murphy asked his partner, "Hey, have you searched that backyard dunny?"

"Of course," said his partner, keen to conclude this terrifying interlude with Murphy. But he hadn't gone right in; he'd just pushed the door. Murphy approached the door and swung it right open and, lo and behold, a pair of boots could be seen between the bottom of the door and the floor. Rather than arrest the man, Murphy shot him in the foot. He knew his bosses would not be impressed by this Wild West-style policing: it was understood that a little gunplay was inevitable, but if suspects were shot, it was a problem for them to explain. So Murphy came up with a story: when he had kicked the dunny door, it rebounded against his hand and caused his gun to go off. The senior sergeant was underwhelmed but his mood softened when Murphy revealed that the man had confessed to fifteen car thefts. And the news from hospital was good too: the bullet had gone straight through the flesh without breaking any bones. How lucky could you be, thought Murphy.

*

Murphy was a useful weapon in the hands of the bosses: he was willing to go where others were afraid to and he was able to get results where others failed. And somehow he managed to stay out of official trouble. One morning, he was serving a warrant on a property in South Melbourne and the resident was a little slow in responding, so Murphy decided to kick the door in. He didn't know a woman was hobbling up the hallway on crutches to answer the door, nor that white ants had eaten away at the door jamb. So when he kicked the door, the hinges broke free from the rotten timber and it fell on the woman, knocking her unconscious. Fortunately, when she came to, she had no memory of the incident and thanked Murphy for putting her to bed.

Officially, Murphy wasn't supposed to be working the pubs, but often the only way he could get out and about was to join uniform officers in the divisional van, responding to all manner of calls. The CIB had its own vehicles but the bosses frequently commandeered the few available cars to go drinking, leaving detectives like Murphy to work the whole afternoon shift on a bicycle. So he would grab a lift from the blokes in the divvy van and gee them up for a battle or two in the pubs. Some of the struggles were epics.

One afternoon, Murphy and another officer went down to the Druids Hotel to break up a minor altercation, only to find a full-scale melee underway. A legendary street fighter named Bobby Dunn was knocking out all comers and threatening to tear the pub apart. Murphy stormed in and with a combination of fist and baton managed to handcuff Dunn's lethal right hand to his own left hand. It seemed a good idea, but Dunn carried on belting anyone near him with his left hand while trying to brain Murphy with his forehead, elbow or anything else that moved. They spilled out into the street and continued fighting for another ten minutes until they reached Moray Street several blocks away. Murphy and his partner were now covered in blood and in danger of being kicked to death if they went down.

Murphy was starting to buckle at the knees when he heard the wail of sirens closing in on the scene. With the cavalry on the way, Murphy's strength was renewed and he belted Dunn senseless before scything his way through the crowd, dragging the hapless prisoner behind him.

Twenty-five were arrested and brought back to the South Melbourne station. There they were forced to run the gauntlet of angry policemen belting each prisoner as they came through the front door. There was no way the cops were going to let that kind of disrespect go unpunished and each copped his medicine without complaint.

Murphy's family would occasionally learn of his fistic exploits in the newspaper or through local legend, but rarely did they see the man in action. His younger brother Brendan, who later became one of Victoria's leading barristers, copped plenty of hidings on behalf of his brother. He was a smaller, easier target and the bullying haunted his high school years.

One summer night, Brendan was working as an usher at a cinema in Albert Park when some local thugs began playing up in the front row. The ringleader was a tough named Thwaites who had been at school with him. Thwaites was drinking beer and making a ruckus for the amusement of his friends. Brendan politely asked the group to leave.

When the movie finished, Thwaites and his posse of ten thugs were waiting for him out on the street. Fearing for his life, Brendan locked himself in the ticket booth and telephoned Brian. Brendan was small and slight and weighed about "three stone five" by his own reckoning. He was recovering from glandular fever, so a kicking was the last thing he needed.

Minutes later Murphy swept in, driving the police Ford Anglia. Brendan heard his brother tell the thugs to piss off but, confident in their numbers, a couple of them had a go. What unfolded looked more like a Kung Fu movie than a Saturday night in Albert Park. Murphy knocked them all out, one by one, displaying a terrifying speed and agility. Soon there were bodies spread across the pavement in various states of unconsciousness. Brendan was speechless. He had never seen Brian in action before, though the stories were getting round by this time.

Murphy was a mess of contradictions. One night he woke Brendan in the middle of the night and declared they were going to cook a meal for a pair of street urchins he had picked up. Maggie had washed and clothed the kids, and now Brendan would feed them. On another occasion, some colleagues from Port Melbourne thought it would be a great joke to charge an old Irishman named Edward Francis Howlin for vagrancy under Murphy's name. Murphy was acting as police prosecutor when the case came up.

"What are you going to do, Murphy? Lock your grandfather up?" mocked the officers, expecting him to blow up with indignation.

Instead, he brought Howlin home and "Duffy" stayed with the family for nearly six months. Murphy set him up in the back shed and bought him a wireless radio and a canary in a cage. He even spent £80 buying him a hearing aid on hire purchase. A former bodyguard to an Irish prime minister, Duffy had become a swaggie in his later years and he regaled the kids with stories of life on the road and tall tales of encounters with banshees and leprechauns as he traversed the countryside. Then one day, Duffy simply upped and disappeared, leaving behind his canary and his wireless. Murphy and the kids were distraught and searched high and low for him, but they never found him.

CHAPTER 11 CHOCOLATE RUN

MURPHY WAS AT HOME HAVING DINNER after a long day when there was a knock at the door. It was two junior officers; they needed a hand with a raid and the senior constable was nowhere to be found. Could Murphy come lend a hand? No matter what time of the day or night, Murphy was always available and he readily agreed. Besides, if Murphy's hunch was right, the married senior connie was enjoying a red wine with his mistress in Port Melbourne at that moment, leaving his colleagues in the lurch. He grabbed his gear and took off, but as he left, Margaret asked him to pick up a block of chocolate. She didn't ask for much – there were few luxuries in the house of a police constable – but she was pregnant and Murphy agreed to her request. The trio raided the house, recovered a quantity of stolen goods and nabbed the crook. Murphy's thoughts returned to the chocolate.

It was now eight o'clock in the evening and Murphy hurried over to a corner shop owned by a friend, Carol Ferguson. He arrived just as she was closing up.

"Mate, I need a block of Cadbury chocolate. I'll pay you back tomorrow."

"Get stuffed! Keep your money," said Carol. "How many do you want?"

"Just one block and I'll pay you back tomorrow," he insisted.

"Suit yourself!" she said, handing him the chocolate. Suddenly, there was a terrific explosion from next door. The windows blew out and Murphy could see orange flames shooting from the back of the second storey as he ran to investigate. The house would soon be consumed by flames, so he had to make a decision: if someone was in there, he would have to go in. Confirming his worst fears, the shopkeeper said she had heard strange noises coming from next door – a loud, anguished male voice and the sound of heavy objects being dragged around.

Murphy kicked the door in and ran upstairs through the gathering smoke. He tried the door handle of the back bedroom where the fire had started. He was expecting a straight rescue, to haul out a frail, elderly man whose faulty gas heater had blown. The door was unlocked but it was barricaded with furniture. He pushed hard against the door, and when it opened a few inches he saw a flash of silver through the smoke. He looked down and noticed a tear in the sleeve of his new gabardine reefer jacket. He pushed the door again and there it was, that flash once more, and another tear in his sleeve. The third time it happened, he realised he was seeing the blade of an enormous kitchen knife. This was not going to be any ordinary rescue – maybe a murder or a vicious rape was underway. He kicked in one of the panels of the door and then threw all his weight against the makeshift barricade. A tallboy perched on top of a table crashed to the floor and Murphy, wild-eyed and furious, burst into the burning room. Through the heat and haze, he was confronted by a truly fearsome sight. This was a greater force of insanity than even Murphy could muster. The man he saw was squat and powerful; he looked like a wrestler with a shaven head. His trapezoid muscles were so over-developed that the man had no neck at all. From the apex of his head there was just a continuous line out to his shoulders. He was grimacing and gnashing his teeth, working the massive muscles of his jaw and shoulders as if trying to stop his body from swallowing his head. In his hand, he held the knife, waving it and shouting in what Murphy later learned was a Polish accent: "I WILL KILL YOU, YOU BASTARD! I WILL CUT YOUR BALLS OUT!"

The man appeared to have doused the room with an accelerant, probably kerosene, and lit it with the intention of killing himself. It was a crazy man's plan and it hadn't worked; it had just created a fireball and, to make matters worse, now there was a copper trying to save him.

Murphy had fought some tough men in his time but this was a new challenge. He thought he could shoot the lunatic right there and then, but it would take some explaining later. ("Yes, Your Honour, the victim survived the blast and the fire, but I shot him in the rescue attempt and that's how he came to be dead.") Murphy took a step back to assess his options, and heard the sirens of a fire truck pulling up outside. Deliverance, he thought, as the burly firemen with their axes and extinguishers raced up the stairs.

"There's a nutter in the back room with a knife – give us a hand with him!" Murphy shouted. But when they reached the threshold of the room, the Pole came rushing forward threatening to gut anyone who tried to save him.

"Forget it!" said one of the firemen, handing Murphy a fire extinguisher. "We're not going in there. He's your problem."

Murphy took the extinguisher and charged into the room, shooting a plume of foam into the Pole's face until he got close enough to bring the extinguisher down hard on the man's head. *KOONG!* But the sickening blow had no effect on the Pole other than to enrage him. He had dropped the knife and was now looking to tear Murphy apart with his bare hands. They wrestled and grappled amid the flames and smoke. Murphy tried to get his arm around the man's neck to choke him, but the neck was so thick and covered with foam and sweat that his hand kept slipping off. He tried a full nelson, a half nelson, an arm bar and wrist locks, but to no avail. A bowline tied off with a half hitch on a steel cable wouldn't have held this slippery Pole. And each time the Pole got a good grip, it felt like Murphy's eyes would pop out of his head. The room was now fully ablaze. Summoning his strength, Murphy manoeuvred the Pole into the doorway, then forced his shoulder hard into his opponent's mid-section, driving him out of the room and onto the landing. They crashed through the balustrade in their death-embrace and Murphy landed, with a sickening thump, on top of the Pole on the first-floor landing. The Pole was temporarily winded and gasping for air and Murphy quickly slapped handcuffs on him with the help of the firemen. It had taken nearly twenty minutes to subdue the furious lunatic; it had felt like an eternity. But now back-up had arrived and three or four officers helped throw him into the back of a divvy van. Carol brought out a cup of tea for Murphy and the firemen as they sat on the pavement. Murphy passed around Margaret's chocolate.

By now members of the press were on the scene. They were asking why Murphy had been the only officer on the scene battling the lunatic. Murphy told them the senior detective had been there but had now gone back to the station. Of course, he had been drinking red wine and enjoying sweet love with his mistress throughout the evening, but if Murphy had said he had taken the Pole down single-handedly, then the senior detective would have some explaining to do to his bosses – not to mention his wife – if the story ran in the press.

And the action was not over yet. The Pole was howling and

screaming with impotent rage in the back of the van. He had braced his massive shoulders against the frame and was kicking the door. Fearing the madman would burst out and run amok in the traffic, they raced back to South Melbourne police station where they backed the van against a brick wall. Murphy ordered the much heavier "brawler" van to be brought around. The divvy van was backed away from the wall and towards the rear of the brawler, which now had its doors open. As the divvy van came to within three feet, Murphy flung open the back doors and ordered the brawler be reversed hard against the van to close the gap. The Pole exploded out of the divvy van screaming and foaming, only to run straight into the back of the brawler. They slammed the door and locked it. The operation was like transporting a wild animal. A mental ward seemed a better place for this man than a police station, so they headed for the Prince Henry Hospital in the brawler. When they got there, a little doctor came out to assess the patient. He took one look at the dishevelled Murphy, then at the bruised and blackened prisoner strapped to a gurney but still trying to escape, and straightaway suspected police brutality.

"What seems to be the trouble?" the doctor asked Murphy.

"He's a lunatic and I've brought him here to be certified," said Murphy, glad to be handing this problem over to someone else. But the doctor was sceptical.

"I, not you, will decide whether this man is of sound mind. And you will not tell me what to do, okay?" the doctor added, contemptuously. "Now take the handcuffs off this man."

"I prefer not to," said Murphy. The Pole may have been a lunatic but he could sense an opportunity to escape. He lay on the gurney, still and quiet for the first time in hours. The doctor was fast losing patience.

"You are no longer a policeman here in this hospital. You are a servant of the public, do you understand? I won't treat him unless you take the handcuffs off. Otherwise, you can take him back to the police station," he said. "He's just drunk and you've bashed him."

"Doctor, I don't think he's drunk," said Murphy. Now an officer turned up and ordered Murphy to remove the handcuffs.

"Okay, doc, okay, boss, I'll take the handcuffs off. But don't say I didn't warn you."

The doctor leaned over the Pole to smell his breath for alcohol. "Hmm, that's strange, there is no—" but before he could finish, the Pole grabbed the doctor's head in both hands and bit off most of his nose. It was hanging by the cartilage when Murphy pulled the doctor away. "HE *IS* CRAZY!" screamed the doctor, holding his nose and running from the room.

With that, the Pole burst the leather straps on the gurney and was set to wreak havoc in the casualty ward. Murphy picked up an oxygen bottle and hit him over the head with it. *KOONG!* Again the blow seemed to have no effect as he continued to advance. I'm going to have to shoot this lunatic dead to stop him, thought Murphy, going for his gun. But the Pole's eyes were spinning in his head. Like a boxer stunned by a knock-out blow, he was running out of legs and he crumpled to the floor. Murphy re-handcuffed him. Everyone had fled with the injured doctor, so Murphy gathered the papers and signed the doctor's name, certifying the Pole as mad. It was unlikely anyone would argue. The cops got him back into the brawler and took him to Royal Park Mental Hospital.

Upon arrival, they faced the prospect of getting the Pole out of the van and into the hospital. They briefed a huge German orderly who happened to speak Polish and he devised the plan. They backed the van up to the door of the hospital and opened the back. The Pole saw the German orderly leering at him, grabbing his crotch and saying in Polish: "Come here, you little sissy girl, come here and suck my dick!" With a bloodcurdling howl, the Pole rushed at him. The orderly stepped aside, tripped the lunatic and, as he fell, whacked a huge needle into his arse.

With the Pole finally subdued, Murphy could turn his attention to the senior detective, who might be reading about the epic tale in the morning's press. Murphy went to the home of the mistress and knocked on the door.

"What the hell are you doing here?" asked the senior detective, standing in the doorway in his underpants.

"Well, you lazy bastard, I know what you're doing here, but I'm here to tell you what you've really been doing before you, and your wife, read about it in the newspaper, okay?" snarled Murphy. He ran through the evening's events as the eyes of the detective grew steadily wider.

Murphy, battered and bruised, arrived home. His eyebrows were singed, his jacket torn, and he smelt of kerosene, smoke and sweat. He crept into the bedroom, wincing as he undressed in the dark. He slipped into bed next to Margaret, thankful the ordeal was over. Margaret stirred.

"Where's my chocolate?" she asked.

CHAPTER 12 HOONS, BLUDGERS AND MEMBERS OF PARLIAMENT

THE TALK ABOUT MURPHY BEING CRAZY did not bother him, and so he did nothing to contradict it. In fact, it suited him for people to think that way. "Why argue?" he used to say. "This way, I can get away with much more. And I'm useful to the bosses."

The hoons and bludgers of St Kilda learned to fear Murphy. He had no problem with prostitutes; after all, the consort of Jesus, Mary Magdalene, had been on the game and the Messiah had not judged her, so why should God's humble servant Brian Murphy be any different? Besides, the girls were very good sources of information. Standing out on a street corner for hours on end, you see things. And if your continued presence on that corner depended on cooperation with Murphy, then a deal could soon be reached. The game was pretty clean and the girls trusted him. They had fantastic memories for dates, times and car numbers, not to mention physical descriptions of blokes down to the most minute details.

As for their hoons (pimps), Murphy would persecute them mercilessly. It seemed that most of the hoons back then were Maltese or Italian. They had been low class in their countries and had sunk even lower in this one. Many had moved from Sydney to escape the heavy competition; Murphy wanted to send them back, so he locked them up or bashed them at every opportunity.

Typically a hoon would have a couple of girls working for him out of a cruddy room in St Kilda, which they would share with him and a kid or two. When the girls were sick, the hoons would beat the shit out of them and put them back on the street.

These men were the lowest form of life; their mere existence offended Murphy. He wanted them to be afraid. They were supposed to be tough guys, swaggering around the streets letting everyone know they were tooled up and ready to kill anyone who crossed them. Murphy would fly at them on sight and drop them with a headbutt for all to see. He loved hearing people laugh at them because it diminished their power and reinforced Murphy's own. But in humiliating them, he gained enemies by the score.

A hoon once decided to take Murphy down in a honey trap. He ordered one of his girls to lure Murphy up to her room on the pretext of passing on some information. Once she got him there, she started to offer Murphy free sex or money, but something was amiss: she kept gesturing towards the wardrobe. Her hoon was hiding there with a tape recorder, planning to entrap Murphy and get him thrown off the force, leaving St Kilda to the bludgers once more.

Without a word, Murphy pulled the wardrobe down and began jumping on the ply-board backing. As his boots were breaking through, the hoon began yelling and howling that Murphy was going to kill him.

"No, friend, you've got it all wrong, I'm not going to kill you by jumping on you," Murphy said, pleasantly. "I'm going to kill you," he snarled, pulling out his gun "by putting one through your head!" He cocked his .32 and held it to the hoon's temple. The hoon cried and snivelled, begging for his life. Murphy slowly squeezed the trigger – but he had already let the 10-shot

86

magazine slip out of the weapon. The hammer fell on an empty chamber; the hoon, grimacing, expecting a bullet through this head, heard instead *click! click! click!* Murphy dragged the hoon back to his room where, after administering another belting, he discovered a hidden, unlicensed firearm. He never charged the girl; although she had set the trap, she had acted out of fear. With the hoon out of the way, she could now pursue her life as she saw fit, even if it meant "hawking the fork" or "hocking the box", in the street parlance of the day. The way Murphy saw it, selling your body didn't automatically mean that your dignity went with it.

The most notorious of all the hoons was Ronny Carbine. A local legend around St Kilda, Carbine had prospered with the help of crooked coppers and desperate women in need of cash. So brazen was he that he called his St Kilda café The Blue Moon, rhyming slang for hoon.

The Blue Moon was the recruiting window for Carbine's brothel, which was little more than a cellar in Footscray, a sub-urb in the city's west. When he needed girls, he would put a sign in the window: *Vacancy Female Staff*, turned upside down. There was a steady stream of runaways, drug addicts and fugitives from girls' homes to choose from.

The brothel itself was a production line: the clients would be lined up and the girls would run along and manually prime "the population pencils", as Murphy called them, then take them into a room for intercourse lasting no more than three minutes. And that would cost them £5 a throw. The clientele were mostly recently arrived Yugoslavs and Italians, who didn't know they were being ripped off. Carbine was so successful that he bought numerous properties on his home street in St Kilda. With police contacts in his pocket, he felt untouchable. He started calling himself "The Carbine" and letting everyone know that he had guns, stolen property and coppers for the asking.

Murphy was called to Carbine's home one night after reports of a domestic dispute. Apparently, Carbine had been belting his wife and kids, screaming and carrying on so much that the neighbours had called the police. When Murphy and his partner arrived, Carbine yelled abuse, telling them this was none of their business.

"Anyway, ya sugar-bag jacks, I can buy every last one of ya!" he shouted as they questioned him in his lounge room. "I can get all youse sacked. Money means nothing to me!"

With that, Carbine pulled out a wad of money so thick he couldn't get two hands around it. With a flourish, he threw the money into the fire. He expected Murphy and his partner to dive in and retrieve it. Some cops were so greedy they would have taken money smeared in dog shit. But Murphy just stood there. Realising his mistake, Carbine lunged toward the fireplace, but Murphy pushed him back in his chair. Soon the elastic bands around the money were going *ping! ping!* while Carbine was forced to sit there and watch it all go up in flames. He was nearly sobbing with anger and fury. He went to a solicitor and wanted to have Murphy charged with the theft of the money. He claimed that by stopping him from getting his money out of the fire, Murphy had dominion and control over the money. Murphy's bosses thought the affair a great joke because they knew Carbine for the rat he was.

*

Murphy felt sympathy for working women of all kinds. They did it tough in a world full of pompous, overbearing men. They were caring for their families and trying to earn a living. While on patrol in Port Melbourne around 1960, Murphy was approached by a woman who ran a little shop next to the Victoria Hotel. She complained that drinkers from the hotel were coming outside and relieving themselves in her doorway. The urine would seep under the door and between the linoleum and the newspaper underlay, so her otherwise spotless and beautifully kept shop smelled of piss; and it got even worse with the heat in summer. The following Saturday night, Murphy sat in the gardens of the Anglican church across the road and watched the comings and goings of drinkers from the pubs. Eventually, two well-dressed couples came stumbling out of the hotel. One of the men stepped into the doorway of the woman's shop and began to relieve himself. Murphy heard his wife say in mock horror, "You're disgraceful, why don't you go inside!" It was all a great joke to them, until Murphy crossed the road.

"Good evening," he said. "What are you doing there, sir?"

The man was shocked at the sight of a policeman and struggled to stem the flow and get his weapon back in his trousers. He succeeded only in pissing in all directions, down the front of his pants and on his shoes. Murphy recognised the man. He was a local Labor member of parliament. "You dirty bastard," he said. "Have you got a handkerchief on you?"

The man, still straightening his clothes, replied that he had two, in fact, being a fastidious sort of person.

"Hand 'em over," ordered Murphy. The MP complied. Murphy took a cursory look at the handkerchiefs and handed them back. "Now you, get down on your knees and clean that bloody mess up," he growled.

The MP was aghast but he knew enough not to argue and set about the humiliating task. When he finished, he looked around for somewhere to dispose of the urine-soaked cloth.

"No, no," said Murphy. "We're not going to throw away your very nice hankies – that would be a waste. Put 'em back in your pocket and go on your way."

"No, I will not. That's an outrageous suggestion," replied the MP. "You are disgusting."

"I'm not the one pissing in doorways," said Murphy. "So put 'em back in your pocket – and if you don't, I'm going to lock you up."

The MP reluctantly took the handkerchiefs and, wincing, stuffed them in his trouser pocket. Murphy grabbed the man by the belt and slapped the pocket vigorously; soon a dark, damp patch was spreading over the expensive cream pants. Even in his humiliation, the MP was still feeling self-important. "I'm going to have your job," he snarled, preparing to walk away.

"Seeing as you are going to have my job, I'm gonna lock you up right now and your molls too," said Murphy calmly, taking out his handcuffs and baton.

The rest of the party began to complain loudly, reciting the names of the important people they knew and the dire consequences that would result if Murphy did not cease and desist.

"Since you're all carrying on and making such asses of yourselves, I'm going to lock the lot of youse up, got it? Let's go!"

The carping and whingeing stopped immediately. The women began pleading so piteously that Murphy relented and issued the MP with a summons to appear on a charge of public indecency, which might mean the end of his career. On the following day, he filled out a summary brief and lodged it with the senior sergeant. But on the Monday, one of Murphy's least favourite inspectors approached him in the station. The inspector was a dapper little man who wore yellow socks and a red tie with a matching handkerchief in his pocket, just like the MP had. He stopped next to Murphy's desk and, in a very official tone, asked, "Senior Constable Brian Murphy?"

Without looking up from his paperwork, Murphy snapped back: "He's not in."

The inspector glowered at Murphy. "I will begin again. Senior Constable Brian Murphy?"

"Yes, what can I do for you, Inspector?"

"You are in diabolical trouble. You have mammoth problems," said the inspector. "You have ridiculed a member of parliament and we cannot have that. Now—"

Murphy was tiring of this and cut him off. "Listen, Inspector," he said, looking the dapper little man up and down. "On Saturday evening, the member of parliament's member made an appearance without notice and he will have to account for that, not you and not me. So he can go and get fucked. And so can you, for that matter. You go tell him that, okay?" Murphy was now on his feet, eyeballing the inspector, who took a step backwards. The station's senior sergeant couldn't believe what he was hearing; he jumped up to intervene but Murphy stopped him with a wave of his hand.

"As far as I'm concerned, he's garbage. If his wife hadn't pleaded with me not to lock him up, he would have spent the weekend in the cells. Now unless you plan to interfere, I intend to charge him by summons for public indecency," said Murphy, picking up the paperwork. "I've got the brief right here. As a matter of fact, while you're here – you *are* an inspector, aren't you? – why don't you sign for the brief of evidence?" Murphy waved the brief in the officer's face. If Murphy pushed this, the inspector would have no choice but to sign the summons or face awkward questions from his bosses.

91

"No, no, no," said the inspector, his face now a deeper shade of red than his tie. "There'll be no need for that."

With this, Murphy was happy to tear up the summons – but only after the inspector had left the room. All he wanted was for the MP to take his piss home with him and for everyone to recognise his lawful authority. Now that had been achieved, there was no point in proceeding. Certainly, the MP would never piss in a doorway again, and deterrence being a large measure of the law, Murphy felt well satisfied.

A few months later, Murphy and another officer were called to a disturbance at a house in Richmond where a local Labor Party function was taking place. They dragged the hoon who had caused the disturbance out of the party and took him back to the station for processing. Again an inspector appeared at Murphy's desk to remonstrate with him as he typed up the paperwork.

"You can't lock this man up!" he said, putting a hand on Murphy's shoulder.

"Why ever?" asked Murphy, shrugging the hand off. His blood was rising because he knew what was coming.

"Because, *Constable*, this man is very well disposed towards Jim Cairns."

Murphy knew who Jim Cairns was: a former policeman who, with the help of some of Melbourne's worst thugs and political heavies, had made his way to a position of power in the Labor Party. He would end up deputy prime minister in the Whitlam government and one of the kookiest treasurers Australia would ever have.

"I don't care who he's tied up with," said Murphy, his eyes widening. But the inspector wasn't to be trifled with.

"If you don't do as you're told, I will pick that typewriter up and hit you with it,' said the inspector, tapping Murphy's

Remington. It was a big mistake; everyone in the room knew The Psych's very short fuse had just been lit. Murphy was turning white with rage, his eyes were standing out on stalks, but he spoke evenly.

"No, I won't let this man go ... and you won't hit me with that typewriter."

"Really? And why is that, Constable?"

"Because I'm going to *throw* the fucking thing at you!" shouted Murphy, leaping up and pitching the typewriter straight at the inspector. It hit him in the chest and crashed to the floor with a clatter of keys and cast iron.

The inspector was shocked, but he said nothing. He merely walked out of the room, shaking his head and rubbing his chest. Even Murphy was amazed that there was no follow-up. He had assaulted an inspector with a typewriter and there was no disciplinary action imposed whatsoever. Murphy's experience on the street had taught him to read people. He knew there was little an inspector could do if a senior constable failed to recognise his authority; and he was learning that just doing his job could bring him into conflict with superiors.

CHAPTER 13 ALL THE WAY WITH LBJ

MURPHY DROPPED HIS GUARD ON the afternoon of 21 October 1966 when he lost his hat. A policeman should never lose his gun or his hat. The value of the gun is obvious, the hat less so. A policeman without his hat can become a figure of ridicule – and he knows it. A small number of police can control a large crowd, but knock their hats off and the mood changes. They can't shoot you – for the most part – and there are not enough of them to arrest you. So they just stand there while everyone laughs at them.

Murphy's hat was being passed hand-to-hand through the crowd on St Kilda Road, over the Swanston Street bridge that crosses the Yarra River, the site where the Victorian Arts Centre would later be built. A few blocks away, the motorcade of United States President Lyndon Baines Johnson was approaching, en route from the airport to South Yarra, and Murphy and a handful of cops were faced with a baying mob of anti-war protesters: *LBJ! LBJ! HOW MANY KIDS DID YOU KILL TODAY?!*

The woman who approached Murphy looked like a school teacher. She was smiling uncertainly, as if she had no business among this unruly company. But as he leaned down to listen, she grabbed his hat and gleefully tossed it into the crowd. As he watched it disappear, the woman drove her knee straight up into Murphy's groin. It was such a direct hit that all the air rushed out of him and he sank to his knees. The woman stood over him with her hands raised in triumph. All he could think of, despite the sickening pain, was getting that hat back. He lunged into the crowd and grabbed it by the visor just before it disappeared forever. But now the demonstrators were surging forward onto St Kilda Road. If they managed to block it before the presidential motorcade passed, all hell would break loose. The secret-service agents travelling with Johnson had lost another president, John F. Kennedy, three years earlier in Dallas, Texas, so the security forces were edgy and heavy-handed. Murphy estimated that about 40,000 people had gathered by the Swanston Street bridge and their number was still growing.

It was the last day of the academic year and thousands of students were getting drunk in pubs up and down the city in anticipation of LBJ's arrival. Earlier that year, many of their number had won the "Lottery of Death" – the conscription ballot that would send them on a one-year tour of duty in Vietnam as national servicemen.

In May 1966, Australian Prime Minister Harold Holt had announced the death of the first national service conscript in Vietnam: 21-year-old Errol Wayne Noack. Holt had travelled to the White House in June to meet President Johnson and, while in Washington, he had given a speech which concluded with the infamous line that Australia would be "all the way with LBJ." Johnson had rewarded his new ally by becoming the first serving US president to visit Australia. The previous day, in Sydney, Johnson had been greeted by anti-war protesters lying on the road, which prompted the New South Wales premier, Robert Askin, to suggest to his driver: "Run the bastards over!"

In Melbourne, a crowd of 750,000 – nearly one-third of the city's population – turned out to greet LBJ. The morning's *Age* newspaper had advised that LBJ's motorcade would pass down

Grattan Street, Carlton, a university hub. The student mob were marshalled in the pubs along the route, ready to spill out and disrupt the motorcade. Police had barricaded the street and military helicopters hovered overhead.

But it was a ruse: instead the presidential convoy headed straight down Elizabeth Street, bypassing Carlton. When the students realised, they surged through the city trying to get ahead of the motorcade before it got to St Kilda Road. LBJ had slowed progress by constantly stopping to get out and shake hands with well-wishers. By the time the convoy approached the river where Murphy and a handful of officers were positioned, the demonstrators had re-grouped. If they broke through here and reached the motorcade, there would be blood and broken policemen all over the road.

Enter Senior Sergeant Keith Ludwig Plattfuss of the Breaking Squad. He saw Murphy go down and, like a charging rhinoceros, he rushed into the mob. By the time Murphy retrieved his hat, Plattfuss had grabbed the female assailant by the head and driven her hard into the hindquarters of a police horse. If he had slammed her any harder, she could well have been wearing the horse for a hat. The horse lashed out with both back legs, somehow missing the imposing figure of Plattfuss and the woman but striking a couple of other protesters. Plattfuss swung around and crashed his fist into a couple of faces, sending bodies flying.

Pandemonium reigned as the burly sergeant and a few colleagues flung themselves into the crowd, leading with fists and elbows. These particular protesters were not the non-violent peace-loving demonstrators of the later years of the Vietnam struggle but rather a rag-tag mix of students and trade unionists for whom bloody confrontation was a terrific day of sport. And

Plattfuss was happy to indulge them. In full flight, he was an extraordinary sight, seventeen stone and more than six foot, but light on his feet, a legacy of his days as the heavyweight boxing champion of the 9th Division of the Australian Imperial Force during World War II.

Plattfuss came over to Murphy, who was still gasping for air, trying to recover from the blow to the groin. Murphy had heard of Plattfuss but never met him. Everyone in the force knew "The Puss", as he was called, but only behind his back. He was a fearsome sight with that massive block of a head, flecked and serrated with scars and sun spots and topped off with big, cauliflower ears. He had hands as big as ham hocks and arms to match. He looked at Murphy, concerned; his eyebrows knitted like bow lines from a ship.

"You alright there, cunty?" he boomed.

"Bit green around the gills, boss, but I'll live," said Murphy.

"Good, well let's pull some of these bastards into gear," roared Plattfuss. Murphy was only too happy to join the fray. At the senior sergeant's elbow, he was like an infantryman picking off stragglers in the wake of the Plattfuss battle tank. Soon there was no-one willing to take up Plattfuss's offer to have a go.

The motorcade got past the choke point without further incident and headed towards South Yarra, where LBJ was to dine at Government House and attend a festival. If LBJ had been looking out his window he might have seen Murphy and The Puss in hot pursuit of protesters across the Alexandra Gardens. It was a battle that would last all afternoon and into the evening. As the motorcade arrived in South Yarra, two protesters, brothers David and John Langley, had thrown green and red paint bombs at LBJ's car and his secret service detail. David Langley later wrote in a book how a US agent had punched him in the face

97

after he launched his paint bomb. His brother was dragged into a laneway and severely beaten by some other agents.

The Puss hated protesters with a passion and drove the men on that day. As befitting a heavyweight boxer, he had a sledge-hammer-like punch. It didn't matter whether he connected with the head or the body, they went down just the same.

He had served in North Africa and Borneo during the war. He believed he had done something worthwhile for his country by fighting totalitarianism. Now these students were rubbishing the men in uniform who were fighting to stop communism from sweeping through South-East Asia. He believed in the Domino Theory, which held that if Vietnam was lost, one Asian country after another would fall to communism. The student radicals had fought pitched ideological battles with right-wing forces like the National Civic Council and the Democratic Labor Party, who advocated increased involvement in Vietnam for Australian forces. The left-wingers were a small force back in 1966; the majority of the population did indeed want to go all the way with LBJ. It appalled patriots like The Puss that any Australians would welcome the communists into the country he had fought for. Now Plattfuss, with Murphy in tow, was doing his best to knock over a few dominoes of his own.

The protesters gave as good as they got. Murphy saw as many as thirty police bashed that day. Force Command had ordered all able-bodied officers to join the fray. Mick Miller, now in charge of detective training, even had his trainees on the job of crowd control. For Miller, it had been a day of drama but he never let his men get out of control for a moment. For him, politics and personal hatred had no bearing on the job he was asked to do. Like it said on the Victoria Police badge: *Uphold the Right.*

Darkness was falling over the Alexandra Gardens when Mick Miller saw two dishevelled characters coming toward him through the gloom – Murphy and The Puss. While every officer had been briefed on his duty that day, here was a pair acting on their own initiative. This looks like a fighting patrol, thought Miller. Murphy's uniform was torn and there were a couple of fresh bruises on his face. The Puss had a thin line of blood trickling down a corner of his mouth.

"Here, Murphy! Come over here!" Miller called as they passed.

"Yes, boss," said Murphy, his eyes wide and wild.

"If you go with Plattfuss, you'll be filling out reports for six months arising from this day. If you stick with me, then nothing will happen to you whatsoever," said Miller.

Murphy was torn. Miller represented all that was good and proper in policing. He had made Murphy believe that it was possible to enforce the law without worrying about whether justice would ultimately be done. Miller had shown him that a man could have dash and not compromise either his principles or the law, and his fellows would accept and support him.

But what Murphy had seen since the Gamers made him believe that Mick Miller was in the tiny minority of bosses. Murphy had seen the weak, corrupt underbelly of the police force, the lazy sugar bags who sold their men out. He had seen guilty men go free. He had seen evil, worthless men get away with standing over women and children. He had seen bad laws make bad policemen. Sure, Miller represented the law, but this rough, tough bastard Plattfuss represented order and maybe even justice, if only in summary form. Order derived its authority from the law, but its force was the policeman wielding it. Here was the great turning point in Murphy's career. Miller would go on to become Victoria's chief commissioner, a force for change. He saw the future coming when the ends would no longer justify the means, a time when men like Keith Plattfuss would no longer have a place. Plattfuss, who had trained with Miller, would end up a detective-inspector, yet even he may have sensed that his time was nearly up. But it would not stop him doing what was right. And Murphy wanted to be there with him.

He looked up at Miller and said quietly, "Thanks, boss, but I'll go with The Puss."

Of course, Miller was right. Murphy was served with six summonses for common assault on protesters that day. Other officers faced assault charges and it was customary for their colleagues to give evidence in their defence. Murphy had agreed to give evidence for another officer, expecting the favour to be returned. However, the officer declined, saying he did not have Murphy in his diary for that day; he had a cushy job running the lost property office at Russell Street headquarters and he saw no reason to put that at risk by helping Murphy. When Plattfuss heard, he marched straight down to the property office. The door was closed and the officer was playing opera on a gramophone, reading the newspaper with his feet up on the desk.

"Here, why didn't you make a statement for Murphy?" snorted Plattfuss, glowering down at the man. "He gave a statement for you. You saw what happened to Murphy, what's the problem?"

"Well boss, he's not in my diary ..." stammered the officer. Plattfuss ground his teeth and pointed a thick sausage finger in the man's face.

"Well, you fucking imbecile, your diary is incomplete then. You might as well get off your arse right now, because I'm going to make damn sure you're on foot patrol when your next shift begins," he growled. Then he stomped out of the property office, slamming the door. That was Plattfuss. Loyalty was a two-way street, no matter the cost of the freight.

And Murphy wasn't cheap. The press on Murphy's LBJ-Day charges gave an insight into his policing. The *Herald* newspaper of 21 December 1966 recorded that:

> an anti-Vietnam sympathiser claimed in South Melbourne Court that [Murphy had threatened]: "I'm going to take you to Port Melbourne and shoot you dead."
>
> Brian Herbert Workman, 36, had been at the front of the crowd at 5:30 pm on Johnson's return from Government House into the city.
>
> "The crowd surged forward and policemen, including Murphy, started throwing punches," Workman told the court.
>
> "Murphy hit me three or four times in the face and I raised my knee near his groin."
>
> He was thrown into a police car and taken to Russell Street headquarters.
>
> "At Russell Street Murphy said, 'You're the b— who kneed me. You put me in the gutter.'
>
> "I heard him say to others, 'Well, whose prisoner is he?'"
>
> "Yours, if you want," came the reply.
>
> Workman claimed that Murphy had handcuffed him and driven him to Port Melbourne Police Station, threatening to shoot him on the way.
>
> "At Port Melbourne we went to a back room and Murphy shut the blinds. I emptied my pockets including some 'no conscripts to Vietnam' pamphlets.
>
> "Murphy would question me, jump up and hit me and sit down and resume questioning. This happened several times. He also jumped on my feet and hit me with a large bag."

Murphy's defence, through his barrister Ray Dunn, was to encourage Workman to begin raving about his activism. Surely the best way to protest against President Johnson was to stop the presidential car, Dunn asked.

Workman answered: "I consider Johnson's policy conducive to war. I am a communist."

That made him an enemy of the state, hardly likely to win an assault case against an officer of the state such as Murphy.

Mr Foley, SM, in dismissing the charges against Murphy and fining Workman $50 for kneeing Murphy in the balls, said, "I do not believe beyond a reasonable doubt that Workman was assaulted. But I am perturbed that he was taken from Russell Street to Port Melbourne and then back to Russell Street."

Workman could think himself lucky that Murphy hadn't taken the scenic route via Williamstown.

*

Plattfuss had made such a strong impression on Murphy that he was determined to show his gratitude. He learned that Plattfuss was an avid fly fisherman, so he went out and bought a top-of-the-line Mitchell reel and went to Russell Street to present it to him.

Plattfuss was sitting at his desk in shirt sleeves typing a report on a big old manual Remington when Murphy walked in. He had his battered trilby hat perched on the back of his head, his tie was askew and one suspender twisted. A cigarette drooped from the corner of his mouth with a long tip of ash. The front of his shirt and tie were dusted with ash where he had let it fall, so intent was he on the task before him. He was slowly and deliberately punching the keys of the typewriter, hard enough to perforate steel.

"G'day, boss!" said Murphy. The Puss cocked one bushy eyebrow.

"What the fuck are you doing here?" he snarled.

"Boss, I just wanted to thank you for your help and support out there at the demo the other week," said Murphy.

"Don't need your thanks, cunty, just doing my fucking job," said Plattfuss, looking back down at his typewriter.

"No, but I wanted to thank you just the same," said Murphy. "I wanted to give you this as a token. I heard you were a top angler." He handed over the package.

"What the hell is this?" asked Plattfuss.

"It's a Mitchell …"

"I know it's a Mitchell, you imbecile! Why are you giving this to me, trying to suck up or something?" asked The Puss, but his voice was cracking. Murphy couldn't believe it; The Puss stood up from his desk and turned away to hide the big fat tears that were rolling down his cheek. "Thanks," he grunted after a moment, pretending to look for something on the shelf behind him. "Now fuck off out of here!"

CHAPTER 14   A PUSS IN HOBNAIL BOOTS

PLATTFUSS HAD MADE HIS name as a policeman on the streets of Richmond in the 1950s and 1960s. This inner-city suburb is gentrified now, and most of the single-fronted, timber workers' cottages have been renovated. *For Sale* signs boast of chic, alfresco entertainment areas and easy access to Bridge Road café society and the picturesque Yarra River. Back in Plattfuss's day it was a squalid slum, full of misery and despair, and home to some of the city's most active villains. Good people didn't like to linger in Richmond at night, such was its reputation. Factories lined the Yarra and poured their effluent into its waters, until the river seemed to run more slowly, just a thick, sluggish ooze of brown and green gunk. Its pubs were the lairs of Painters and Dockers, fences and petty crims, pickpockets from the pony track. To survive here, a policeman needed to be strong or to stay behind his desk at the station. Plattfuss waded into the human tide of Richmond like a blue centurion. The criminal class of the area may have felt respect for him, but for Plattfuss, fear was good enough.

Stories abounded about his exploits. Back in the mid-1950s, Joseph Patrick Turner, alias Joseph Patrick Monash, had been a fizz – an informer – on the rise. He had graduated to armed robbery and other criminal lurks largely on the strength of his special relationship with bent police. But to Plattfuss, Turner was a treacherous cur, a double agent willing to give his mates up to protect his own interests.

One day, when stationed in Richmond, The Puss picked up Turner and another head, Miles Patrick O'Reilly, on suspicion of breaking and entering. Turner was an angry little man and as Plattfuss questioned the pair in his first-floor office, he told the detective he was nothing but a big German bastard. The Puss swung around and hit him, knocking him clean out of the window and onto the driveway below. Turner lay there motionless but Plattfuss thought he was playing doggo.

"Get up off the ground. If you don't, you're going to be sorry," Plattfuss bellowed from the window. But Turner wasn't interested in returning to the first floor and said he would lie there as long as he wanted to. So Plattfuss took his old, heavy Remington typewriter and threw it at Turner. It crashed onto his chest. Plattfuss shut the window. He ordered the watch-house keeper to pick up the typewriter, or as many pieces as he could. "But leave that other bastard there, I'll look after him later. I'm dealing with Mr O'Reilly at present," he said, turning to his remaining prisoner.

O'Reilly, having seen all this, immediately caved in and signed up for two or three armed robberies he'd committed, putting in every other villain he could think of. Turner, meanwhile, was still lying on the driveway, groaning, whimpering and gasping for air. The young officer in the watch-house was concerned he was going have a dead body on his hands and called an ambulance. He dragged Turner to the front of the police station and told the ambulancemen he had found him lying there – it appeared he had been hit by a car.

When he had finished with O'Reilly, Plattfuss came down and asked who had called the ambulance. The young officer reluctantly owned up, saying that he didn't want to wear one of his boss's mistakes. All The Puss said was: "Good job, laddie."

The following day, The Puss went to visit Turner in St Vincent's Hospital, where he was nursing a broken sternum and several cracked ribs, courtesy of The Puss's touch typing. He leaned in close to Turner: "That's only the start of your problems, cunty. You've busted your sternum and five or six ribs. But when you get out, I'm gonna be waiting for you and I'm gonna give it to you again. And it won't be your sternum next time, it'll be your spine. You'll never walk again. Do you understand me?"

Turner nodded his head and asked The Puss to come back tomorrow. Then he gave up every one of his mates – sparing himself, of course – and The Puss ended up solving every break-in from Richmond to Bendigo to as far away as Portsea; a good day's work.

*

By the late '60s, Plattfuss was running the Breaking Squad and Murphy was his right-hand man. Murphy was the only one who could control his ferocious boss. They were a team of fifteen men who worked tirelessly around the clock when a job needed to be done. It was nothing for the Breakers to work three days straight, taking catnaps in their offices or on benches outside the Supreme Court as they waited to give evidence against suspects they had brought in. The Puss had something to prove. The squad had previously been run by crooked bosses who could only nab a safebreaker when they knew where he was going to strike – and that was usually because they were in on the job. The Puss was honest and morally upright; he was going to show the crooks how policing ought to be done.

Once he and members of his team followed a team of breakers for nearly five hours into Victoria's high country. Concerned that they might slip over the border into New South

Wales, Plattfuss gave the order to open fire on the highway. When the villain's car slewed off the road and into the undergrowth, one of the young cops was exultant.

"Hey, boss, I aimed for the bloke's tyres and I hit 'em," he trilled.

"That's good, son. I aimed straight for his fucking head and I hit him in the fucking head," deadpanned Plattfuss.

These kinds of stories filled Murphy with righteous purpose, if not common sense. In mid-1969, the squad was called to a break-in underway at a store on the corner of Glenferrie and Barkers roads, Hawthorn. Murphy approached the scene in a squad car with two other officers, Laurie Pitts and Jack Grey, just as the three villains were about to make their getaway. The squad car screeched to a halt and Murphy jumped out, lined them up with his .38 and let a shot go that ripped through the car door and into the leg of the driver, Aubrey John Carter. But the bullet didn't stop Carter and he tried to run Murphy over, narrowly missing him as he dived to one side. Adrenalin was pumping through Murphy now. He always told his kids not to worry about taking drugs; they had the best drug in the world coursing free through their veins. In moments like these, Murphy was as high as a kite on the stuff.

He jumped into the back seat and shouted at Pitts to give chase. "FASTER, FASTER PITTSY!" he yelled into the young officer's ear when the villains looked like getting away.

"Murph, I'm driving as fast as I can!" Pitts shouted. Murphy jammed his gun into the back of Pitts's neck and drew the hammer back.

"Pittsy, you drive faster or you won't be driving anywhere again," said Murphy, his eyes standing out on stalks. Jack Grey couldn't believe what he was seeing; they were supposed to be chasing crooks and here he was, about to witness a murder in the squad car. Grey, showing enormous courage, jammed his thumb between the hammer and the firing pin. He was calm but insistent.

"Brian," he said, "just let it off … gently, let it off and settle down!" Murphy looked wildly at Grey and then at the gun against his colleague's neck. He was so pumped, he felt like he could have shot everyone there and then. The red mist slowly cleared and Murphy came back to reality. He let the hammer off and pinned Grey's thumb. The chase continued.

The villains ditched their car in North Fitzroy but with a bullet wound in his thigh, Carter wasn't getting far and his accomplices were soon rounded up by the back-up units that had joined the mad chase. Carter was losing blood at a great rate when the ambulance men got to him. He was lucky: the bullet had just missed his femoral artery. One millimetre was the margin between life and death for him that day. But Murphy, still flying on adrenalin and anger, ran over and punched Carter as he lay on the gurney, which was being wheeled by an ambulance man.

"Turn it up!" cried the ambo. "This man's seriously wounded!"

"This man just tried to kill me with a bloody car!" said Murphy, grinding his teeth.

"Fair dinkum?" asked the ambo.

"Yeah. Correct weight!" replied Murphy. The ambo flipped the gurney up on two wheels and Carter dropped onto the road with a sickening thud.

"Prick!" said the ambo.

*

The success of the LBJ protests sparked a wave of demonstrations denouncing Australia's involvement in Vietnam. When called to man police lines, Murphy would wear a badge under his lapel, *Make Love Not War.* When confronted by protesters, he would flash the badge, smile and wink as if to say he was on their side. This ruse allowed him to get among the demonstrators, whereupon he would poleaxe a ringleader or two and drag them out. But by 1970, popular opinion was changing on the Vietnam War. In 1966, the protesters at the LBJ visit had been a tiny minority. The anti-war movement was now a broad-based coalition of students, left-wing unionists and workers. The spectacle of police brutally putting down demonstrators was alarming to the general public, who had previously supported Australia's involvement. Television images of baton-wielding police creasing the skulls of nice middle-class kids made people think twice about the war.

In September 1970, a small group of students from La Trobe University tried to march down Waterdale Road, Heidelberg, from the university to nearby factories, hoping to rally the workers with their anti-war message. Until then, the Maoist faction had been a small, uninfluential group within La Trobe's Labor Club and had struggled to gain much support for their "Anti-Imperialist Week". The march had been the centrepiece of the week's activities, but the New Left – La Trobe's dominant political grouping – had sabotaged proceedings by deliberately scheduling an anti-war movie at the same time. Consequently, only seventy students had turned up for the march. They had walked just two blocks when police, wielding batons, chased them back onto the campus. There was outrage at the police tactics and 400 students and staff joined forces for a follow-up march.

Plattfuss was the inspector in charge that day when police confronted the mob again. He planned "to pull the bastards into gear", just like when LBJ came to town in 1966. He led a full-scale baton charge worthy of anything he had seen in North Africa. The students had taunted Plattfuss to bring out the batons again and he didn't disappoint. "If it's baton they want, it's baton they'll get," Plattfuss said before giving the order.

There were reports that police had pursued students onto campus with guns drawn, threatening to shoot those who tried to escape. At least one student was reportedly arrested at gun point.

When they had beaten the students back, Plattfuss, completely impervious to the changing political winds, told the press: "They got some baton today and they'll get a lot more in the future." The Battle of Waterdale became an enduring cause among the Left, helping consolidate the different factions against the so-called brutality of the capitalist state.

A third march was held; this time, the numbers swelled to 800. Builders' labourers, wharfies and plumbers joined the students and, defiantly, they all headed down Waterdale Road. The police, chastened by a storm of criticism of The Puss's baton charge, softened their tactics and failed in an attempt to push the march off the road.

There was nothing personal or political in Plattfuss's actions; he was no capitalist stooge. He wasn't anyone's stooge. What he saw coming towards him down Waterdale Road that spring day was not a threat to the capitalist hegemony but a breakdown of public order, a mob blocking traffic and showing disrespect to police, even threatening them with violence. And that could not be tolerated.

When the protesters who were charged came to court, The Puss was there to give evidence for the Crown. When they saw him, they jeered and cat-called, yelling out he was a fascist. It affected him deeply – he had seen how real fascists had operated in World War II and there was no worse insult you could hurl. The students were amazed when they saw tears rolling down The Puss's cheeks as he sat in court. A couple of the students approached to apologise for upsetting him and, at lunch, they joined him for a cup of tea. When they returned after lunch, they changed their pleas to guilty.

Back then, police rarely revealed their inner thoughts about politics and religion. Such talk was actively discouraged for the divisions it created. The bloke sitting next to you in the muster room in the morning could save your life later that day. If you were a Catholic and he a Protestant and you argued over religion, then you could never be sure whether he might leave you for dead. So you never heard debates over such things inside a police station. In The Puss's mind, there were only two sides: the men and the crooks. Even the bosses became the enemy when they penny-pinched on resources or failed to back the men.

A cop could never let an enemy get over the top of him, not even for a minute. If they got away with belting a copper, there was no telling what they would do to ordinary members of the public. One night in mid-1969, Plattfuss sent Murphy and another officer, Paul Higgins, to arrest a group of safebreakers. Diplomacy having failed, a wild brawl broke out in the house. Murphy was in the hall when one of the crims came running at him. Murphy jumped up and grabbed the fretwork of a timber frame that divided the hall of the house. He kicked him flush under the chin but the timber gave way and he fell hard to the wooden floor, damaging his back and ribs. Hearing the commotion, Higgins ran in the front door with a shotgun but tripped on the step and the gun discharged, blowing the Christmas cake out of the light fitting. Taking control of the situation, the cops gave the robbers such a terrible hiding they ended up in hospital.

The next morning when Murphy went to work, he could hardly move. The Puss spotted him and shambled over. "How did you go last night, cunty?"

"Fine thanks, boss, but I've got a shirt full of sore ribs."

"Someone gave it to ya last night?"

Murphy recounted his disastrous acrobatics display and Plattfuss nearly wet himself laughing. Then his face hardened.

"Now listen you, when you got over the top of him, did he scream?" Murphy replied that the man had gone to hospital. Plattfuss came close and stood right over Murphy. "I'm not asking if he went to fucking hospital, I'm asking if he asked you for mercy!"

"Well, yes, he did," replied Murphy.

"Did he shout and scream? Did he beg you long for mercy?"

"As a matter of fact, he did."

"That's good," said The Puss, well satisfied with Murphy. "He'll learn a lesson from that."

This authority was all important to Plattfuss's image as a policeman. Respect for the police was waning as the 1960s wore on. The "clip over the ear" and the "boot up the arse" had been a long-accepted part of policing. The constable delivered summary justice on the run; that way, the state was spared the expense of court and incarceration for minor offences. Villains never complained, because they knew they couldn't win; but the anti-Vietnam protests had brought police brutality into the open, focusing the attention of the middle class on its civil rights and obligations. The age of "the bash" was drawing to a close just as a golden era of armed robbery and violence was beginning in Victoria. In 1970, armed robberies had nearly tripled to 144 from just 56 in 1969. In 1971, there were 171 stickups, and this figure steadily rose over the 1970s. The crims were losing their fear of the cops. But Plattfuss and Murphy were notable exceptions to this new dispensation.

CHAPTER 15 THE BREAKERS

To The Puss, there was no such thing as a shift or a roster. When there was a job, he was on duty and so was everyone else. This never bothered Murphy in the slightest. During his first holiday in 1955, Murphy had spent every night hiding in a park, for a week, in an area where a cat burglar had been breaking houses. He got his man (who turned out to be a woman). Now The Puss offered Murphy a whole new world of adventure and it could start at any hour.

It would begin with a knock on the Murphys' front door from a local policeman any time between midnight and dawn. They didn't have the telephone connected until 1971.

"Mr Plattfuss asked me to pass on an urgent message: Get out of bed and get your gear on. I will pick you up in twenty minutes." The Puss would round up two carloads of detectives and set off to some undefined destination.

On this night in 1969, The Puss had woken up at 2 a.m. with a nagging thought. There had been a string of unsolved break-ins at grocery stores and other merchants' premises in the Prahran area. Suddenly, an idea struck him and that was the end of sleep for the night.

"Where are we going, boss?" asked Murphy eagerly, already firing up. At moments like these, the promise of a big adrenalin rush would set his stomach rumbling like a goods train going through the mountains.

"Why do you want to know? I'll tell you in ten minutes. All shall be revealed," Plattfuss replied. He puffed his massive chest out, grinning at his oracle-like power. The two carloads of detectives pulled up outside a house in Prahran.

"Right, cunty," said Plattfuss. "Have you ever heard of a head named Ivan Alfred Kane?" Murphy knew of him but had never been to his home. Earlier that year, Ivan had tried to break into a leather-goods warehouse. Police were called and he tried to escape by climbing onto the roof. One of the cops had shot him in the buttock, knocking him off the roof.

"Well, this is his place. Let's pay him a visit!" said Plattfuss.

When Ivan Kane, in his underwear, opened the door, it was his size that first took Murphy aback. He was even bigger than Plattfuss: over six foot two and twenty stone. He was as powerful a man as Murphy had ever seen. With The Puss leading the way, the cops followed Ivan down the corridor to the kitchen. There was a large amount of meat sitting on the table: all kinds of cuts from steak and veal, chops and spare ribs through to sausages and fancy sweetmeats, spread out on butcher's paper on the table.

"What the fuck's this?" snarled The Puss.

"It's meat," replied Ivan.

"I know what it is. What's it doing here?"

"Well, I am a butcher," said Ivan.

"Is that right? Well, cunty, show us how a butcher would deal with this lot," he challenged.

"No problem," said Ivan, throwing on an apron and expertly sharpening his carving knife on a whetstone. He proceeded to slice half a dozen perfect steaks from a side of beef. He carved like a pro – and the Puss thought that maybe he had this one wrong after all.

"Since I've got all this out, why don't I cook you blokes a meal?" asked Ivan. It was nearly 4 a.m. and the idea of a cooked breakfast was welcome. Soon Ivan had set out a feast: steaks, sausages, chops and sweetmeats topped off with fried onions, garlic and tomatoes. The detectives and Ivan sat around the table eating and chatting amiably about all manner of things. It was after 5 a.m. when The Puss pushed back the table and motioned for his men to return to Russell Street.

"Well, that was very nice of you, laddie. I'm feeling very full indeed," he said. It was dawn when they pulled into the garage at headquarters. On the radio, the despatcher at D24 was calling for units to attend a job at Dingley on the edge of the suburbs. A butcher's shop had been broken into and a large amount of assorted meats, as well as cash, had been stolen.

The Puss's face darkened to a furious shade of puce. "Don't you turn that fucking ignition off," he snarled, grinding his teeth like millstones. When they got back to Ivan's place, all the meat was gone; there was not a trace, the kitchen was spotless, and there was no sign of the meal the police and Ivan had enjoyed just half an hour earlier.

"Where's the fucking meat?" growled The Puss.

"What meat?" asked Ivan.

"I bet you could find some of it if I punched you in the guts," said The Puss, drawing one hammer fist back. Ivan flinched visibly. He might have been bigger than The Puss but Murphy could tell he was a big softie, a gentle giant. He took a shine to Ivan from that moment on. He admired the coolness and dash of a bloke who could get caught red-handed with stolen property and end up feeding it to the police. But for duping The Puss, Ivan was going to get a thorough going-over once they got back to Russell Street.

On the ride back to town Murphy sat in the back seat with Ivan while Plattfuss rode in the front.

"Couple of things you should know, Ivan," whispered Murphy. "Remember, his name is Mr Platypus, okay?" Ivan nodded. "Secondly, when Mr Platypus is interrogating you, watch him very carefully. If he comes and sits on the corner of the desk and pushes his hat back on his head with his right hand and takes a drag on his cigarette, you are about to get the best left hook you've ever had, right under the ribs, okay?"

Ivan's eyes widened. The Puss threw Murphy a dark look over his shoulder.

"What are you two bastards talking about?"

"Nothing, boss, just what a good bloke you are," said Murphy, winking at Ivan.

When they got to Russell Street, The Puss took Ivan to an interrogation room almost in the basement.

"Now, you're in a lot of trouble, laddie," he said, taking a long powerful drag on his cigarette.

"Yes, Mr Platypus," said Ivan meekly. The Puss spun around in an explosion of smoke and spittle.

"WHAT DID YOU CALL ME?"

"Mr … P-Platypus," Ivan stammered. The Puss leaned across the desk until he was eyeball to eyeball with Ivan.

"THE NAME IS PLATTFUSS … NOT PLATYPUS! DO I LOOK LIKE A PLATYPUS TO YOU, SON?"

"No, Mr Platypus, I mean Mr Plattfuss." Ivan was trembling. The Puss flashed a dark look at Murphy. He had pulled this Mr Platypus routine before with other prisoners, but the cheeky, bald-headed bastard could wait. He sighed and moved around the table. Ivan was watching every movement.

Just as Murphy had predicted, Plattfuss sat on the edge of the table, pushed his hat back with his right hand and took a long drag on his cigarette. Before The Puss had even time to expel the smoke, Ivan had flung himself to the floor and rolled up in a ball. This made The Puss even more furious.

"Get up off there, you. I haven't even taken a swing at you yet and you're already taking a dive! Get up!"

"I might be mad, but I'm not going to get up to cop one of your left hooks," said Ivan from the safety of the floor.

By about 11 a.m., Ivan had signed up for the butcher break-in and three other jobs. It turned out that Ivan had hidden the stolen money under the paper that had been on the table where the cops had eaten.

Ivan was processed and behind bars but Plattfuss was not finished for the day. He had been pursuing a breaker named Ferdie Thomas, who lived out in Oakleigh, and now he rallied the troops for a raid on his house.

When the Breakers kicked the door in, Thomas scarpered out the back and over the fence. The Puss sent an officer after him and calmly pulled out his .38, waiting to draw a bead on Thomas as he scaled the next fence. But every time he had Thomas lined up, the cop in hot pursuit would bob up in the line of fire.

"Get after him, cunty! He's getting away, you lazy bastard!" roared The Puss in frustration. But the cop was a plodder and Thomas showed him a clean pair of heels. Relaxing a little, Thomas decided to double back to get his car in the driveway of his house. Surely the coast would be clear. But when he turned the corner into the driveway, still running full tilt, there was Murphy and Plattfuss. The Puss planted a huge right hand on Thomas that stopped him dead – he crashed to the ground, knocked clean out.

"Handcuff this one, would you, Murphy," ordered Plattfuss.

It was a typical day with the Breakers. They had mustered at 2 a.m. and they were still going at 8 p.m. that night. They brought their prisoner back to Russell Street, processed him, and still Plattfuss wasn't finished. He called Murphy into his office.

"Good job today, laddie," he said, cigarette ash falling on his shirt for the umpteenth time that day. "Get the blokes in here, there's something I want to discuss with them, okay?" Murphy reached over the desk and brushed the ash off the boss's shirt, to the Puss's irritation. Only Murphy could get away with something like that.

"I would, boss, but I've already sent them home," said Murphy.

"You did what? I was going to do that! How dare you, you baldy-headed presumptuous bastard!"

"Well, they've gone home to their wives and so should you. I'll drive you home, boss," said Murphy.

"Don't you bloody tell me how to run this squad, you cheeky prick," he grumbled, but he was putting on his coat. Even this blue centurion knew when it was time to call it a day. And even after a day and a half like this, Murphy knew there was no guarantee there wouldn't be another knock at the door at 2 a.m. the next morning.

CHAPTER 16 RAISING KANE

DESPITE FALLING FOUL OF THE PUSS, Ivan Alfred Kane would keep the Breakers busy for the next few months. He was running hot; he couldn't help himself. He enjoyed the thrill of stealing stuff as much as Murphy enjoyed locking him up. One of his favourite larks was to break into homes, creep into the bedrooms and lift the jewellery off the bodies of sleeping residents. He would return flushed with excitement from these expeditions and wake up his wife.

"Look what I've got, love!" he would exclaim.

Two nights after being released on bail, Ivan went down to Portsea, a beach-side holiday playground for the rich, but he had forgotten it was a holiday weekend and that all the owners were in residence. So he stole a forty-foot boat from a marina instead and towed it all the way to a buyer in Albury – eight hours' drive north – on the New South Wales border.

A week later, Murphy heard over the radio that police were chasing a man suspected of a smash and grab on an electrical appliance shop. Disturbed by the owner, the thief had run off with a television set. The owner had let fly with a shotgun and thought he had wounded the thief. Murphy got on the radio and asked what model the car was – it was a red utility, just like Ivan's. Damn, thought Murphy, I could lose a good fizz here; he asked the police to take it nice and easy. Since saving him from The Puss's heavy hand, Murphy had taken a shine to Kane and an important relationship was developing.

At that moment, the police were chasing Ivan at high speed, firing shots at his tyres to slow him down. He nearly managed to outrun them on the rims of two flat tyres, but he gave up and they dragged him out of his ute. The store owner had peppered him with the shotgun and he was oozing blood from sixty pellet holes in his back. They threw him in the police car and one of the officers cracked him over the head with a torch. He complained loudly, saying if they just got Brian Murphy he would confess everything. But they didn't want Murphy sticking his oar in, so the officer hit him over the head again to shut him up. Handcuffed, shot and torch-whipped, Ivan exercised the only protest remaining to him – he stuck his fingers down his throat and threw up all over his tormentors. They stopped the car with a screech and called Murphy. When he got there, Ivan was hand-cuffed and lying on the footpath. The police were standing around disconsolately, splattered with the contents of Ivan's voluminous stomach.

"Mr Murphy, am I glad to see you," cried Ivan. "I kept telling these blokes to get hold of you and they kept hitting me!"

"C'mon now, Ivan, behave yourself and tell them whatever they want to know and they'll look after you," said Murphy.

"Fair dinkum?" asked Ivan.

"Fair dinkum." And with that, Kane went quietly away with the other police and made a full confession.

The doctors left most of the pellets in Ivan's back and Murphy visited him in hospital as he recovered, even smuggling in a can of beer to quench Ivan's considerable thirst. Ivan felt so bad about vomiting on the cops that he paid for their dry-cleaning out of his own pocket: a villain with a conscience.

Not that it stopped him from conducting hundreds more of his "midnight shopping" trips. Another night, as he was fleeing from the scene of yet another botched robbery, the police fired a volley that startled him so much he ran straight out of his size-16 moccasins. As soon as Murphy heard about the moccasins, he called Ivan.

"How do you know they're mine?" asked Ivan, a little indignantly.

"There's nobody we know with feet that big. The Puss says if your feet were any bigger you'd be paying land tax," replied Murphy. Ivan laughed and admitted they were his.

Ivan eventually got five years in jail on Murphy's testimony. He wrote to Murphy from inside to thank him for the way he had treated him and promised to repay Murphy's kindness. And so it was that, largely on the strength of his relationship with Murphy, Ivan agreed to give evidence to the Beach Inquiry into police corruption in 1976. Villains were lining up to give evidence against policemen like Murphy who were prepared to do deals with criminals. Barristers didn't like such deals; it brought down their acquittal rates and made them look like fools when their clients, after deep and meaningful dialogue with police, would return to court and change their pleas. Deal-making was a stock-in-trade of policing back then – not over murders, as occurred during Melbourne's recent gangland wars, but over break-ins and armed robberies.

If you cut a good deal, you might clear up a couple of hundred break-ins and get a lot of property back for the victims. If Murphy arrested someone for a break-in who then told him about a murder, he would often just let him go. The problem with such deals was that the language used in these confessions was strikingly similar from case to case. Many of the briefs

used the same words; lines such as "Oh shit, you got me copper" made them appear to have been produced from a pro
forma. Barristers got together and agitated for an inquiry and
every crim jumped on the bandwagon, telling stories about
being assaulted, verballed or framed on false charges. A crim
named Sammy Hutchins gave evidence against Murphy, and
the inquiry's chief, Barry Beach, QC, recommended that Murphy be charged on thirteen counts of conspiracy to pervert the
course of justice. But he never was. Thirty-three of the fifty-five
officers named in the inquiry were charged, but none was convicted. The Police Association held a public rally to protest and
under political pressure the Hamer Government established a
review of Beach's findings; most of his recommendations were
overturned. Ivan was the only villain to jump the box and give
evidence for the police; magnificent, truthful testimony, according to Murphy. However, it made him plenty of enemies in the
underworld: if Ivan Kane would give evidence for the coppers,
what would he say about fellow crims to get himself out of jail?

Before he went inside, Ivan had been at Joey Turner's place
and had learned that he and his gang were planning to kill a
bloke named Cosi Costello, who was later found at the beginning of the F19 freeway – before it became the South-Eastern –
with his face and hands blown off. Ivan told Murphy that Joey
Turner had done it. Murphy told the Homicide Squad but they
did nothing.

The day before Ivan was due to be released from Dhurringile
Prison near the northern Victorian town of Shepparton, Murphy received a call from Inspector Mick Patterson, who was in
charge of the CIB statewide.

"Murphy," said Patterson, "you'd better go and get that fizz of
yours out of there. The Kane brothers [no relation to Ivan] and

a crew of villains were looking for him last night." It was a minimum-security facility for non-violent prisoners close to release, and the Kanes had run through the jail, firing shots and threatening warders while searching for Ivan.

Ivan had heard them approaching and managed to wedge all twenty stone of himself into a broom locker no more than eighteen inches wide. Patterson told Murphy that the Kanes had vowed to come back. If he wanted to continue his relationship with Ivan, he better get to Dhurringile immediately.

So Murphy clambered out of bed at 4 a.m. for the journey to Shepparton. When he got to the jail, Ivan was standing in the governor's office, looking like a naughty schoolboy waiting for his parents to pick him up.

"Brian, am I glad to see you. Get me out of here!" said Ivan. By 7 a.m. they were back in Melbourne waiting for the parole board to open in order to process Ivan's documents for his release. The chief judge of the parole board walked in and found the pair sitting in the hall.

"What the hell are you doing here?" he asked Murphy.

"I brought him down from jail, Your Honour," said Murphy.

"Get in here," said the chief judge to Ivan, motioning for Murphy to remain outside. "What are you doing with that arsehole?" he asked Ivan behind closed doors; it was a strange question for a judge to put to a convicted robber about a cop.

"Well, he most probably saved my life last night," replied Ivan.

"Oh really," said the judge. "Well, you're out now, and you would do well to be careful of the company you keep."

Ivan had promised Murphy he would stay out of trouble. In return, Murphy had helped find him a job at a bakery on the Mornington Peninsula. In the days ahead, Ivan worked hard and the baker was thrilled. He said he was the best worker he had ever had: he could weld, fix conveyor belts, make bread and perform any task he was assigned. He didn't have any trade tickets but all those skills he had picked up breaking safes were now coming in handy.

When Murphy's eldest child, Reg, finished school, Ivan got him a job at the bakery. Ivan would drive forty minutes from his house in Frankston to Middle Park to pick up Reg, then drive another forty minutes to the bakery at Tyabb. Murphy was never concerned that Ivan would be a bad influence on Reg; on the contrary, Ivan would reinforce everything Murphy told his son at home: who to avoid in the bakery because they were playing up or smoking dope, who were the decent people. Occasionally, Ivan would come and cook dinner for the family, making his own pasta and whipping up a three-course meal.

Some police believed that Ivan was up to his old "midnight shopping" tricks. There had been a surge in the number of unsolved safebreakings and Ivan was the prime suspect. Murphy was ordered to sit off his house and watch his comings and goings. When Ivan didn't appear at the house, senior police accused Murphy of tipping him off about being under surveillance. Murphy didn't have the heart to tell his superiors that Ivan had long vacated the property; he wasn't going to help police put his best informer out of business.

This relationship went much further than a cop and his informer. Ivan and his wife, Gail, were regular visitors to the Murphy home in Middle Park. They yearned for the kind of family life that Brian and Margaret enjoyed: closeness between parents and children, absence of conflict, communication to resolve disputes. Ivan and Gail had never seen a family like this, where, as Gail liked to say, "the members of the family just seemed to like each other." Ivan used to wonder what he could have made of himself had he lived a life like this. Though neither was Catholic, Ivan and Gail had their children baptised; they figured if they turned out like Murphy's kids, they would have done them a good turn.

Certainly, Ivan was one of the most intelligent people Murphy had ever met, barristers and judges included. If he hadn't been out "midnight shopping", Ivan would rise early and read all the newspapers by 9 a.m., cover to cover. Ask him any question from the day's press and he would invariably get it right. Murphy was always urging him to consider an occupation befitting his intelligence. Ivan had more dash than any crim he had ever known, but he was so prolific that the odds were against him staying out of jail for long. He carried sixty shotgun pellets in his back and a .38 slug in his arse; how long would it be before his luck ran out and some copper or shopkeeper shot him dead?

It was around this time that Ivan began a new career in dodgy finance deals. Melbourne quickly became too small for him and in the mid-1980s he took off overseas for one of the most outlandish crime sprees any Australian head had ever embarked upon. For years, Ivan would call Murphy from the four corners of the globe. He would be in Jakarta doing deals with the sons of Sukarno in Indonesia; he set up investment companies in the United States with mysterious Filipino partners.

One night in the late 1980s, he called Murphy from a pub in Bow Street, London. He was with a policeman waiting to meet an agent from the British intelligence agency MI6. He wouldn't tell Murphy what he was doing with MI6 other than to say that whatever he was mixed up in was too big for the ordinary wallopers. He was moving in a higher clique of criminals now and openly made fun of the cop who was handing him over to MI6.

"Imagine, Brian, this bloke's forty-seven and he's only a first constable," he said in front of the bobby.

The regular letters and calls continued for years. Ivan sent Murphy memorabilia from his travels: hats from China, Hong Kong, Thailand, the Philippines and South America, a menu from Mexico with grasshoppers à la carte, a matador's cape from Spain. Then, around 2001, the letters and packages simply stopped. Ivan also stopped sending money to his now ex-wife, Gail. Even today, Murphy still expects to pick up the phone and hear his cheery voice. He's buried a number of his informers and he hasn't got the heart to consign Ivan to the expired list. That's the thing about The Skull. Once in, he never lets go, no matter what.

PART 2

WAYS AND MEANS

CHAPTER 17 BILLY AND ME

IT WAS JULY 1968 AND BILLY "The Texan" Longley was in his pomp. Police regarded him as one of the most dangerous and cunning villains in Australia. He was all the more notorious for his new and unlikely confidant, Brian Francis Murphy. Theirs was a friendship that would last more than fifty years.

Longley was the most powerful man on the waterfront, though he didn't look the part. In those days he could easily have been mistaken for a stockbroker or a bookmaker, at least without his Stetson hat. Always immaculate in tailored one-button suits – he had never bought a suit off the peg in his life – he had a well-lunched, prosperous look about him. He had a wry, quiet countenance, never the kind of bloke to make a fuss: too much depended on things going nice and smooth. But at the first sign of trouble, the picture would quickly change. In a single movement, Longley would undo that suit button and from his belt "Matilda" would make her fearsome appearance. Matilda was a .45 calibre Colt automatic hand gun with a walnut grip. Early on in his career, Longley had realised he couldn't shoot everyone who crossed him; but the .45 wasn't just for putting holes in people – it was like carrying his own iron bar. Whipped straight from the belt in the firing position, Matilda's heavy barrel could be brought down on a rival's head in a flash. She had nipped many an argument in the bud, and probably saved a few lives at the cost of a mild concussion.

The police-issue .38 calibre Smith and Wesson was too light to be effective for this purpose. Others had tried the German-made 9-millimetre Luger, but when you belted someone over the head with it, invariably the 7-shot magazine would fall out, drastically limiting your options if things went further. And there were sharp edges on the Luger that would open up a man's head in a very non-surgical manner. So by the spring of 1968, with a war raging on the docks, Billy Longley and Matilda were rarely apart. Except for one particular night at the Rose and Crown Hotel in Port Melbourne, when she was in the glove box of Longley's car.

The trouble had started when a rival from the Port Melbourne push had backed up in the crowded bar and stepped on Longley's three-year-old daughter, Lisa. She wasn't hurt and Longley hadn't cut up rough, but an associate had remonstrated with the offender and the pair had come to blows. The Port Melbourne man, who was in the hotel with his two sons, was dealt a flogging and left, promising to return with a gun. Accounts of what happened next vary widely, but the most popular has it that the man returned with a big team of blokes chanting, "Kill Longley!" One of them lashed out with a boot and kicked a heavily pregnant woman who was with Longley flush in the stomach. Showing great perspicacity, Longley's wife fetched Matilda from the car and threw the gun to Longley, who was now under physical attack. Witnesses say that Longley caught the .45 and as he fell to the ground, jacked a cartridge into the chamber and shot one of his rivals in the groin. Seconds later, the Port Melbourne man was shot in the face; the bullet blowing out a good number of teeth before exiting under the chin and lodging in his collarbone. A third man was wounded before the volley of shots ended.

By the time police got there, everyone – bar the victims – had scarpered. Murphy and a team of detectives were searching for shell casings and other clues to what had taken place when the telephone rang behind the bar. Murphy picked it up.

"Rose and Crown, hello?"

A deep voice answered. "Is that you, Leo?" Leo McCann was the publican.

"Yes," said Murphy. He had no way of knowing for certain, but he thought the voice belonged to Billy Longley. "Is that you, Bill?"

There was a pause. "Are the bobbies still there?" the voice asked.

"Yeah," said Murphy. "When they go, come back and see me."

The line went dead. Longley knew he hadn't been speaking to Leo McCann; their friendship went back to the 1940s. Leo had been the barman at the Royal Hotel in Essendon, where Longley was a regular. Leo had once stopped him from drowning a bloke in the horse trough outside the hotel.

Until now, Murphy had never met Longley. Eight years earlier, Longley's first wife had been murdered at home in South Melbourne in mysterious circumstances, and Murphy was detailed to guard the house in case Longley – the prime suspect – came back. When Murphy saw a figure creeping through the darkened house, he let fly with a haymaker. The victim wasn't Longley but a fellow policeman, who spent the rest of the night nursing a broken jaw.

Though Murphy suspected the voice on the telephone was Longley's, he couldn't swear to the fact. But this hunch was enough for Murphy's colleagues, who wanted him to testify that Longley had tried to find out what evidence police had gathered from the scene. It was going to be a tough case to win. While the victims were sure Longley had shot them, every other witness was either looking the other way or had their eyes closed when the half-dozen shots rang out.

When Longley was charged, Murphy refused to play along. The two cops who had laid the charges came to Murphy and piled on the pressure. "Now, you're going to say that you knew it was Longley's voice, right?" said one detective.

"No," replied Murphy. "If I'm going to commit perjury, it'll be to get myself out of trouble, not some other bloke into trouble."

The detective was furious. What sort of cop wouldn't back the boys up? By telling the truth, Murphy was backing a villain against the police. It shouldn't matter that he had to lie; Murphy's allegiances were to the cops, not Longley.

The committal hearing was held at the Port Melbourne courthouse. When Murphy arrived, Longley was standing out in the street.

"How are you going, Bill?" Murphy asked, but Longley ignored him. He had no love of policemen. In 1960, the Homicide squad had given him a terrible four-hour kicking at Russell Street headquarters trying to get him to confess to the murder of his wife. He had maintained, as he did all his life, that his wife had died from a tragic accident: she had been hit by a stray bullet. But the cops had belted him relentlessly, throwing cold water over him when he lost consciousness. He couldn't walk by the time they had finished with him and had crawled back to his cell on his hands and knees. Even so, he never squealed. He lived his life by the maxim that a thoroughbred never stumbles and a good man never tumbles. And that meant never telling on coppers too. Longley had suffered at the hands of the police since as far back as the Great Depression.

He remembered getting a clip over the ear from uniform cops if they caught him scrounging for a feed in the streets. At eighteen, he gave a local copper in Ascot Vale such a flogging he ended up in hospital. It felt good at the time, but he soon learned that you can win a round with the cops but you never win the bout. They had never left him alone after that.

In 1960, Homicide cops picked Longley up and stole a large sum of money from him. He had planned to use this money to buy a corner grocery store in a new housing development south of the city. Before the advent of shopping malls, it would have been a licence to print money, but the theft put paid to his plans. No one but a fool would ever choose to be a villain, he used to say. His life of crime had already caused him untold grief. The police had a way of knocking a bloke down just as he was trying to bob up, over and over again. Crime was a cop-out, but it often seemed to be the only option left when your card was marked. Longley had encountered the sugar bags down the docks who would let Painters and Dockers take whatever they wanted off the ships as long as they got their cut. In fact, every successful knockabout had a cop or two in his back pocket.

But Murphy was a curiosity to Longley. He had heard that Murphy was mad – he had once bust into the house of a prominent unionist, kicking in the door and chasing the bloke up the corridor firing shots into the roof and walls. He had also heard that Murphy couldn't be bought off. He knew of Murphy's brother, Pat, and his generosity and willingness to help knockabouts and their families. But that didn't mean he had to like him, especially now that Murphy was trying to lock him up for attempted murder. But when The Skull took the witness box, Longley glimpsed something he had never seen in a copper before: integrity.

Longley's barrister, Frank Galbally, asked Murphy about the telephone call he had taken on the night of the shooting at the Rose and Crown Hotel. No doubt Murphy had believed the caller was Billy Longley, but had he ever spoken to the accused?

No, he had not.

So he couldn't be sure that the caller was, in fact, Longley?

No, he could not be sure.

Murphy felt the hateful stares of his colleagues from South Melbourne CIB as he left the box. At lunch recess, as he was coming out of the courtroom, he ran into Longley.

"I'm very well, thank you," said Longley, to answer Murphy's inquiry of several hours earlier.

"That's good," said Murphy. He hadn't given his testimony to help Longley; it was simply the truth. He didn't want Longley to be under the misconception that he deserved special treatment. "Longley, you know where you're going to finish up, don't you?"

"No," said Longley. "Where am I going to finish up?"

"Shot dead in a back lane," he said, staring hard at him. But Longley stared back just as hard.

"Well, if that's the case, tell 'em not to miss – because I don't." Longley held Murphy's gaze, as if challenging him to be the one.

"It won't be me that gets you," said Murphy. "Not unless I have to."

When the detectives from South Melbourne CIB saw Murphy talking with Longley outside the court, their hatred only deepened. Longley had been committed to stand trial for attempted murder but was acquitted as a result of sloppy police work. The cops had shown one of the witnesses the mug shots of only three villains, one of whom was Longley. By law, they should have shown him at least a dozen shots. The judge dismissed the case almost immediately and Longley was a free man.

From this time, a kind of respect, if not a friendship, began to develop between Longley and Murphy. It was more an acknowledgment of each other's right to exist than any strong notion of fellowship. Murphy knew enough not to bother a crim like Longley unless he showed open disrespect towards police. If Murphy walked into a pub on Longley's turf and there was any sign of a blue, Longley would wave his finger at the bloke as if to say, "Don't mess up where I am. I don't want this jack interfering. If you mess up here, chances are he'll grab me." Not a word passed between The Texan and The Skull, but their understanding was perfect. Longley could control a whole pub with just one finger; Murphy could bring Longley's world crashing down in a heartbeat. Restraint defines the extent of a man's power.

On 4 March 1970, four heavily armed men pulled off the largest payroll robbery in Australia's history until then, making off with $587,000 from a Mayne Nickless armoured van in the Sydney suburb of Guildford. But the robbers – Steve Nitties, Alan Jones and Frank "Baldy" Blair – had more to fear from their mates than the cops. New South Wales police had tipped off the leader of Sydney's feared Toecutter Gang, Kevin Gore, to the identity of the robbers in the hope of recovering some of the loot. Gore kidnapped and tortured Blair to make him hand over the cash, cutting off his toes with bolt-cutters before killing him.

The police alleged that, somehow, $6000 of the Mayne Nickless loot had found its way into the hands of Billy Longley. When the case came to court, Longley's barrister, Frank Galbally, subpoenaed Murphy to give character evidence for his client. Over the objections of his bosses, Murphy fronted for Longley. He had been subpoenaed – what else could he do? He testified that Longley was what he was, but that he had not given police any trouble in recent years; in fact, he wasn't a bad sort of bloke. This sent Murphy's bosses into orbit with rage. Here was one of their own testifying that Longley wasn't a bad bloke! They had officers and lawyers go through the transcript line by line to see if they could pin Murphy for anything – perjury, false testimony, anything at all – but Murphy had told the truth as he saw it. The character reference didn't help much: Longley was still found guilty and did more than a year in jail.

But now Longley was full of admiration for Murphy. He did not doubt his ferocious reputation, but in all his dealings with him, Murphy had been as good as gold; he just kept coming up as fair dinkum, as Longley told his sceptical fellow Painters and Dockers. From that point on, Longley never tried to hide his friendship with Brian Murphy; and this friendship was soon to be tested in a very public way.

CHAPTER 18   ONE THING LED TO ANOTHER

THEY WOULD COME IN THE STILLNESS of the night, in the darkness between sunset and sunrise. During the day he was too busy to worry. But when he got home he had to be a different person. He couldn't tell his wife the thoughts that went through his mind – he couldn't tell anyone. It was like being in a different dimension. So at night he would lie there thinking of all kinds of things: what had gone wrong, what could go wrong, what will tomorrow look like – will someone come to this house?

Sometimes he would see the faces of the men who had died on the Westgate Bridge on 15 October 1970, or worse, their body parts: a signet ring on the finger of a severed arm, a tattoo on a battered leg. On his days off, and on the sly, Murphy had been doing security work at the construction site. On that day at 11.50 a.m. a 2000-tonne section of the half-built bridge collapsed, killing thirty-five construction workers. Murphy was on his way to the site, to the exact spot where the span of bridge had fallen, to hand the workers their wages. He had been late leaving home, having lost track of time fixing the radio in his old Falcon sedan. He had gotten to know most of the seventy or eighty workers through handing their pay packets to them. Many were recent migrants and he would field endless questions about everything from marriage licences to the immigration of distant families. He identified twenty-eight of the bodies that afternoon. Men like 23-year-old Jouzaf Ozelis, who had been planning to marry his girlfriend, or 32-year-old George Tse-hilios, who had sold his blacksmith shop in Greece to come to Australia, saving for eight years to buy a house for his wife and two kids. There was Tony Falzon, the Maltese carpenter, and Charlie Lund, the foreman, who was just about to leave the bridge. Murphy helped lay out their bodies as the rescue workers brought them from the rubble; he identified them, tied little toe-tags and covered them. He went home feeling numb. Margaret asked him what he wanted for tea – steak or spaghetti bolognaise? "No thanks, love," he murmured. "I'll just have a coffee and a biscuit and go up to bed." In his bedroom, Murphy felt the emotion wash over him as he stared at the ceiling. The next morning, he was invincible once more and soon to walk, without any hesitation, into the greatest controversy of his career

*

On Friday 26 March 1971, Murphy was driving into Russell Street to pick up some papers when he heard another member checking three names over the radio: Ian Revell Carroll, Thomas Joseph Connellan and Neil Stanley Collingburn. The officer, 26-year-old First Constable Carl John Stillman, and another officer, Max Gosney, had intercepted the three in Collingburn's car on Nicholson Street, Carlton, with a set of golf clubs they suspected were stolen. Murphy heard the names and suggested Stillman go to another channel.

"Listen, be careful of those three," he warned Stillman. "They will kick you to death if they get the chance." Stillman was unconcerned – what would Murphy know? They were his prisoners and all was under control. At thirty-seven, Murphy was already a seventeen-year veteran of the force and, to officers like Stillman, a relic from an earlier era. To Murphy, Stillman was a smartarse with some very tough lessons ahead. He was already making mistakes in this arrest: rather than bundle all three suspects into one police car, they had divided the prisoners. Carroll had gone in the police car with Gosney, Stillman rode in Collingburn's car as a front-seat passenger, with Connellan in the back. En route to Russell Street, Collingburn and Stillman argued – Collingburn produced an iron bar and threatened to cave the constable's head in.

At twenty-eight, Collingburn was universally regarded as "a good crim", staunch and full of courage – a villain on the rise. He was a Painter and Docker drawing a wage at the waterfront, but like many of their members he rarely set foot on a dock, much less worked on a ship. He was a ghost-worker who listed his occupation as waterside worker to cover his true vocations: breaking, entering, stealing and standover.

Collingburn was gaining a name across Australia in the right circles. He believed he deserved respect, even from the police. He was of medium height but nuggetty and strong and never one to back down from a fight. In street parlance, he had "a ton of dash".

A little earlier in 1971, the Armed Robbery Squad had arrested Collingburn and another villain in connection with a series of thefts. When they got them to Russell Street, a detective rang down to the Breaking Squad: they were short-handed; they needed a couple of men to go with Collingburn and search his house in Elizabeth Street, Richmond. It was a strange request, Murphy thought as he went upstairs; perhaps they were expecting trouble and simply didn't want to be in the firing line.

Murphy arrived at the Armed Robbery office to find Collingburn making a scene, screaming abuse at detectives as they struggled to put handcuffs on him. Murphy asked why they were cuffing the prisoner. One of the detectives replied that if they didn't, he would just as likely jump out of the car.

"Well, don't bother with the cuffs. If he jumps out of the car, I'll shoot him stone fuckin' dead," declared Murphy, glaring at Collingburn. This caught Collingburn's attention. He stopped struggling and stared hard at Murphy.

"Would you really shoot me dead?" he asked, looking Murphy up and down contemptuously.

"Yeah, sure. Try me," Murphy replied. "I don't know you, I don't have any trouble with you, and you don't want any trouble with me. But if you play up on me, you'll discover that I'm a different kind of person than you think, okay? And I'll kill you without a moment's hesitation. Understand?"

Collingburn nodded.

"When you come back, they'll charge you with whatever it is you've done. If there's nothing in your house, there's nothing in your house. No-one's going to plant anything in there. You have my word," said Murphy. Collingburn quietened down and they made the trip to Richmond without incident. As they approached Collingburn's house, the prisoner asked Murphy for a favour.

"If the baby's asleep, please, will you promise me you won't wake her?"

"No, I can't promise that. I don't know what type of reception I'm going to get there. You could have guns, you could have anything in the bassinette," said Murphy. But Collingburn wouldn't let up.

"Look me in the eyes, mate. I'm telling you, man to man, there's nothin' in the baby's room. I'm telling you, there's nothin' there. I've never met you before, you should take me as you find me," pleaded Collingburn.

This struck a chord with Murphy. No matter how rough and violent his raids might be, he would never leave a place more of a mess than he found it; it demeaned and humiliated the woman, already paying for the sins of her man.

He decided to reserve his judgment until he got inside Collingburn's single-fronted worker's cottage. They began to search the house. When they got to the baby's room, Collingburn's wife, Rae, begged Murphy not to go in because the baby was sleeping. There was nothing in there, she and Collingburn insisted. "Okay," said Murphy, "we won't go in there." I'll take a chance this time, he thought. His change of heart touched Collingburn; there were tears in his eyes. No copper had ever taken his word for something before. But there was a rider to Murphy's generosity of spirit.

"If any other policeman comes back and finds anything in that room, I'll make it my business to wreck the both of you, okay?"

Murphy went back to the office and filled in his diary. His new boss at the Breakers (The Puss had moved to Heidelberg CIB by this time) was sceptical. Collingburn was a dead-set villain, he told Murphy. He was part of a big network of villains who were brash and bold and getting away with murder. His brother, Keith Albert Collingburn, had been liberated from a police van by men armed with automatic weapons while being moved from one prison to another. Murphy had been crazy to give this dangerous head any leeway at all.

Collingburn had been found with stolen property on that day, but he would walk on the charges, a result of either corruption or sloppy police work. The detectives from the Armed Robbery Squad had failed to officially caution him, so the arrest had not been lawful. To Murphy, cautioning a suspect on arrest was as normal as putting his underpants on every day, but for some unknown reason, they had not done it that day.

If Collingburn had been processed correctly and locked up, he never would have been at Russell Street on the afternoon of 26 March 1971. Murphy arrived not long after Constable Still-man had taken all three suspects into a muster room where the Crime Cars Squad was stationed. He was coming down the stairs with another officer when he heard a clamour of voices and a struggle. Someone ran out from the Crime Cars office and shouted, "Collingburn's running amok in there!"

Murphy could have kept walking. Collingburn wasn't his pris-oner, so he had no business in that muster room. But seventeen years of experience weighed heavily on him. A small group of onlookers had gathered; the senior officer on hand, an amiable character who was forever smiling, wanted nothing to do with the commotion and was talking on the telephone.

All the things Murphy had learned from his heroes and mentors Jack Meehan, Mick Miller and Keith Plattfuss were now second nature. He knew that none of them would have hesitated to go into the muster room. Though the outcomes would have been different in each case, the rationale was the same. Someone's got to take control here, Murphy thought, and because I can cope, it had better be me.

*

In the intervening thirty-seven years, there has not been a single day when Murphy hasn't thought of that moment or the few minutes that followed. He has lost count of the number of times he has prayed for Collingburn and his family. Every time he passes the cottage he searched in Richmond with Collingburn, the sequence of events flashes through his mind again: the moment that affected the course of his life.

It is January 2008 and we are sitting in Murphy's lounge room in bayside Middle Park. After thirty or forty hours of tape-recorded discussion, we have not discussed "the Collingburn incident", as Murphy calls it. We have danced around its part in the story. It seems that Murphy, in his calculating way, has decided that today we will address the ghost that has lurked at the edges and in the silences of our dialogue. I mention Collingburn's name and Murphy reaches under the coffee table and produces an envelope of post-mortem photographs. The corpse in the shots is that of a man of less than thirty years of age. He is swarthy and his full head of brown hair is tousled and matted. One dead eye stares, almost accusingly, out of the picture at Murphy as he holds it in both hands. He flips over to the next picture, a full-length shot, showing Collingburn's naked torso; there's a big, ugly incision running right down his stomach to his groin. It's roughly stitched, like the mortician has closed it with a baling hook. There are what seem to be bruises and blotches all over the body. He looks like the very image of someone who has died amid savage violence.

It's an oddly disturbing moment for both of us. Murphy is welling up with tears. I'm not sure whether they are for Collingburn or himself. For reasons I cannot explain, I'm less certain of Murphy's innocence having seen the post-mortem pictures: how could Collingburn go into that muster room a healthy, 28-year-old man and end up like this? How could the two police officers in the room with him not have had something to do with this? The thought nags away at me. Have all the hours we've spent discussing his career been leading to this moment? Perhaps this is an exercise in absolution for a man who is not guilty yet not innocent enough. He puts the photographs down on the table and begins to tell the story once more.

*

As Murphy entered the room, he saw Carroll sitting on the right, Connellan sitting on the left and Collingburn standing at the extreme left of the room. Collingburn was remonstrating loudly with Stillman, who was sitting opposite on a swivel chair, behind a table with a typewriter in front of him. The situation was about to blow up like a string of penny bungers.

Seconds later, Collingburn lunged at Stillman and hooked him hard in the face. Recoiling from the blow, Stillman toppled backwards with the chair to the floor, raising his boots as he fell. Murphy saw Collingburn loom over Stillman, looking set to hit him again, but Stillman lashed out with both feet, driving his heels into Collingburn's mid-section and pushing him back into a row of lockers. Murphy grabbed Collingburn and threw him back into his chair.

"You fucking lunatic, what are you doing?"

"Mr Murphy, I'm sorry, but I'm not having this young cunt putting shit on me!" said Collingburn. With that, Carroll jumped up and Murphy punched him hard on the jaw. Then he gave Connellan one for good measure. He turned to Collingburn.

"You aren't going to win here. Behave yourself!"

"I'm not having this young cunt putting shit on me," Collingburn repeated. "You never put shit on me."

"I don't have to," replied Murphy.

"I know," said Collingburn, appearing to calm down a little.

"Are you okay now?" asked Murphy.

"I'm okay. Sweet, sweet," mumbled Collingburn. Then Connellan and Carroll started mouthing off again.

"You've already had a serve! Do you want another?" barked Murphy. Then he turned to Stillman and ordered him to separate his prisoners: he should have known better than to question a prisoner in front of others. Stillman seemed unimpressed with this advice. His balls are too big for him to listen, the fool, thought Murphy as he walked out. He was hardly out the door when the fighting resumed. He ran back in and put a headlock on Collingburn to cut off his air supply. After a short struggle, Collingburn sank to his knees and, finally subdued, agreed to behave himself. He was bleeding from the nose and mouth. There was the beginning of a lump over one eye and a slight swelling of his lip. Less than two minutes had elapsed since Murphy had entered the muster room. When he left, Collingburn was very much alive.

Another prisoner, Wayne Leslie Franklin, was being held in a smaller cubicle adjoining the muster room. Later, he remembered hearing swearing and a male voice shouting: "Get up, you cunt!" Half an hour later, Franklin was moved to the muster room where he found Collingburn sitting by himself in obvious pain. He had bruises on his face and a big lump above his right eye.

"He didn't look too good to me," Franklin later testified, recalling that one of the detectives had said something about taking him to hospital. "He could hardly walk by himself. He walked out very slowly, as though there was something wrong with his hip or his kidney region. He leaned to one side." Franklin later testified that he had heard two police officers discussing the incident, claiming to hear the following exchange:

"How do you think we'll go on this one?"

"We'll get out of this one for sure."

Gas gangrene is a ruthless killer once loose inside the human body. A ruptured duodenum, as Collingburn suffered, allows *Clostridium perfringens* bacteria to pass from the small intestine into the peritoneal cavity, where all the vital organs are located. The duodenum is like a tube from a bicycle tyre; once ruptured, excreta pours out and the progression to toxaemia and shock is often very rapid. Antibiotics alone cannot stop the spread of the infection as the toxins destroy nearby tissue, producing gas. The most effective treatment is surgery without delay, involving excision of the tissue and debridement of the wound. Amputation is often required where limbs are involved to get ahead of the galloping infection.

Stillman and Gosney took Collingburn to St Vincent's Hospital at 4.30 p.m. that day, after he complained of abdominal pain. Although he was severely injured, Collingburn refused to make any complaint to the police duty officer before he went to hospital. On admission, he told medical staff he had been injured falling from a chair. It was only after doctors told him he would require an operation that he told staff that Murphy and Stillman had bashed him.

Collingburn carried on loudly that he didn't want the nurses – black crows, as he called them – fussing over him. Accordingly, they put him down the back room. That was effectively a death sentence, with his ruptured duodenum leaking toxins into his system. His condition steadily worsened over Friday night.

Surgeons did not operate to repair his ruptured duodenum until 10 a.m. the following day. By that time it was far too late. And his cause had not been well served by his last meal: a big lunch of bacteria-laden oysters kilpatrick followed by steak dianne.

On Saturday morning, a resident surgeon examined Collingburn. He told a senior nurse that the patient was suffering from gas gangrene and that he needed emergency surgery – an exploratory procedure called a laparotomy. The nurse had not regarded the case as serious. The night before, a surgical registrar had diagnosed him with nothing more serious than bruised abdominal muscles. Collingburn's belligerent attitude had not helped his cause and staff had apparently paid more attention to other patients as Collingburn's condition steadily worsened overnight. The surgeon told nurses that if he didn't receive surgery he would die and they would have to answer for that. He died the following day, after the surgery. The official cause of death was peripheral circulatory failure following septicaemia.

Murphy had been oblivious to what was happening inside Collingburn's gut as he got on with the job that Friday afternoon. He and two other Breakers carried out raids on premises, searching for evidence linking Collingburn and his partner in crime, Ray "Chuck" Bennett, to the theft of $125,000 worth of leather coats from a city retailer. They found a van with rolls of wrapping paper used by the villains to package the coats for transport to Sydney. They interviewed the owner of a barber shop, who confessed that Connellan and Collingburn had sold him a quantity of razor blades. It was business as usual. He spent most of the weekend at home alone. Wife Margaret and mother Maggie were away on holiday in New Zealand and the kids were in Ballarat for the day, visiting the Eureka Stockade. It wasn't until Sunday afternoon, when Murphy went into Russell Street to fill in his diary, that he began to learn of Collingburn's fate.

The telephone rang on his desk. "Breaking Squad, Sergeant Murphy speaking."

"You dirty bastard," said a muffled voice. "You killed my mate. Now I'm going to blow your head off!" It wasn't the first time he had fielded such a call, but he still thought it strange.

"Go fuck yourself, you idiot," he said, slamming the phone down and returning to his diary. Then a police colleague came over, shaking his head.

"You're in very big trouble," he said. "The bosses are looking for you, and they're going to charge you with murder."

"What are you talking about, you imbecile?" Murphy barked.

"Collingburn is dead. The bosses are looking everywhere for you. You're number-one cab off the rank."

"That's got nothing to do with me," replied Murphy, but inwardly he knew this was trouble. He rang Stillman at home and found him in no mood to discuss police business.

"Before you go any further, Sarge," said Stillman, "I'm on leave and I'm not coming in for anyone." Murphy felt the heat rising in him.

"Let me tell you something," he began quietly. "You either come in here or you're by yourself, okay? I'll say that I saw nothing and you're going to be charged and convicted of murder."

He had to frighten Stillman into coming into work that instant. He needed to know what had taken place if they were going to beat this. He had no idea that Stillman had taken Collingburn to hospital on Friday afternoon. He did not know whether Stillman or anybody else had given it to Collingburn after he had left.

Stillman agreed to come in but they didn't stay long at Russell Street. Murphy, Stillman and Gosney went to Murphy's house, where they went over what had happened in minute detail. Murphy asked Stillman whether he had sustained any injuries. Stillman said he had a chipped tooth and a bruise inside his lip where Collingburn had punched him. Murphy rang the police photographic department and got a snapper to take pictures of Stillman's minor injuries. He helped Stillman write his statement of what had happened in the muster room and asked if he was happy with it. Stillman replied that he was, it was the truth; but he couldn't understand why Murphy had dragged him from leave for this.

"This is going to blow up bigger than the atomic bomb," said Murphy. "The department thinks they've got me. The Painters and Dockers think they've got me. And you're in the shit with me."

Stillman couldn't see how he was implicated in Collingburn's death. He told Murphy he was just big-noting himself; this would blow over and life would go on.

That night after work, Murphy procured two shotguns for his own protection: one for the back door, one for the front. If the Painters and Dockers came looking for revenge, he wanted to be ready. Next morning, he got the kids off to school and went straight into Russell Street. Much would depend on the officers who had been around the muster room in the two-minute period of the fight. The sergeant who had shouted "Collingburn's running amok!" could help establish the fact that the prisoners had been the aggressors, not the police. But this sergeant was due for promotion to inspector; writing a statement for a renegade like Murphy and a low-ranking officer like Stillman could jeopardise his career.

"Go get stuffed," he said. "I'm not going to do my promotion for any bastard – especially for the likes of you and Stillman. I saw nothing, I heard nothing and I wasn't there, right? And if you have any brains, you weren't there either."

But Murphy *was* there. He hadn't killed Collingburn, but he was there and nothing could change that. More than that, he was supposed to be there. Someone had to take control, otherwise a policeman, namely Stillman, could have been in the morgue, not Collingburn. But Murphy could not make others feel that way, much less stand over them to give evidence on his behalf, so instead he shut up about it. By Monday morning, the pressure was building up like a blocked sewer pipe. Bosses were rushing in and out saying he was a lunatic and in diabolical trouble; he would be very lucky if he wasn't charged with murder; it was a miracle he hadn't killed anyone already.

It seemed there was a lot of glee at the idea that Murphy had finally come unstuck. And the death of Neil Collingburn soon left the realm of law and order to become a symbol of broader struggles and tensions in Australian society. Two senior police, former Homicide bosses Inspector Jack Ford and Superintendent Jack Matthews, were on trial for running an extortion racket – standing over illegal abortionists operating in Melbourne. It was a sensational trial that struck at the heart of Melbourne's complacency on corruption. Columnist John Larkin wrote in the *Age* newspaper in April 1971:

Beneath the grey flannel, the politeness and the slow sell, beneath the belief in its infallibility, there has developed a growing realisation that Melbourne is as vulnerable as anywhere, is ethically no better, nor worse, than any other city.

The abortion situation was the beginning of this fright leaking out of the walls. You trust it will not be the end.

Times were changing. The violent struggles between police and anti-war demonstrations from 1966 onwards had polarised public opinion. Men like Murphy and Plattfuss were now cast as the brutal lackeys of an oppressive, unpopular ruling class, hell-bent on enforcing its corrupt and venal interests, not just in Australia but across the globe. The federal government, under

Murphy had been a trainee auctioneer and an apprentice watchmaker, but when he pulled on the uniform, he knew he had found his calling. While many cops called the job a brotherhood, Murphy knew he was always alone.

Above: Growing up in South Melbourne in the 1940s, a kid had to be handy to survive. Many of Murphy's classmates ended up on the wrong side of the law.

Above: The Skull's father, Reg "Snowy" Murphy, was almost killed by police in the wharfie strike of 1929 but he knew a good cop from a bad one.

Left: Murphy's mother, Maggie, was always there to share the hate. There was nothing he could get past "The Commandant".

Above: Margaret Blanchfield wanted to marry a man of action. Murphy told her little of his adventures, lest one day she had to lie for him.

Left: Murphy, disguised as a railway conductor, took down the SP bookies of South Melbourne in the mid-1950s.
Below: Another uniform. Murphy became a feared bouncer at Melbourne pubs, such as the Oxford Hotel, in his spare time.

Left: Valour Badge. One minute Victoria Police were trying to pin the manslaughter of Neil Stanley Collingburn on Murphy, the next they were pinning a medal on him.

Left: Corporal James Gardiner, a casualty of war played out in the suburbs. He met Murphy for a quiet chat over a gun one night in December 1975.

Right: The Boss. Sinclair Imrie "Mick" Miller was a highly effective policeman as well as an ethical and moral leader.

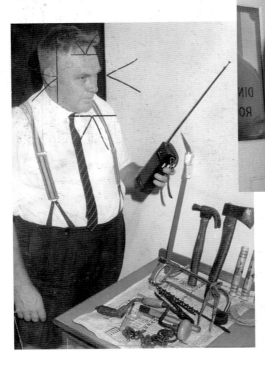

Left: The Puss. Sergeant Keith Ludwig Plattfuss believed order was as important as law. And if crims belted coppers, they should be made to beg for mercy. (Courtesy of Herald & Weekly Times Ltd.)

Left: Janas Tuingla. The sex monster escaped the law's judgment but got his right whack in the end.

Right: Irish swaggie Eddy Howlin came to Murphy as a prisoner and ended up a house guest.

Left: Murphy wanted to kill gangster Freddy "The Frog" Harrison in the name of the law. He was soon to croak anyway.

Above: The Consorter. In the 1970s, the Consorting Squad was alleged to be running a murder squad. Bent or straight, the working day for the Consorters looked much the same. Bad laws made bad policemen but did they become killers?

Below: The Marauder. Murphy could pop up anywhere, anytime. A non-drinker, he could stand in a pub with drunks and still blend in.

Left: Armed robber Raymond "Chuck" Bennett was the one man Murphy feared. He swore he would kill The Skull but someone else got him first. (Courtesy of Newspix)

Right: Gunman Billy "The Texan" Longley hated police but Murphy kept coming up fair dinkum. The unlikely relationship between cop and crim lasted more than fifty years.

61/391 Billy Longley, P1.6.72:B8.5.25

Left: Les Kane. His murder in 1978 set off a deadly chain of events that destabilised Murphy's world. But Murphy refused to help avenge his death.

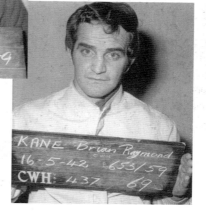

Right: Brian Kane once dreamed of being a cop. With police help, he became a killer when he took out Raymond "Chuck" Bennett inside the Melbourne Magistrates' Court in 1979.

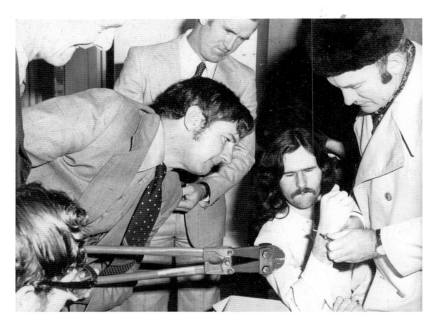

Above: Unorthodox methods. In the 1980s, Murphy (right) was a dinosaur to his colleagues but he continued to catch crooks, even while the cops chased him.

Right: Christopher Dale Flannery would become Mr Rent-a-Kill, but to Murphy he was just a good bloke. That is, until he started killing people for money. (Courtesy of Newspix)

Right: Ivan Alfred Kane was a loyal fizz to Murphy for nearly thirty years until he mysteriously disappeared.

Liberal prime minister Billy McMahon, would soon welcome the all-white Springbok rugby team from apartheid South Africa. Police would break up the protests against one of the most vicious, iniquitous regimes ever seen. To ordinary people, the police tactics were becoming more of a threat to society than the demonstrators. On 3 April, one of Melbourne's biggest anti-Vietnam War demonstrations to date was smashed by over-zealous police in the city centre, right in front of shocked weekend shoppers. *Struggle*, the "Revolutionary Newspaper of the Worker–Student Alliance", denounced the violence:

> They attacked from all sides. Indiscriminately bashing. Horses thundering and spinning: clubs crunching on bare heads. The two vans that had pulled up were stuffed full of special police bashers who belched forth into the crowd. They poured out of the vans and went to work, bashing in formation. Superbly coordinated, skilled fascist murdering thugs. Hitler would have glowed with pride.

The Collingburn "murder" was more evidence of "the vital role played by the police force in the apparatus of state repression in bourgeois societies".

In the 9 April edition of *Struggle*, the editors apologised for holding over an article on the Cultural Revolution, instead running two full pages of coverage on the Collingburn killing under the headline "WORKER MURDERED BY POLICE".

Collingburn's demise was "a class question", the newspaper claimed. Though he was rarely seen down the docks, his membership of the Painters and Dockers qualified him as "working-class youth".

[Members] of the working class and radical youth expect to be beaten up when "questioned" in police stations but the blatancy of this murder is a new element in the bourgeois armory.

Collingburn's life history is typical of many working class youths.

From this political crucible, Collingburn had emerged re-alloyed. A petty villain had become a working-class martyr. Four days after his death, 400 students and workers marched from the Victorian Trades Hall to Russell Street police headquarters bearing two cardboard coffins, one with Murphy's name and the other with Stillman's. A chant went up that echoed through the streets for blocks around: "WHO KILLED COLLING-BURN? THE POLICE KILLED COLLINGBURN!"

Murphy was in the Breakers office at Russell Street when he heard the mob approaching. A boss suggested he leave the building, go home and take the kids away immediately. There was also word that the Painters and Dockers were going to kill him. A mate of Collingburn's, Bert Kidd, had offered notorious gunnie Brian Kane a contract worth $30,000 to take out Murphy. Now students and workers were threatening to storm the building; an ugly confrontation was brewing. The bosses wanted Murphy to slip out through the police canteen onto La Trobe Street.

"I'm not sending my kids anywhere because of the Painters and Dockers," Murphy declared. "If I go home, it's going to be in a police car from outside this building. This mob's not going to dictate where I go."

Before the bosses could stop him, Murphy walked out of the front door and into full view of the chanting mob, which had gathered in front of the building. Well, if you want me here I am, thought Murphy. He waved to the crowd and they waved back, apparently not realising the object of their fury was standing right in front of them. He got into a police car and was driven home. The bosses suggested he take a fortnight off. By then, everything would have quietened down and he could come back to work. He asked if there was any likelihood he would be charged. The bosses assured him there was not.

But barrister Frank Galbally was acting for the Collingburn family and they were out for blood. Despite the fact that Murphy had twice assisted the barrister when he was acting for Billy Longley, the stakes were higher now. If the police did not charge Murphy and Stillman, Galbally threatened to take out a Supreme Court civil warrant alleging the pair had murdered Collingburn. If Galbally was successful, Murphy and Stillman would immediately be locked up in Pentridge Prison – there was no bail for accused murderers. And a series of riots at Pentridge that autumn made the jail a very dangerous place indeed for a pair of cops accused of killing a Painter and Docker. To be on remand awaiting trial would effectively be a death sentence for Murphy and Stillman. To make matters worse, Galbally had visited the morgue and inspected the body, declaring to the press that Collingburn's injuries were so severe that he looked like the victim of a road accident. In fact, the body Galbally viewed *had* been in a road accident – it was not that of Neil Stanley Collingburn. Galbally had been shown the wrong body, an embarrassing oversight the barrister never bothered to correct. Such disinformation fanned the flames of the controversy.

For the first time in his career, Murphy felt his destiny was in the hands of others. A doctor friend dropped by on Monday night with some pills: anti-anxiety medication and some sleeping tablets. Murphy said he didn't need them, but the doctor insisted. He needed all the rest he could get, and during the day, the anti-anxiety pills would take the edge off, preventing a volcanic eruption of rage if things went from bad to worse.

He took the pill that night and fell immediately into a deep, dreamless sleep. The next morning, he woke feeling like a zombie, but he followed the doctor's orders and took the anti-anxiety tablet after breakfast. Soon, on top of the grogginess, he felt detached and vague, as if he were a player in a movie shot out of focus with the sound muffled and distant. The pill had lifted the deep sense of foreboding, but now a kind of languid whimsy had taken over, as if nothing mattered anymore.

His sister-in-law drove him into town and all the way there he sat in the car with a half-smile on his face. He felt like a drooling lunatic. As they sat at the traffic lights on Swanston Street in the morning peak hour, Murphy turned to his left and saw a well-known Painter and Docker pull up alongside. When he saw Murphy grinning at him, the man reached into his coat, pulled out a hand gun and shoved it straight into Murphy's face.

"You murdering dog, I'm going to wipe that smile off your face! I'm gonna blow your fucking head off!" he snarled.

In his impaired state, the possibility of getting shot on the way to work seemed absurd. Murphy began laughing and waved at the gunman. "G'day, how are you going?" he said, cheerily. Inside, he knew his response was bizarre, but he just couldn't help it. His sister-in-law did not share the amusement. Fortunately, the lights turned green and she launched the car to the left, blocking the would-be assassin's vehicle and running him onto the footpath. When she had cleared the intersection, she turned to Murphy and shouted at him.

"You imbecile, what are you doing?"

"I don't know," he replied, still in the grip of this pleasant delusion. Later in the office, after wandering around in a daze, he took a call.

"Why are you letting sheilas take care of you? You're a weak arsehole," said a voice, strikingly similar to that of the gunman he had met in the traffic. Perhaps there was an orchestrated plan to stalk him, he thought. In this state, he would be easy pickings. When he got home that night, he took all the pills and flushed them down the toilet. If he was going to survive the next few weeks, he would need to be sharp like never before.

Murphy suspected the department was about to leave him for dead, and all doubt was removed the following night. A Geelong-based superintendent had been given the job of investigating Collingburn's death. He turned up, with two Homicide detectives, at Murphy's house, drunk and belligerent.

"Murphy, you'll do ten fucking years for this killing," he said, staggering around the living room so errantly he nearly knocked over the television set. One of the Homicide detectives was shaking his head, as if to let Murphy know that he shouldn't cooperate. So he ordered the trio to leave, refusing to answer any of their questions. After they had gone, Murphy telephoned a mate in the Surveillance Unit, otherwise known as "the Dogs". They owed Murphy a few favours and readily agreed to help. The Dogs followed the Geelong superintendent all night. Later, he made a sworn statement that he had gone straight from Murphy's house to Russell Street to make notes of the confrontation, but the Dogs told Murphy a different story. The superintendent did not go to Russell Street but straight to the police club, where he resumed drinking. Several hours later he drove his police car, blind drunk, all the way to Geelong, a forty-five minute journey. When he got home, he opened the car door and spilled into the gutter, where he spent the rest of the night. So much for an impartial, sober investigation, thought Murphy.

Across town that night, Neil Collingburn's father was sitting in Billy Longley's kitchen. Keith Collingburn was a knockabout unionist who had established a strong reputation in the underworld with his sons Neil and Keith. Collingburn senior was relaying the conclusions of his brief investigation into his son's demise and the death sentence he planned to impose on Murphy.

He told Longley he had got himself a gun. He knew that Murphy and his wife went to the South Melbourne Market early every Saturday morning. He planned to be there next weekend and shoot Murphy dead. If Margaret Murphy was in the way, then so be it. Villains had learned to cop it sweet if police bashed them in custody; and if what Galbally and the press were saying was right, then Neil had undergone a systematic, ferocious kicking that could not go unanswered.

Longley knew that if Keith Collingburn had his heart set on killing Murphy, then Murphy was a dead man. It's impossible to evade a killer who does not fear the consequences. Collingburn would kill Murphy in broad daylight in front of dozens of witnesses. Or he would wait until Murphy got in his car, where a man is most vulnerable – with the engine off and fumbling with a seatbelt, Murphy would be a sitting duck.

This might have been a conflict of interest for Longley. He had known Neil Collingburn and they had got on well. But Murphy had been the first cop who had ever been straight up with him; he had helped Longley avoid a long prison stretch for the Rose and Crown shooting in '68. It would be ironic if Longley, a union man, stood in the way of revenge for the death of a Painter and Docker – and for a cop, no less. But there was another angle he could pursue.

"Keith, have you thought about your wife?" asked Longley. "She's already lost a son. If she loses you, where does that leave her? Your family will be destroyed, for the sake of revenge. A war will ensue that no-one can win." This line of argument seemed to forestall, if not discourage, Collingburn senior's murderous intentions.

There were other Painters and Dockers plotting to kill Murphy. Longley knew there were plans to make "a sneak go" on Murphy outside his house or even to plant a bomb under his car. Like Murphy, Longley had his own little army of enemies but few were game enough to front him. His house had been strafed by machine-gun fire and bombed by rivals in his own union. They were cowards, these men who struck at a man's home. And Longley told them so to their faces.

"You can't take it out on the kids and the wife," he said. "If you have something to say to the bloke, say it to his face. Don't go throwing bombs or firing shots through his windows."

So much had happened in a week of Murphy's life, he scarcely seemed the same man. He had hardly eaten and the weight had fallen off him – the best part of a stone. When he went to the airport to meet Margaret and his mother's plane arriving from Auckland, he looked gaunt and stressed. A couple of carloads of Dogs were following as he drove along the freeway to the airport. Margaret was so happy and excited to be home she didn't notice a thing; but Maggie knew her son too well. She kissed him, took a step back and looked him up and down.

"Here, what's wrong with you?" she asked sharply.

"Nothing's wrong with me, Mum."

"Bulldust," said Maggie.

On the way home, Maggie noticed that some police officers she knew were following them.

"What are they doing out here, eh?"

"Oh, Mum, they must've had a job out at the airport," said Brian, unconvincingly.

"Bloody liar," muttered Maggie.

When they arrived at home in Middle Park, the police cars were still on their tail and they parked a little up the street on either side of the house. Maggie pointed to the cars again.

"Right," she said. "What's wrong?"

Murphy could delay no longer and he explained the events of the past week. When he had finished, Margaret sighed and said, "Oh well!" Maggie's face flushed red instantly.

"What do you *mean* 'Oh well'?" Maggie stared hard at Margaret, her pale blue eyes blazing. "He's guilty of nothing! Do you hear me? He's guilty of nothing!"

Margaret never meant to suggest he was guilty, only that what would be, would be. But to Maggie, this was an intolerable show of disloyalty. Though Margaret had delivered five children into the Murphy clan, her membership to the family was still contestable with Maggie – maybe this redhead would cause them grief after all. It wouldn't have mattered to Maggie if Murphy had murdered Collingburn right in the middle of Russell Street, she would never condemn him. Now that Reg was three years gone, Brian was her man of the house. There was hardly a day when Brian didn't drop by Maggie's house in South Melbourne. As did all her children, but theirs was a special relationship.

Whenever he needed to share his hatred of someone, his mother was always there. Maggie would hate anybody that Murphy hated, only more fiercely. He liked to say his mother had the Irish Alzheimer's disease: she forgot everything but the hatred. And she kept it long after Murphy's had died down. If she heard her son had begun talking to someone again, she would castigate him.

"You're a weak-gutted individual," she would say.

"But Mum, you can't carry it on forever," he would say.

"Says who?" she would say, ending the discussion.

Margaret was a different soul, full of forgiveness and love. She wanted to see the good side of everyone. That was fine for the sanctuary of peace and family values she had created in her home, but outside was a different world altogether. Hatred had helped Murphy survive until now in his career. Maggie had used it to exorcise any vestige of weakness she saw in him; and, if Maggie held sway, hatred would get mother and son through this crisis. But in the end, it was Margaret's love that would keep their household together through this, the sternest of tests.

Murphy had taken a fortnight off work on the department's advice and he and Margaret went to stay at a friend's house at Lakes Entrance on the coast of south-east Victoria. At 7.30 on the evening of 8 April, there was a knock on the door. No-one outside of the family had the address, so Murphy was on guard. He carried his service revolver and hid another .38 in Margaret's handbag, just in case he needed it. But when he opened the door, there were three police officers he knew – Vic Anderson, Harry Kramme and Rex Hornbuckle – all colleagues in the Breaking Squad.

"What's going on?" asked Murphy.

"They've just locked up Carl Stillman," said Harry Kramme.

"Poor bastard," said Murphy. "Is there anything I can do for him?"

"Don't fucking worry about him, Brian. We've come here to lock you up too."

CHAPTER 19   IN THE DRY DOCK

MURPHY WAS IN THE LIVING ROOM at home when he heard his eldest son, Reg, running in from the street calling for him. He had always been a protective father but now he was hyper-sensitive to the slightest hint of danger to his kids. At the sound of his raised voice, he gritted his teeth for the umpteenth time that day and hurried to the front door.

It was early May, 1971, and Murphy had been on bail for man-slaughter for about a month. To most experts on the street, he and Stillman were as guilty as sin. The bosses hadn't even waited for the coroner's verdict on Collingburn's death to lay charges. The inquest, initially scheduled for 19 April, would not begin until the second week of June. This left Murphy and Stillman swinging in the wind, on $1000 bail each and suspended with-out pay.

The bosses had done them no favours. Acting Chief Commis-sioner Reg Jackson, or "Judas" Jackson as Plattfuss called him, had done nothing to quell the storm. Just a week after the death of Collingburn, Jackson had told the *Herald*'s chief police reporter, Seaton Ashton, that "the bulk" of the investigation was now complete. "But certain avenues of investigation still have to be finished." In short, a few loose ends needed tying up before they locked Murphy and Stillman up for ten years apiece. Ash-ton quoted Collingburn's father, Keith – a "bootmaker" – who said that "his son had told him that he ... had been detained over the ownership of two sets of golf clubs." It was an open and shut case: Collingburn was killed because two over-zealous cops did not believe a worker could be a golfer, so they beat him to death. To make matters worse, it came out that Connellan had bought the golf clubs at Northland shopping centre a few days earlier. It seemed only a matter of time before the courts brought judgment down upon them; that is, if the Painters and Dockers didn't get in first.

Neither cop had been "slotted" – locked up – after they were charged. Superintendent Frank Holland had processed Murphy and released him on bail immediately. Murphy had called Billy Longley to ask for a favour – a limited guarantee. Murphy himself was fair game, but he asked that his wife and children be off-limits. He added a chilling coda. "Billy, if anyone so much as looks at or talks to my kids, I'll kill four Painters and Dockers for each one of my kids. It'll be four to one, you tell 'em that! Then I'll tie their corpses to the back of my car and drag the bastards into Russell Street. They can charge me with their murders and I'll plead guilty," he said.

"Righto, chief," said Longley, in no doubt that Murphy was as serious as cancer.

Longley agreed to put Murphy's request to a meeting of the union members. This was a delicate matter for Longley. Securing a deal for one of the union's most hated adversaries would be no easy feat. In fact, it could get a bloke killed. Little wonder then that Longley had tucked Matilda – the aforementioned .45 calibre Colt – into his belt. Not only that, but an associate brought along a 9-millimetre Owen submachine gun, with twenty-five rounds in the clip.

There were no minutes taken at this meeting and no printed agenda, but it's fair to say the motion to provide Murphy with a limited guarantee was passed with acclamation, without resorting to the casting votes of Matilda and Owen. Longley rang Murphy with the results. He could not guarantee Murphy and his car, but Margaret and the kids would be safe as long as they stayed in the house. No-one would go near the house. That was it, but it meant a lot.

But Murphy, of course, was never one to leave well enough alone, and his actions precipitated Reg's dash in from the street a few weeks later.

"Dad," said Reg, breathlessly. "You know the man in the hat? The one who's got the big white car? He's out the front and he wants to talk to you."

There, in the evening shadows, stood Billy Longley, resplendent in his Stetson hat, leaning against his brand new Ford Fairlane ZD sedan.

"G'day, buddy, how you going?" said Longley.

"Not bad, Bill."

"You were working down the dock today, were you?"

Murphy admitted he was. Longley had been at a Painters and Dockers pub that evening and had heard a remarkable story of Murphy's appearance down at the Port Melbourne dry dock. Murphy was happy to fill in the details. Suspended without pay, he needed to feed his family. John Link, the boss of Link Industries, a major pump business, had offered him work. That morning a manager of the Duke and Orr dry dock was having trouble with a pump used to drain the water from the dock when a ship was in. Link sent an engineer, "Frenchie", to fix the problem and he asked Murphy to accompany him. Murphy readily agreed. So they went down there, walked straight into the engine room at the dry dock and climbed down a ladder to the main pump forty feet below ground level. Stacked all around the hole were heavy pig-iron ingots, at least a couple of hundred-weight each. Murphy was scurrying up and down the ladder, to and from the car, getting tools for Frenchie. Steadily, a number of dockies began to gather at the top of the dry dock, looking down on Murphy and Frenchie. He could hear them talking to one another. "It's that jack who killed Collingburn, isn't it? Yeah, the dog. What's he doing here?" Murphy started to feel extremely vulnerable at the bottom of the dry dock. If one of those pig-iron ingots toppled down onto them, they would be finished. Accidents happened all the time on the waterfront. There would be little sorrow and even fewer witnesses if Murphy met his doom down there.

Halfway through the job, a delegation of Painters and Dockers led by Jack "Putty Nose" Nicholls and the manager of the dry dock, a Scotsman named Bill Shorten (father of the federal Labor politician Bill Shorten) came to the top of the ladder.

Shorten called down: "Are you Brian Francis Murphy?"

"You know very well I am, Bill, what are you talking about?"

"I have these men with me, they are the delegates, and they say unless you leave the dock area immediately there will be a national strike of the Seaman's Union and the Painters and Dockers," he declared.

Murphy climbed the ladder to confront them. He was angry; here were unionists trying to deny a man a day's work. Painters and Dockers were at the lower end of the union food chain. They were the workers who scraped the barnacles off the ships below the waterline in the dry dock and cleared the jellyfish out of the ships' sea drains. There were some skilled workers – scaffolders, crane drivers, ship riggers and painters – but no-one had tenure; they were all unemployed when the ship left the dry dock. It was also a dirty, dangerous occupation and many workers died from asbestos-related illnesses or cancers caused by the organic compounds in the paint. The Federated Union of Shipwrights, Painters and Dockers, formed in 1900, had successfully fought to improve wages and conditions, but now the union was riven with thugs and gangsters who saw the docks as a venue for criminal opportunity. The union had complained long and hard about police harassment leaving the families of dockies on the breadline, and here they were doing the same thing to Murphy. He looked with scorn at "Putty Nose" Nicholls, who would later become secretary of the union and for a brief time the most powerful Painter and Docker.

"Listen, Jack, what about when you were in jail? Who got the city mission around to feed your family? Who was it that got St Vinnie's around to bring clothes for the kids? Whose brother was it came around to fix the copper when there was no hot water? It was me and mine, you weak bastard," said Murphy.

Nicholls lowered his head and shuffled his feet. "This is a union matter, nothing to do with me," he muttered.

"Is that right, is it? Well, if it's nothing personal, I know the score now. One day I'll be back in the police force and I'll come and get the whole bloody lot of you – but nothing personal, okay?" Murphy said.

No-one said a word. No-one had the balls to take him on. If a despised copper could go there with no back-up, without a gun in each hand, there was no telling what else he could do. In a mob, these Painters and Dockers were a force to be reckoned with, but there was not a man prepared to stand one-out against Murphy. It was only Shorten's threat of a strike that made Murphy leave the dry dock that day and he left with his head held high. When he got in his car and turned the ignition, he half expected it to blow up. When it didn't, he reckoned he had a chance of getting out alive, so he drove right past the ship in the dry dock. About eighty workers had gathered along the deck of the ship, all booing and hooting. Murphy lifted his cap, pushed it to the back of his head so they could all see his face and kept driving. Once out of the dock, he went to change gear and found his legs were shaking so badly he couldn't operate the clutch, so he kangaroo-hopped all the way up the road.

People were dying on the docks all the time. Jacky Twist had blown Freddy "The Frog" Harrison away with a shotgun back in 1958 on South Wharf in broad daylight in front of dozens of workers (and no-one saw a thing). Forty dockies would be murdered before the dock wars ended in the 1980s. It had been extremely foolhardy of Murphy to set foot on the docks, but he had turned a negative into a positive. When he had finished the story, Longley let out a deep, rumbling chuckle.

"I'm telling you, mate, if your guts were on the stock exchange tonight, there wouldn't be enough money in the entire country to buy 'em. You've stuck it right up their arse. The only one you've got to worry about killing you after today is some low-life druggie, paid by one of those cowards to knock you off. None of those blokes had the balls to take you on."

CHAPTER 20 THE VERDICT

THE STATEMENT THAT MURPHY WROTE concerning his part in the events of 26 March 1971 was just a page and a quarter long, double spaced. Few of the statements he took from men he charged were longer than that. Truth, he found, was always simple and unadorned. Lies were complex, elaborate constructions that collapsed under their own weight in court. But in politics, lies are expedient. A lie told in the service of expediency can gain favour from a wider group, including when that lie involves sacrificing one member for the benefit of the group.

In the weeks before the coroner's inquest into Collingburn's death, two detectives came to see Murphy at work with a proposition. They told him that if he changed his statement to say that Stillman had bashed Collingburn, causing his death, Murphy would be exonerated. He wouldn't even face trial. A deal would be done to tidy up the mess before the inquest. They said barrister Frank Galbally, acting for the Collingburn family, would not attack the new statement. The Crown and the police would support a motion to dismiss the manslaughter charges against Murphy. He simply had to lay the whole thing at Stillman's door to walk back into the job. There would be back pay. There would be a promotion from senior constable to sergeant. Stillman was nothing to him after all, said the detectives. The police, the press, the politicians, the courts and crims all wanted a scalp for the death of Collingburn, and Stillman's would do. Then everything would go nice and quiet again. No need for inquiries and reform; it would be business as usual. And all it required was a new statement.

Murphy listened as the detectives laid out the plan, occasionally remarking, "Is that so" or "You don't say." But inside he was boiling. Finally, he spoke. "You go back and tell the police department, Galbally, the Crown, the press or anybody else to go fuck themselves. I'm not changing anything for anyone, I'm innocent and so is Stillman," he said. So the die was cast. And in any event, changing his story would have been a high-risk strategy; if he came unstuck, it would look like he was just trying to save himself, and no-one would believe an accused killer who claimed the police had cut him a deal.

Murphy never told Stillman about the approach. The young constable was already doing it very hard. Though they had little in common, Stillman began calling Murphy at home almost every night before the trial. Murphy had been Stillman's first senior constable and he had learned a lot from him. Stillman knew that he was more responsible for their predicament. He had failed to follow procedure in the arrest and the interview back at Russell Street, and now they were on trial for his mistakes. One night, Stillman rang Murphy in a particularly despondent mood. It almost seemed to Murphy that Stillman was contemplating doing away with himself, or worse still, running away before the trial. Murphy decided to nip this in the bud.

"If I go down as a result of something you've done," he told Stillman, "I'll do the time and then I'll get out and hunt you down and kill you and your fucking family – your family first so you can watch, okay?" Margaret was in the kitchen at the moment Murphy let fly and she turned white; she nearly fainted.

She rarely saw this side of her husband's personality, his basic instinct for survival, and it was terrifying. It hinted at the other world he lived in, the world he kept away from her.

The coroner's inquest, held before a jury in the second week of June, 1971, was the low point. When it began, fifty members from three trade unions demonstrated outside. Speakers addressed the mob with a loud hailer, which was clearly audible inside the court.

In the witness box, Collingburn's co-accused, Ian Revell Carroll, testified that Murphy and Stillman had carried out an unprovoked and savage attack on Collingburn. Smartly dressed in a checked overcoat, the 23-year-old Carroll told the court that Murphy had led the assault.

The *Herald* reported that Carroll said the following: "During the bashing, Murphy shouted, 'The bash is on.' There were other police looking through a window and chanting 'Yeah, yeah' and laughing." Carroll said he had tried to punch Murphy to defend his mate Collingburn. He said Murphy had run up the room and punched him in the face, saying: "Assault me, will you?"

Murphy's counsel, Ray Dunn, asked Carroll if he was suggesting Dunn's client was running around like a raving lunatic. Carroll said Murphy had screamed all the time. Meanwhile, Stillman had stomped on Collingburn's mid-section while he was prone on the floor. Stillman had then shook Collingburn by the shoulders, telling him to get up.

"Stillman then smashed Collingburn's head on the ground," Carroll said. "Murphy and Stillman got either side of Collingburn and threw him into the lockers." He said Murphy had yelled out: "From now on, the bash is on."

Connellan's version was even more disturbing. He told the court that Murphy had said: "The bash is on for you fucking cunts who bash policemen. I'll kill you all." He added that Murphy had previously threatened to kill two other associates, Julian Fabris and Bobby Johansen.

The medical evidence seemed to back up Carroll's and Connellan's claims. Dr Roy Fink, a surgeon at St Vincent's, testified that the only patients he had seen with ruptured duodenums had "been run over by cars". To produce the half- to three-quarter-inch tear, he would have had to lay Collingburn on his back "and, if I didn't have any other weapon ... jump on his abdomen."

Government pathologist Dr James McNamara told the court he had only seen such injuries in plane crashes and after people had fallen from high buildings. The duodenum would have to be pressed up against the backbone with tremendous force.

Margaret did not attend the inquest; perhaps she couldn't bear to hear such savagery. She listened to radio reports and watched the TV news, which highlighted the most sensational and damaging claims. On TV, Murphy and Stillman looked as guilty as sin. When Murphy came home, Margaret would calmly inquire as to the day's proceedings. He would give his version and Margaret would look puzzled and say: "But that's not what was on the news." He would calm her, telling her he would never lie to her about anything he had done.

Once he woke in the dead of night to find Margaret crying beside him. He felt about as big as a louse on a flea's arse.

"What are you are crying about?" he asked.

"Why us?" she sobbed.

"It's got nothing to do with us, nothing whatsoever. This is the card we've been dealt and we have to play it," he said. "Do we have any kids that are handicapped?"

"You know we don't," she replied.

"Well, what would be worse? Me going to jail for ten years or having to cope with kids that have to suffer with disabilities?" he asked. There was silence. "We are blessed. We have a good, healthy family. Your sister is living here and she earns more than me now, so she can run the house for you. If I get ten years for this, you might be without a husband but you will never be without family. So thank God it's only this," he said.

When Margaret finally went to sleep, Murphy lay awake. He felt a crushing guilt. Margaret had never questioned his innocence, never questioned what he said, even when she should have on the evidence. She had gone to Mass every day and prayed fervently for God's will to be done. She had offered Masses for the soul of Neil Stanley Collingburn. But she had never asked her husband if he was innocent. To entertain such doubts would have brought her world crashing down. And without her, heaven knows where Murphy would be.

The jury committed Murphy and Stillman for trial. On the morning of 9 March 1972, Murphy called his two eldest children, thirteen-year-old Reg and twelve-year-old Bernardine, into the shed. He had a watch that he had intended to give Reg when he was twenty-one. But the morning of the verdict now seemed the best moment for this.

"I'm going to court this morning and I may not be back for ten years," he said. "Have this watch, Reg. You're the head of the house now; don't be standing over your mother, just take care of things," he said, trying to be practical and unemotional. "And Bern, you have to back up your brother …" Then big, hot tears began welling in his eyes and in those of the kids too.

*

After a three-week trial, the jury retired to consider its verdict at 12.05 p.m. The trial itself had been an anticlimax for Murphy's enemies after the sensational evidence presented at the coroner's inquest. Carroll and Connellan had given the same evidence and the Crown's medical experts had supported their version of an almost ritualistic police murder. The image of chanting officers watching Murphy and Stillman stomping on Collingburn on the muster-room floor would linger. But Murphy's team had responded with its own medical experts, including one Professor Hughes. Hughes's evidence condemned hospital staff for failing to provide Collingburn with adequate treatment. Had surgeons acted sooner, he would have survived. But he had also been the architect of his own demise: the final meal of steak and oysters had primed his system with bacteria. And then he had picked a fight with someone he shouldn't have.

The case would turn on Ian Revell Carroll. On the day of the arrest, Carroll had been charged with possession of an offensive weapon, namely a sheath knife. Stillman's partner, Gosney, said that on arrival at Russell Street, the prisoner had wanted to use the toilet. Gosney saw Carroll hiding the knife in a waste bin under the sink. Carroll claimed police had framed him; the knife wasn't his. He told the court he had merely stood in front of the urinal, did his business and that was all.

One morning, Murphy woke with a start at 4 a.m. with a thought: Carroll's a liar – and I can prove it! He rang his barrister, George Hempel, and, without explaining, asked to meet him at Russell Street immediately. At 7 a.m. he met Hempel, who was less than impressed to be dragged out of bed during a trial.

"This had better be good, Brian," he said as Murphy led him to the second-floor men's toilets at Russell Street. "What are we doing in this toilet?" he asked, getting slightly irritated.

"We're looking at the urinal that Ian Carroll pissed in," said Murphy.

"What urinal?" asked Hempel. There were only cubicles in the bathroom.

"Precisely," said Murphy. "This was a female toilet but now it's used by men. Carroll lied about what he did in here. He never stood in front of any urinal because there aren't any," said Murphy.

"Point taken, Brian."

Hempel recalled Carroll to the witness box and efficiently destroyed him. If he had lied about the knife, then what credibility did he have? This was a convicted thug against two police officers and at least two other police bystanders. Even when faced with damning medical evidence, juries in these days were reluctant to convict police.

Having taken an hour for lunch, the jury came back three hours and forty minutes later with a verdict. Stillman and Murphy were called from the cells below the court where they were served their last meal before judgment. Murphy was fit and ready. He had given up smoking – a sixty-a-day habit – and trained his body hard by kayaking and manual labour. He had resolved that if he went down, no-one was going to stand over him in jail. He would make a statement early by flogging the first lag that looked sideways at him.

As they rode in the lift, he looked at Stillman. He didn't begrudge this big, soft kid his mistakes. Murphy had cleaned up the mess as any senior constable would.

And he had given good evidence – better than he had ever given before. Even if found guilty, he had the satisfaction of that. Here was a man who had never passed an exam in his life until he joined the police force, matching wits with every learned soul in that august chamber. From the witness box, he would only lose five trials in thirty-three years. From the dock, he didn't want to lose this one. Now the attention to detail was paying off. It was reported that on the night of Collingburn's death, Murphy had summoned Stillman and Gosney to Russell Street and then to his home. They were together from 4.30 until 9.30 p.m. discussing the events of Friday night, getting every aspect straight. Murphy and the others had given flawless testimony. He hadn't gone off like a lunatic, been sarcastic or smart-arsed – all the things his barrister had heard he was. When he left the box, he asked his barrister how he had gone.

"Brian," said Hempel. "I have a friend at Twentieth Century Fox and a friend at Kevin Dennis Used Cars – who would you like to me to call?"

But a select audience was about to give its verdict.

"You look like shit," said Stillman.

"You must be looking in the mirror, pal," replied Murphy.

"If this goes wrong, I'm sorry," Stillman said, as the lift reached the court floor. They walked through a holding cell and into the court. The first person he saw was Margaret, rocking back and forth, clutching her rosary beads. At that moment nothing, even being found guilty, could compare with the grief he felt for putting Margaret in this position. He was still thinking about that in the seconds before the acquittal came. On hearing the verdict of not guilty, Murphy and Stillman left the dock and rushed over to embrace their wives and supporters.

"Get back in the dock!" roared Judge Leckie.

"I think he is only going to his wife," said one of the barristers.

When the pair came out of court, Murphy made a point of remembering Collingburn.

"Someone's lost his life here. There's a mother and father without a son, a wife without a husband and a child without a father," he said, earnestly.

That night, 337 nights after he was first charged, was the only night that Murphy could not sleep. He was afraid that his acquittal was all a dream and if he fell asleep he would wake up and still be living the ordeal. The bosses who had left him for dead now rushed back. He and Stillman were to be promoted: Murphy to detective sergeant and Stillman to senior constable. There would be back pay and no loss of privileges. "They are back to the same position they were when suspended," said the acting chief commissioner A.L. Carmichael the day after the acquittal. Murphy was back in the Breakers.

*

A few days later, Murphy was called up to the superintendent in charge of the CIB.

"Brian, sit down, mate," he said. "You've been through a lot."

"Meaning?" said Murphy.

"The Collingburn thing ..."

"I don't give a fuck – finished. So tell me, what's happening today?" he asked.

"I tell you, if we had a dozen detective sergeants with the get up and go that you've got and the nous for speaking to people, we'd be so far in front." He paused. "But you're going back to uniform." He braced himself for an explosion.

"Well that fucks you," said Murphy. "Is that all?"

"Isn't that enough?" asked the superintendent.

"It doesn't matter," replied Murphy. "I'm still gonna get up tomorrow morning and go to work and do my job. What about you?"

"I'm going to send you home with a detective sergeant to make sure you don't do anything stupid," said the superintendent. When Murphy got home, he told Margaret he was back in uniform.

"What's Murray doing here?" she asked.

"They've sent him home with me to see I don't do anything stupid like shoot a superintendent."

"Yeah, that's right," said the detective sergeant.

There was also a fear that the acquitted men were still in danger. A handbill had circulated around the docks, vowing that Collingburn, the martyred worker, would be avenged:

Amongst this gang of fascist thugs Murphy is a shining example. Even within this violent and corrupt police force he has a long record of violence. Collingburn was killed. He was killed by the police. He is not the only one who has been killed in this way. Nor will he be the last. He was a simple worker but he has not died in vain. His death and its consequences have left a lasting lesson. It will not be lost.

For nearly a year after the acquittal, there was graffiti on a red brick wall of St Brigid's Catholic Church in North Fitzroy in vivid white paint: MURPHY IS A MURDERER. He drove past it for months until, fed up, he called the priest and asked for it to be removed. The priest refused, saying it was part of history now.

Certainly, the Victorian Government was keen to bury the affair, having failed to quell public concerns about accountability for police brutality. Six months before the verdict, on 15 September 1971, the chief secretary of police, Rupert Hamer, announced the appointment of a retired stipendiary magistrate to review the action taken on complaints against police. But the police ombudsman had no real power. He had no staff, no budget, no vehicle and no premises. He had no recourse to any data other than that provided by police. Victoria's Office of Police Integrity commented on the wisdom of the reform in a report thirty-five years later:

> Unfortunately, like any system of accountability based simply on paper review, it proved less than effective. Some years later when inquiring about the progress of long-delayed reviews, it was found he (the ombudsman) had died. His widow expressed relief at the fact that the growing mass of files taking up space in her lounge room could be removed.

*

On 8 January 1974, Senior Constable Norman Curson was on foot-patrol duties at the main entrance to Flinders Street Railway Station in Melbourne. He was approached by a young woman and, as he turned to speak to her, a man named James Belsey walked up behind him, produced a knife and cut Curson's throat. Belsey then calmly walked across Flinders Street into Young & Jackson's Hotel, where he was arrested a short time later. In the meantime, Curson had been rushed to Prince Henry's Hospital but died a few hours later.

After Curson died and the identity of the murderer was established, one of Murphy's colleagues came in to see him at Russell Street.

"Murph, that bloke came in looking for you twice, you know," he said.

"Well, why didn't you tell me?" asked Murphy, incredulous.

"Well, I just thought he was another nutter. I didn't worry about it."

Apparently Belsey had a long history of mental disorder and had made frequent threats to kill police. He was charged with the murder of Senior Constable Curson but was subsequently acquitted because of his insanity. As a result, he was sentenced to be detained "at the Governor's pleasure".

The incident rocked Murphy. It was nearly two years after the Collingburn verdict, but perhaps there were people who would never be convinced. Perhaps in Belsey's fractured mind any officer was Brian Murphy, or perhaps he thought, in vengeance, any officer would do. Either way, the fracas in the muster room three years earlier had indirectly claimed another victim. Lucky it wasn't me, Murphy thought.

CHAPTER 21 THE TUNING OF THE BELL

IN MID-1972, SOON AFTER the Collingburn acquittal, Billy Longley rang Murphy with a piece of wisdom. A full-scale war was raging down the docks and Longley was up to his neck in blood, but he always had time for such musings.

He had been reading a book which discussed the process of making church bells from bronze in the Middle Ages. The trick was to get the proportions of copper and tin in the alloy just right. Too much copper and the bell would be soft, losing its resilience and tonal quality. Too much tin and it would be too hard, liable to shatter. So what gave the bell its resonance and sustained vibration could also be its greatest flaw. You couldn't tell until the bell tolled. The bell maker would take the bell from the furnace, and let it cool over night. The next day he would take a sixteen-pound sledgehammer and strike it as hard as he could. If it didn't crack then, it never would. That's what Murphy had been through, said Longley, and they hadn't broken him. They would never get him now. But they were trying their best.

He was sent back to Russell Street and placed in charge of a group of officers who had all fallen from grace. One had been a suspect in the murder of his wife, while another had been implicated in a string of factory break-ins. The bosses believed Murphy would eventually stuff up again, taking everyone near him down as well. Better that decent men be spared his perfidious, violent influence, they reasoned.

It was back to the beat on night patrols with his young miscreant officers for Murphy. Cruising round darkened streets, he taught them to how to catch crooks. As they drove through blocks of factories in Collingwood, Abbotsford and Richmond down to the Yarra River, he would say: "Look for the nice car parked in areas like this. Crooks will reconnoitre this area in their own cars, then leave them and go to the job on foot. Head up this way a quarter mile till we see a laneway or a break in the factories that leads to the next street. We'll speak to anyone we see at that end, especially if they're carrying a sports bag, and we'll lock 'em up if they can't set us straight. They just shouldn't be hanging round factories at night."

In residential areas in the early hours of the morning, they would drive slowly, playing a torch light over parked cars. "Be looking for the car window with the dew rubbed off by hand and then follow the trail to your car thief. Arrest anyone carrying a torch, especially if it's masked with brown paper with a small hole cut out of it. Take special note of car doors left ajar. Good crims know that residents always remember the sound of a car door closing, even from a deep sleep."

Then they would cross the river into leafy middle-class Kew and park by the Yarra. "What's a bloke doing paddling a kayak down the river fully clothed at 2 a.m.? He's probably coming back from a spot of midnight shopping in those homes up there. Probably paddling down to where he's left his car in Richmond with the goods stuffed in the kayak. Let's meet him there.

"Later, a few hours before dawn, take a swing through Toorak, where the burghers feel so secure in their self-importance they don't have fences before their expansive lawns. There's a set of footprints leaving the pavement and across the front lawn of that house …" They would follow the trail of prints in the frost to the home.

"And it goes to that bedroom window … there's a handprint here, where they've had a look in." So they would follow the trail to the next house, the next window, and on up the icy street for a block or two. "We either have a peeping Tom or a house-breaker, maybe even a rapist." Each shift they were guaranteed to make at least two arrests. Often the charge was only loitering, but the intent was clear, and it stopped a lot of crime.

Through Murphy's stories, they learned to use the full range of their policing powers, not to mention their cunning and native intelligence. One of his favourites came from the mid-1960s, from his days on the beat in Port Melbourne.

A phantom flasher was operating at Clark Street State School. He had been exposing himself to children at lunchtime but would disappear by the time the teachers were alerted. Murphy worked out that the man lived in one of the adjacent homes across the street and set a trap. He borrowed his brother Pat's truck, emptied all the plumbing gear out of the back and parked it near the school. He and another cop concealed themselves in the back tray under a tarpaulin. A third officer was posted on the other side of the school with a pair of field glasses trained on the suspect's house. Sure enough, the flasher emerged from the house and walked up to the cyclone fence at the front of his house. He checked there was no-one with authority around and then, with a sick grin, pushed his erect penis through the wire and began waving it at the kids. At the appearance of the offen-sive weapon, a signal was given from the lookout and Murphy crept up stealthily. The flasher was having a great time, smiling and laughing as the kids ran off in terror. Without a word, Murphy reached across and seized the flasher's penis in his right hand. The man tried to pull away but Murphy had a vice-like grip and yanked him hard against the fence. The offending member became a useful handle as Murphy delivered a series of stunning headbutts. In shock, pain and confusion, the offender began to urinate wildly, spraying Murphy and the other cop who had come to help, but Murphy was not about to let go and they hauled him down to the station.

A couple of days later, Murphy received a call from the man's solicitor warning that the flasher was planning to plead not guilty and that shocking allegations would be made against the police in court. They had indecently assaulted his client and there would be retribution, if not compensation. Murphy replied nonchalantly that he was bringing two children to the station that day to get their statements. Their fathers were big-time crims – gunnies from the Painters and Dockers – and he was going to tell these men who the offender was and where he lived. The phone went dead. When he got to court, the flasher pleaded guilty without a murmur. He lived by the school for another twenty years and, though Murphy always kept an eye on him, there was no chance of him re-offending.

It was the birth of "slychology", as Murphy called it: a blend of street smarts and police method, with some carrot and an awful lot of stick.

He had become more reflective about violence since the Collingburn affair but by his own admission he still loved a fight. And at forty he was in his prime: cyclist, kayaker and all-round action man. And trouble followed him. Even a trip to the fish'n'chip shop could leave the kids feeling like extras in a Chuck Norris flick.

On one afternoon in particular, Murphy, in his jeans and tight T-shirt, had left the kids in the blue Valiant to pick up the egg-and-bacon sangers. As he stood in the shop, he noticed in the greasy mirror that one of the two blokes behind him had pulled a knife. They're planning to rob the joint, he thought. A bead of sweat ran off his tanned pate and onto a prodigious sideburn. In a flash, he reached down and produced his .38 from a holster on his right ankle (tailor-made from the finest leather by a Franciscan monk; it was, at the time, the must-have accessory among Victorian detectives). He spun around and it was on. The one with the knife lunged at him – but missed – before fleeing the fish'n'chip shop in terror and running up the stairs to the pool joint next door. Murphy, passing his wide-eyed kids, followed at a gallop, pistol in hand, into the crowded hall. The villains had forgotten all about stabbing Murphy now and were scrambling wildly around the pool tables trying to escape the armed lunatic in hot pursuit. They made a dash for the stairs but Murphy cut them off. He clubbed one on the back of the head with his gun so hard that he crashed down the stairs, sprawled across the bonnet of the Valiant and onto the road. Meanwhile, Murphy had the other would-be bandit in his clutches. He jammed his .38 into the man's mouth, the gunsight scraping skin from the roof of his mouth. But the man slipped the barrel and dashed after his mate, desperately calling for him to wait up. His mate was now fifty metres away, running up the middle of the street. "Get fucked!" he called, looking back over his shoulder as he sprinted, before running smack into a tram pole and knocking himself unconscious. By this time the other bandit couldn't care less: he hurdled his fallen comrade and made his escape, lest Murphy shoot him in the back.

The kids, witnesses to all this, were sitting speechless in the Valiant when Murphy came back with the egg-and-bacon sandwiches. He panicked, knowing they would tell Margaret of these highjinks and cause a drama. "Back in one moment, children," he said jauntily. He ran back into the shop and bought them each a Coke. A bribe would surely buy their silence. But it didn't. It's hard to keep quiet when you realise your dad is a superhero.

Margaret worried every time the phone rang in the night – as it did a month after this.

They were on patrol in Victoria Street, Abbotsford, watching the slime of the night oozing out of the pubs and card clubs on that strip. Murphy had the window down and his gun tucked between his legs on the seat as he drove. A pair of mad, drunken Yugoslavs lurched past the car at a set of traffic lights.

"Who do you think you are, dog-fucking cop!" spat one of the men. Murphy just smiled. The Yugoslav pulled a razor-sharp boning knife from his coat and stepped towards the car.

"Cyril, he takes another step, I'll shoot him straight in the guts," snarled Murphy, levelling his gun at the Yugoslav.

"Oh no, boss … don't shoot him," pleaded his terrified constable.

While the attention was on his gun, Murphy opened the door, slamming it into the knifeman's guts. His arm came spearing through the window and Murphy smashed it with his gun to dislodge the knife. Then both officers leapt out of the car and gave the pair a sound flogging right in the middle of the street before locking them up.

Murphy knocked off and went to bed. At 2 a.m., he was woken by the telephone. It was an inspector.

"Murph, you're in diabolical trouble. That bloke with the knife has gone to the hospital and he's vomiting blood everywhere."

"So?" said Murphy, a million thoughts running through his mind.

"Did you give him a hiding?" the inspector asked.

"He got a couple of good whacks, but that's it!"

"Well, you'd better lock your front gate. If this bloke dies, you'll be getting another visitor."

"My front gate is staying open. I've done nothing wrong," said Murphy and hung up on the inspector. Margaret woke up in horror.

"What was that all about?" she squeaked, the panic rising in her voice.

"There's something wrong at work. It's got nothing to do with me," he said.

"Are you sure?" she asked from the darkness.

"Yeah," he said, quietly. If I go down this time, there's a street full of witnesses, so I'll be alright, he thought. They both lay there listening to the sound of each other's breathing for a minute or two, then went back to sleep.

At 5 a.m. the phone rang again. This will be Homicide, thought Murphy.

"Is everything alright?" he asked, turning away from Margaret.

"Yeah, Murph, he was chucking red wine, mate. It was red wine."

"Sweet," said Murphy, and went back to sleep.

*

All things considered, life was going smoothly for Murphy back at Russell Street. He knew in his heart that he should never have been reinstated after the Collingburn acquittal. There were too many enemies, and even friends, who still believed he had killed

Collingburn. Young coppers idolised him and fought to get on his crew; they believed he had gotten away with murder and wanted to be like him. He was no longer The Psych of his earlier days; he had become The Skull. It was as much for his brains as for the bald head that the name stuck.

Since Collingburn, he was infinitely more sneaky and he gave himself free rein to plot and scheme. He was forever solving problems, using the bosses' own systems to defeat them. He saved the job of one constable over two inspectors, swearing a statement in court that described the bosses as "weak arseholes". The judge accepted the statement in full but kept it off the public record as it would have "caused disaffection".

Mick Miller, now assistant commissioner and a few years away from the top job, had always had a soft spot for Murphy. After the acquittal, Miller had offered Murphy an early retirement, a "psych pension" for life. All that was needed was to get three shrinks to say he was mad. How many would it take to say he was sane? Murphy had countered.

Murphy sat the senior sergeant's exam in mid-1972. He thought he had done a ball-tearing paper and he went to see Miller.

"How do you think you went with the senior sergeant's exam?" Miller asked.

Murphy was confident he had passed.

"Maybe so, but you won't be getting it this year," said Miller. "I think there's a bit of discipline coming your way, Murphy."

"It won't do much good," Murphy replied. "I'm not sitting the exam again, and they can go stick it up their arse. I'm not going to play their stupid games."

Thus Force Command's last opportunity to control The Skull was forfeited. As a senior sergeant behind a desk, the bosses could have observed, if not controlled, his activities. Now

Murphy would spend the rest of his career in the field enforcing his own version of law and order. He was a darker character than before the Collingburn affair; he kept more secrets, and the contrast between his home life and the job was sharper. His informer network included some of Melbourne's best crooks and he didn't mind if they thought he was up to no good. It made them relax and tell him more. Just how far he was prepared to go, he never let on.

It was as well to keep Murphy active on the job as try to control him, so the bosses assigned him to a small special-duties squad, where at least he was in plainclothes again. By 1974, his purgatory was over and he applied for readmission into the CIB. A meeting of the regional CIB chiefs was convened to consider the matter. No-one wanted him except Plattfuss, now an inspector and boss of Heidelberg CIB. On his first day, Murphy turned up in The Puss's office for duty.

"Now listen, cunty," said The Puss through a cloud of cigarette smoke. He waved one meaty fist. "If you want to stay here, you keep your cunt scratchers in your pocket, right? And your Bungaree boxing gloves on the ground," he added, pointing to Murphy's boots, "and all will be well."

Unlike The Puss, the senior sergeant was of a more nervous disposition.

"We run a nice quiet station here," he said gravely. "We don't want any bravado, you understand? We want no-one belted. If they haven't done it, they don't get locked up. Frankly, Murphy, you come here with a pretty bad reputation." Murphy exploded and immediately went to leave the office.

"If that's what you think of me, you can go and get stuffed," he shouted. The Puss came shambling out of his office when he heard the row.

"Where are you fucking going?" he roared at Murphy.

"He's given me a lecture, boss!" cried Murphy.

"For Chrissake, Sergeant, give this bloke something to do," ordered Plattfuss.

Within a few hours, Murphy was back in the station after apprehending a serial offender wanted for up to thirty rapes. It had been a long, violent pursuit and arrest. The suspect – who eventually got ten years' jail – was battered, bruised and covered in blood. In the struggle, Murphy had pulled a knife from the back of the man's trousers and managed to open up his buttock like a tender piece of rump steak. When he hauled the bloody culprit in, the senior sergeant had his feet up on a chair, smoking. He took one look at Murphy's prisoner and gulped. He opened the drawer, grabbed a handful of pills, swallowed them and left for the day. Plattfuss was rapt.

"About time you got off your arse! What took you so long?"

That set the tone for Murphy's two years at Heidelberg. With a free rein, courtesy of The Puss, he could do what he did best – catch crooks.

CHAPTER 22 IN SMOKE

BY MID-1974, BILLY LONGLEY was tropical. That is, he was hot on the underworld's hit list. A battle for control of the waterfront was underway inside the Painters and Dockers, and Longley, it was said, had taken decisive action.

At 9.55 p.m. on 17 October 1973, Longley's rival, union secretary Pat Shannon, was gunned down in South Melbourne's Druids Hotel. A man carrying a .22 calibre rifle walked in and pumped three shots into Shannon at the bar, killing him instantly.

Everyone was nominating Longley as the shooter, though he would always claim he was in bed hours before the shooting. For the next year and a half, Longley was "in smoke" – in hiding – as the Shannon faction sought revenge. He rang Murphy at Russell Street a couple of days after the shooting.

"What's doing?" he asked Murphy, nonchalantly.

"What's *doing*?" Murphy replied. "The cat's among the pigeons, that's what's doing!"

Longley started laughing. "It certainly is," he chuckled.

At Longley's trial for murder in 1975, the Crown submitted that police had sought him day and night throughout the entire time he was in smoke; a 21-member squad was tracking him relentlessly, the court was told, but the dangerous, cunning Longley had managed to stay one step ahead. In reality, there had been only a cursory search. On the day of Pat Shannon's funeral, police had searched Murphy's house, suspecting him of hiding Longley. Murphy had snuck up to see who attended the Shannon funeral and returned home to find some detectives had been through his house. Having not found Longley hiding in Murphy's closet, they ceased any further inquiries. Perhaps the bosses reckoned the Shannon forces would eventually catch up with Longley, saving the state the cost and inconvenience of convicting him of murder.

It was hardly a secret that Longley was staying in a little house with his wife next to the post office in Monageeta in central Victoria. Murphy had even given police the address. He had visited Longley with Margaret, and their gracious host and his wife had served them tea with scones and jam.

There had been one abortive attempt to bring him in. The Puss had asked Murphy to organise a meeting where Longley would submit to questioning. Longley agreed to the meeting, but he knew that Plattfuss had a terrible name among crims. Sure enough, on the appointed evening, The Puss, with an entourage, arrived at the Oxford Hotel like he was leading a legion of Roman soldiers. Longley, who was sitting off watching the venue, changed his mind. He couldn't be sure that Plattfuss wouldn't double-cross him. Plattfuss had always said he got the best information from people behind bars. Jail, where Painters and Dockers could get at him by bribing the screws, was not an option for Longley.

The Puss was furious at being stood up.

"When I catch that fat bastard, I'm going to rip his head off his shoulders and piss in the hole," he roared.

"And you wonder why he didn't come?" quipped Murphy, risking a punch in the head.

So for the next few months, Longley would call Murphy at

Russell Street on night shift for a chat, finding out the latest news on the street. Murphy had eyes and ears everywhere and kept Longley up to date with the latest scandals.

It wasn't until 13 February 1975 that Longley finally gave himself up to Detective Jimmy Fry after negotiating with police through his lawyer. He told authorities that he only surrendered because he didn't want people thinking he was evading justice by staying on the run. He feared getting his head blown off by rival unionists much more than being nicked by police. At Longley's trial, the Crown was desperate to prove the police had been seeking Longley throughout his time on the run. One police witness after another attested to their earnest efforts to catch Longley. One Homicide detective, when asked how he knew of the manhunt for Longley, pulled Murphy's name out of thin air. The judge ordered that Murphy appear in court and verify this important element of the Crown case.

The detective rang Murphy at Heidelberg CIB to tell him he had dragged him into the case. He was apologetic. "I've done the wrong thing – what'll I say to them on Monday? You'll have to give evidence to save my arse," he moaned.

"I'll tell you what to say – tell them you've lied and that you'll plead guilty to perjury!" Murphy shouted. "That's what you can say!" He slammed down the phone.

The Puss heard the exchange and strode over.

"Who the hell were you talking to?" he demanded.

"Nobody, boss," said Murphy, feigning absorption in some typing. The Puss loomed over him, grinding his teeth.

"Don't you bullshit me, cunty!"

"Alright then, boss, it was a bloke from the Homicide Squad. He wants me in court on Monday to back up the lies he told to save his arse, okay?" Plattfuss smashed his fist into his palm.

"I'm glad you told him to go fuck himself. You aren't going to court like that! I don't care who it is, you can tell them from me to go fuck themselves. The damn cheek of them even asking," said Plattfuss.

"Okay, boss, let's agree to agree then, shall we?"

"My bloody oath!" said The Puss, greatly satisfied.

At 11.30 on the Sunday night, the phone rang at Murphy's home. It was Plattfuss.

"You're going to court in the morning and don't you fucking argue with me!" said The Puss and hung up.

The next morning, Murphy was on hand for the start of proceedings in the Supreme Court. Across the corridor was a police room, where members could sit and wait to give evidence. As he walked into the room, he saw the Homicide detective who had nominated him the previous Friday.

"Well, Murphy, you've graced us with your presence," he said, emboldened by the bosses' directive that Murphy appear. "You're going to have to decide today whose side you're on, the police or the criminals," he sneered. Even if he realised he had just lit the fuse, there was no time to avoid the explosion. Murphy launched himself across the table at the detective, grabbing two handfuls of his shirt, tie, coat and throat.

"You bastard," he roared as he shook the startled detective. "Don't you dare tell me whose side I'm on!"

Then he went berserk, screaming that he was going to kill the detective. Two Homicide cops tried to prise Murphy off but he wouldn't release his grip. Two other cops grabbed him by the waist to drag him away but succeeded only in helping the first pair pull Murphy's coat inside out over his head. Suddenly the doors swung open to a full courtroom. The prosecutor and the defence counsel walked in, saw the fracas and quickly shut the doors before scurrying back to the bar table. The judge was ascending the bench while this wrestling match continued. It only ended when the clerk of the court called Murphy to give evidence. Murphy, red-faced and sweating, was still struggling back into his coat as he hurried into the court.

"Are you Brian Francis Murphy?" the judge asked him.

"Yes I am, Your Honour," said Murphy.

"When you are finished getting dressed, please go into the witness box," said the judge.

It was easy enough for Murphy to deny telling the detective that Longley was being sought. But Longley's counsel never directly put the key question: had the police actually been seeking Longley for Shannon's murder? Had he been asked, his answer would have been an emphatic *no*. But he was never asked. It seemed a minor point, but for many years later Murphy felt that lapse had contributed to Longley's downfall.

Longley got a life sentence for Shannon's murder and served thirteen hard years; but he never blamed Murphy. He hadn't killed Shannon, there was no doubt about that, he said, but there had been damning evidence. One of his co-accused, Kevin Taylor, testified that Longley had stepped from the shadows that night, grabbed the .22 and shot Shannon personally. It was a pack of lies, but perhaps the scales of justice had now come into balance. Longley had killed many others, maybe up to a dozen people, and had gotten away with it. There was a kind of rough justice to going down for Shannon, so he could cop it sweet. And perhaps jail was a safer place than the streets of Melbourne. Dozens of men would die in the struggle for control of the union, which raged for another decade. There were numerous plots to kill Longley inside jail but they never succeeded. He formed an alliance with the notorious standover man and criminal psycho Mark Brandon "Chopper" Read, which probably saved his life. But Longley left the best part of himself in Pentridge Prison's maximum-security H Division. He outlived all of his enemies, despite the hardships of jail, but it was a mixed blessing: it gave him too much time to ponder his mistakes.

CHAPTER 23 THE VALOUR BADGE

By December 1975, Murphy's rehabilitation was virtually complete and soon he would return to Russell Street to join the Consorting Squad. He was excited by the prospect. Just one more quiet Christmas in the northern suburbs, he thought, and he would be back in the action downtown. But trouble found Murphy no matter where he was.

Shortly after 7 p.m. on 16 December, Heidelberg police received a report of gunfire in Hyacinth Street, Greensborough. Ida and Rob Aughton were playing cricket in the street with their two kids. They had set up the wicket in front of their house, 7 Acacia Court, at the top of the cul-de-sac, and the bowler was coming in from the bottom corner at number 1, adjoining Hyacinth Street, where Corporal James David Gardiner lived with his wife and two small children. Ida thought she heard someone cracking a stockwhip; she had grown up in the country and was used to such sounds. The frequency of the cracks increased. Someone's going crazy with that whip, Ida Aughton thought.

She glanced back at her own house and heard a fizz past her ear – then one of the terracotta tiles on her roof shattered. She suddenly realised someone was shooting at them from the bottom of the street near the Gardiner house. Ida and Rob grabbed the kids, ran into the house and lay on the floor. They heard intermittent volleys for the next three hours that broke windows and street lights in Acacia Court and Hyacinth Street.

When Murphy started his night shift at 9.30 p.m., the siege was still going on. Over the radio, the D24 despatcher suggested he take a look, as a stalemate had developed.

Peering over the windowsill of her front room, Ida Aughton could see a dozen police cars parked here and there. The street was cordoned off and officers were creeping through neighbouring gardens, guns drawn, trying to get a clear view of the Gardiner place. The gunman was in the front bedroom, propped on the windowsill to watch the street, his .22 calibre rifle at the ready. He commanded an extensive field of fire. From his house on the corner, high on the hill, Hyacinth Street dipped away steeply, putting a dozen homes in his direct sight.

Corporal Jim Gardiner was only thirty-three but already he felt like an old man. He had joined up in 1966 and was sent to Vietnam in June 1969 with the 110 Signals Squadron. He spent his tour at Vung Tau "back beach" where signallers operated a major communications hub for the war. Information on his war service is sketchy but it appears he left Vietnam in October 1969 after falling ill. He came home bitter and disillusioned, just as public opinion was swinging heavily against the war. Like many vets, he wondered how he had survived and why so many Australians hated him for it. He stayed in the army on his return and was attached to the 6th Signal Branch at Watsonia Barracks in Melbourne. He had a wife and two young children but depression and perhaps undiagnosed post-traumatic stress had pushed him to the edge. Over a period of months, in small amounts, he had stolen $1800 from the army mess at Watsonia. He feared he would be exposed and court-martialled. Earlier that day, he had tried to commit suicide with a rifle in the hills behind the Healesville training camp but was interrupted. He returned home in an agitated state after several hours of drinking. His wife, Joy, was babysitting for some neighbours across the road. Jim came to her with his rifle in hand and told her that an intruder was prowling inside their house. At 6.30 p.m. the firing began from inside the Gardiners' home and his wife called the police. Corporal Gardiner was making his last stand.

When Murphy arrived, he saw as many as twenty officers taking cover behind their vehicles as Gardiner took pot shots, blowing out the headlights of the police cars. He ordered every light in the street be turned off and then, through the darkness, Ida Aughton saw a lone figure stand up from behind cover.

"Jim, I want to talk to you," she heard Murphy say.

"Get fucked, any closer and I'll put one through you," shouted Gardiner, looking through the rifle sights at Murphy.

"Eh, eh, Jim, just give me a chance," said Murphy confidently. "I'm coming to talk to you. I won't be armed. Just want to talk to you, mate."

He handed his gun to his partner, Griff Morris.

"I'm going over, but if he shoots me, kill the bastard with my gun, would you, Griff?" Morris had the heart of an ox; he would follow orders.

Murphy approached the house up the sloping front lawn. Ida could hear him pleading with Gardiner in the most plaintive, compassionate tone she had ever heard.

"Jim, come on, put down the gun. You want to see your kids again. I want to see my kids again. Please, Jim, I'm begging you, please put down the gun." She watched him edge his way right to the house and then up the steps to the front door. He sat on the rail. To his right, twelve feet away, Gardiner sat on the windowsill of the front bedroom, the rifle trained at Murphy's head.

Murphy pulled out his tobacco and tried to roll a cigarette, but his hands were shaking so badly he couldn't manage it.

"Hey, Jim, can't seem to roll a smoke with you pointing that thing at me; why don't you give me one of yours?" asked Murphy.

"Well, you would be a mean bastard, wouldn't you? Rolling your own! Make one yourself," snorted Gardiner.

"I would but I'm shitting meself," said Murphy. Gardiner laughed, lowered the rifle and tossed over a cigarette from a packet in his shirt pocket. Murphy resisted the urge to lunge over and pull Gardiner off the window. "Hey, I know what, Jim. Let me come in and we'll have a talk about this."

"If you have a gun or handcuffs, I'll kill you, you understand?"

"Sweet, sweet, just let me in."

Gardiner opened the front door and pushed the rifle straight into Murphy's mouth, forcing the muzzle between his lips. Murphy could feel the warm steel of the recently fired weapon on his tongue. The front gunsight scraped the roof of his mouth. With one hand, Jim frisked Murphy up and down and, satisfied he was unarmed, pulled him inside.

"What about a cuppa?" Murphy suggested, his legs shaking as they walked into the kitchen. Still holding the rifle, Gardiner put on the kettle. His wife had made a hedgehog cake and he offered some but Murphy refused – his mouth was so dry with terror he couldn't swallow. Gardiner's anger flared again.

"What? Are you crook on me missus?" he snarled.

"No, no, give us some of that cake then." Murphy took the cake and tried to eat it. It stuck to the roof of his mouth and he blew crumbs when he tried to speak. He had to get inside this man's head, or neither of them would walk out of there alive.

"Jim, no matter what's gone on, your kids and your wife, they love you," said Murphy. "And no matter what you've done, we can't hang you and we can't deport you, so already you're way in front. And you know what, Jim? If you kill me, my kids will be terribly disappointed because I'm supposed to be taking them fishing tomorrow."

"How many kids have you got?" asked Gardiner.

"Five," said Murphy, running through the names and ages.

"Well, I've only got two," said Gardiner, sighing.

They talked about their kids and the burden of fatherhood. It was sometimes hard to live up to the man his kids thought he was, said Murphy. Life was full of mistakes, disappointment and sorrow, but a child's love was unconditional. There would always be forgiveness. Soon the corporal was crying, saying he had made a mess of everything for his family. But there was always time to begin again, Murphy said. Redemption could begin right there.

Then, quite unexpectedly, Gardiner unloaded the rifle and laid it on the floor. There was no talk for a moment, just the sound of Gardiner's crying. Murphy never made a move towards the gun.

They began to talk about everything that had happened, from Vietnam until that moment. Gardiner told Murphy a story of seeing innocent civilians killed in urban attacks and of seeing the aftermath when a vehicle carrying American and Australian troops had hit a landmine. Compared with others' experiences, what he had witnessed had been minor, but somehow he had taken on the guilt of the survivor. He had walked away, unin-jured, while so many others had died.

He should have gone too, he said; his life was worthless. Soon after Gardiner arrived home in Christmas 1969, he attended a function at Sydney University. Officers had warned veterans not to wear their uniforms on campus to avoid antago-nising the students, but Gardiner was too proud to go in civvies.

The students spat on his uniform, called him a baby killer, and he never forgot it. Everything in his life was wrong; the system was against him, picking on him.

Everybody lives by the system – you can't buck it, Murphy told him.

"What's affected you is something that happens to perhaps one in 100,000 people. You're special."

"Don't fucking give me special," said Gardiner.

"Whether you think you are or not, you're special," said Murphy, fixing him with a stare. "How many other blokes have survived in a war zone, got back here and have a wife and children that love them?"

Murphy promised he would make sure Jim was well treated if he came out and gave himself up. Shortly after 11 p.m. the Aughtons watched the two men walk out of the house and to the waiting policemen.

"That was the longest twenty minutes of my life," said Murphy when he got back to his partner.

"You were in there for over an hour and a half," said Morris, handing him back his gun.

The next day, Murphy, through his contacts, arranged for the National Bank to extend Gardiner a loan to cover the money missing from the army mess. Gardiner later pleaded guilty to using a firearm to prevent arrest. Judge Byrne of the County Court released him on a $50 three-year good behaviour bond. On Murphy's evidence it was clear, the judge said, that Gardiner would not re-offend and therefore he would not jail him. He had been diagnosed with psychotic depression.

"It is plain to see, in this case, the sheer unselfish bravery of Detective Murphy," the judge told Gardiner. "He put your welfare before his own life."

The following September, Murphy was awarded the Victoria Police Valour Award "for outstanding courage, restraint and devotion to duty".

"With grave risk to his own life, he confronted and subsequently arrested an armed offender, who threatened to kill anybody that came near him," wrote Chief Commissioner Reg Jackson. This was the same chief commissioner who, five years earlier, had sanctioned Murphy's prosecution; the same one who had rejected Murphy and Stillman when they tried to recoup their legal expenses of $1500 from the Collingburn trial.

Murphy received the Valour Badge on 21 September 1976 on the parade ground at the Glen Waverley Police Academy. As he pinned the badge on Murphy, a deputy commissioner, J.R.G. Salisbury, began to laugh.

"Well look at you, Brian Francis Murphy. It wasn't so long ago we were trying to pin a murder on you, and here we are pinning a Valour Badge on you!"

"Funny how things turn out, isn't it?" Murphy replied.

Of course, Murphy had not put himself in the firing line to win awards. He had seen a man in need and had answered the call. He had taken control of a situation, just like he had with Collingburn, but this time they had both walked out alive. A week after the siege, Murphy went back to the Gardiners' with presents for the kids and Christmas cake. It was as much as anyone else had done. There had been a visit from the army chaplain but that was the extent of the military aftercare.

In May 1978, Murphy was on interchange duty in Perth when he received a call from a bank manager in rural New South Wales. He told Murphy that Jim Gardiner had taken his own life at home with an overdose of sleeping pills.

"Get fucked," Murphy said in disbelief and hung up the phone.

*

On 4 January 2009, I drove out on the Eastern Freeway to find the house on Hyacinth Street, Greensborough, where the siege had taken place. Murphy had given me a precise description but not the house number. In thirty-four years the street had changed; gum trees had since grown tall and now obscured the scene that Corporal Gardiner had commanded from his window.

I started knocking on doors but most of the residents were new; the old families were gone. Finally, there was a lady who knew the house. It was directly across the street, but the block had been subdivided and another house sat on the sloping front lawn. The front door now looked onto Hyacinth Street. I knocked and a tall, rugged man in his mid-sixties answered. I explained what I was doing but he said he couldn't help. He had only recently leased the property and he hadn't heard of the siege.

When I mentioned that Gardiner had been a Vietnam veteran, he looked at me, suddenly interested. "I served in Vietnam, too," he said softly. He would have been the same age as Jim Gardiner had the corporal lived. He folded his powerful, tattooed arms and looked down, contemplating, as if a powerful surge of memory was passing through him. He would never look at this place in the same way again, he said. He knew exactly what Jim Gardiner and his family had been through inside these walls. I asked him how he felt about his war service.

"You have your days. I'm up and down with it, I guess," he said. "And your nights, too."

Later that day, I found Ida Aughton, now living in a small town in central Victoria. She remembered Murphy. "He was a beautiful man. It still brings me to tears when I think of him and the way he spoke to Jim that night."

Then, after days of research, I located Gardiner's widow living in New South Wales. She had remarried seventeen years ago and now enjoyed a quiet coastal retirement, playing golf and enjoying life with her new husband, a local businessman. December 1975 was a time she didn't care to relive. Jim had never spoken of his tour in Vietnam. Something had happened there, she didn't know what. She couldn't help me, or didn't want to.

But then she rang back, anxious and upset. She said she had never told her new husband the full circumstances of Jim's passing. The coroner had extended her the dignity of a verdict of accidental death, not suicide. She revealed that she had asked the bank manager – her neighbour – to call Murphy. He wasn't family but it seemed important to let him know what had happened. It was heartbreaking to see what Jim was going through but at least Murphy had given him two more years with his kids.

CHAPTER 24   THE THUNDERCLAP

"HAVE YOU ALWAYS DONE THAT?" I interrupted Murphy, mid-stream.

His left hand, clenched into a fist, was resting, fingers inward, on the light aluminium café table. He was tapping it with his right hand, punctuating each point that he made. It was only a light touch but it sent vibrations through the flimsy table right into me. At seventy-six years of age, he was long retired but the habits of non-verbal communication were so ingrained he was unaware of them. It was just a casual conversation over a coffee but still he controlled the tempo and the mood; he could connect with me, or even manipulate me, without ever touching me. It set me thinking about how he had beguiled me in the five years we had been talking, how he subtly tuned me to his way of thinking. Though his legend had been built on the bash, perhaps the implied threat of violence, or indeed the absence of it, had been his most effective weapon.

"When I did belt someone, it was because I'd failed to connect with them. I'd failed to get inside their heads," he said. Frustration would suddenly boil over and he would lash out with a back hander. Or he might deliver his trademark "thunderclap", an open-handed double strike to the ears of the hapless suspect. Murphy's thunderclap may have nearly burst the eardrums of the victim but it rarely secured a confession. More often, violence just sparked defiance.

"They might say to me, 'Does it make you feel good, belting me like that?' and I'd say, 'No, it makes me feel like a failure because I can't get into your mind.'"

I tried to imagine the emotional temperature in those tiny interview rooms, just two metres by two metres, at these moments. How frightening he must have been to the suspect – this wild-eyed cop teetering on the edge. Every crim thought they knew how Murphy had killed Neil Collingburn, how he had frothed and raved, jumped off the tables onto Collingburn and rammed his head into steel lockers while the other jackals stood laughing and cheering him on. This was his turf – this little room with just the two chairs and a table was the lion's den. The softening up began long before they even got there. He would arrest the suspect and drive him back to the station in complete silence. There would be no radio, no chatter between the cops. The suspect would be alone with his thoughts, wondering how much Murphy knew. At the station, they would be put in the interview room and left alone, sometimes for hours on end. Murphy wanted their blood pressure to rise, the sweat to pour out of them. Some would burst into tears under the pressure and "open up like a watermelon falling off a truck". If they started mouthing off, he would leave them to stew even longer.

"They might say, 'If you aren't going to charge me, I'm walking out of here.' I'd just stick my head in and reply, 'If you leave here now, you'll be carried out, okay?'" So the screw would be turned tighter and tighter. When he finally began the questioning, most people would say anything to get out of there.

"I'd just sit there, never taking my eyes off them, leaning forward and closing the space between us. They felt they couldn't afford to look away because they were expecting a slap, but most often it didn't come," he said. And finally when he spoke, it wasn't a question but a statement.

"I know what you've done. There's plenty of proof," Murphy would say. Then more silence. And if the answers weren't forth-coming, he would change tack. He'd say: "I know exactly what you're feeling right now. You're wondering if someone's coming to bail you out. You're thinking about your wife and kids, you're wondering if someone's going to come by your house tonight to hurt them. In the dock you'll be wondering what's to become of you, how your life's come to this, how long you're going be away for. And who's waiting for you in jail."

If there was any defiance left in them, they might say, "How would you know, you're just a copper!" and Murphy's eyes would bore straight into them.

"Because I've been right where you are now," he would say, and even if they didn't know Murphy, they would have heard of the Collingburn case. "Yeah, that case, that's right. I'm the cop-per and I know what you're going through right now," he would say. "Because I've been there."

At that moment, he wanted them to believe that he had done what the Crown had alleged, that he had gotten away with kill-ing a man with his bare hands and boots – that in this small space, there were no rules, no mercy and no escape. He wanted the fear to take hold, to see the man mentally stripped bare. Whatever awaited in jail could never be worse than this ordeal. The confession would be a relief.

Even from a distance of twenty years, the psychological power of the man was obvious. People in the café looked over to see what this old man could possibly be talking about, steadily tap-ping his fist on the table.

And when he had flayed their skin and they had spilled their guts, the mood would change again. He had to leave them with some dignity, even a shot at redemption. Murphy had rarely seen love openly expressed at home as a child, though he knew it was there. He only ever saw his father kiss his mother twice: the first time when Reg went for a trip to Tasmania, the second just before Murphy carried him out for his last journey to the hospice. Murphy sometimes wondered where his compassion came from, but he let it flow at these moments. He had cried many times as a suspect told the sorry story of his life. His mother Maggie would send him up when she heard of these moments, saying he must have bladders behind his eyes, such was the torrent of his tears. None of it made sense to others: one moment he was bashing a suspect senseless, the next he was offering to give evidence on his behalf or sharing his lunch with him. It was draining to hear him recount those interviews.

In 1975, the bosses sent Murphy to a psychiatrist by fooling him into thinking he was seeing a physician. They ran through the first few years of his career: the shootings and dead bodies, the treachery and danger. On just the first four years, the doctor said he could get Murphy a disability pension for life; it was an outrage that he had never received any counselling. But Murphy told him he didn't believe in counselling. When things troubled him, he would have a conversation with himself. He would ask a question and if the answer came back right, he would press on. But he sometimes couldn't fathom his own emotions; he would laugh when he should cry and cry when he should laugh. It was a half-hour appointment with the psychiatrist, but after talking for almost three hours, they were no closer to an answer.

CHAPTER 25 THE CONSORTER'S PUSH

THE *Vagrancy Act 1966* WAS A LAW that had been written with Murphy's freedom in mind, he used to think. It gave the policeman almost unfettered power to control the streets and the behaviour of the criminal classes. It was an offence for a thief to be in the company of other thieves, even at home. They could not consort in any public place, whether it be a railway platform, a park, a race track, a church or even a punt on the river. A first offence brought one year's jail, the second a two-year stretch. For real vagrants, the new law wasn't all bad; it meant they could sleep rough in summer and then be nicked and locked up for six months over the winter months.

But for professional crims, the Act was a major impediment to business. It meant a two-up cheat with a two-headed coin in his pocket could not be within a block of a pub. A housebreaker could be nicked for possession of a drill bit. Even a fortune teller could fall under the heavy cosh of the Consorting Squad.

Any person who pretends or professes to tell fortunes or uses any subtle craft, means or device by palmistry or otherwise to defraud or impose on any other person or pretends to exercise or use any kind of witchcraft, sorcery, enchantment or conjuration or pretends from his skill or knowledge in any occult or crafty science to discover where or in what manner any goods or chattels stolen or lost may be found shall be guilty of an offence.

Penalty: 5 penalty units.

The law, which critics regarded as one of the key indices of a police state, brought a lasting judgment upon citizens for the company they kept. Once convicted under the Act, an offender would be referred to as "an idle and disorderly person", "a rogue and vagabond" or even "an incorrigible rogue".

For all its negative connotations, the *Vagrancy Act 1966* was like handing Murphy a key to the city. No longer was he restricted to one area of town or type of crime. Armed with its sweeping powers, he could do virtually as he pleased anywhere in the state.

Wherever and whenever villains met, Murphy and the other Consorters would be there. If publicans were foolish – or paid – enough to allow villains to run two-up or SP bookmaking from their premises, police could have the place declared a common gaming house and arrest any head they saw coming or going. It forced the sale or closure of some pubs, for want of honest drinkers. Crims were forced to leave Melbourne and meet in secret locations to plan their activities. And even then Murphy might turn up.

In Murphy's town, the only legitimate excuse for consorting was to gather good mail for him. Then you might get some small latitude. But if you defied him, the persecution that followed was ferocious and endless. Murphy exercised a kind of mind control. For instance, he had been regularly encountering Thomas Joseph Connellan, who had tried to sink him at the Collingburn trial.

"Are you going to make my life a misery?" Connellan had bleated.

"It's not me you should be worrying about, Tommy, it's Stillman. He's stalking you, mate," Murphy had replied, gravely.

He said that his co-accused, Carl Stillman, had been sneaking into Connellan's house and watching him while he slept. Stillman planned to knock Connellan off when he got bored of this nightly game. Connellan promptly installed $15,000 worth of security at his house, terrified of the night-stalking Stillman. Connellan later died of a drug overdose, while the star witness, Ian Revell Carroll, was shot dead by Russell "Mad Dog" Cox at his Mount Martha hide-out in 1983 after a squabble over money. Murphy didn't shed a tear but he said prayers for both of them.

In addition to his official duties, Murphy moved freely among crims as a bouncer in pubs and nightclubs. It began as a way of paying off debts from the Collingburn trial but soon became a way of life. Most nights he would start at the Oxford Hotel, then move to the Beverley Crest, finishing at 3 a.m. after a stint at St Kilda's notorious Whiskey-A-Go-Go. He would then front up for the day shift at 5.30 the next morning for another 21-hour day. Only on Sunday afternoons would he rest. After waterskiing all day with the kids, he had a dangerous habit of falling asleep behind the wheel of the Valiant. But the money was welcome and the fighting was good, even amusing. He was kept in tune by the thugs who would come, half cut, to the pub to take on the jack bouncer they had heard about. He would get in a fight every night of the week and he was never vanquished.

But there was one man who intimidated Murphy, a man he feared could get over the top of him. When Murphy looked into Raymond Patrick "Chuck" Bennett's cold, black, beady eyes, he saw no fear. It was unnerving to consider that Bennett's dash might match his own. In 1976, Ray Chuck was running around Melbourne, having engineered an amazing escape from prison on the Isle of Wight, where he had been incarcerated for a £140,000 robbery in England. Murphy was told that he had been in a holding cell with a drunk. The warder had come to release the drunk and Chuck, having threatened his cell mate, assumed the man's identity and walked free. He had snuck back into Australia to mastermind the Great Bookie Robbery, when armed villains stole a reported $15 million (the real figure was probably much higher) from the Victoria Racing Club, where bookmakers met on settling day. Chuck had shown himself to be fearless and smart, as well as utterly cruel and ruthless. He had pulled a big team behind him.

Murphy went back to 1971 with Ray "Chuck" Bennett. He may have been a dashing villain, "the armed robber of his generation", but his nickname had far less glamorous origins. It had come from his habit of celebrating big heists by getting smashed on red wine. Sometimes getting up to vomit was such an effort that he would just chuck up on the floor by the bed and go back to sleep. It drove his wife, a fastidious housekeeper, half crazy.

Murphy had found the customary "Mark of Chuck" by the bed when he was searching his house in Kensington one day in early 1971. It was just weeks before the fateful afternoon when Stillman brought Neil Collingburn and his associates into Russell Street.

Chuck and Collingburn were suspected of stealing $125,000 worth of leather coats from a city retailer, and the Breakers were hot on the trail. When they burst into Ray Chuck's place, his little boy was terrified, yelling for his mother, who was in the bedroom attending to Chuck's gastric juices on the carpet. Murphy had scooped the boy up, saying they were friends of Mummy and Daddy's. He remembers passing the writhing kid over the bed to his mother. Chuck wasn't there so they moved on to an address in Clifton Hill, where they found the Myer van used in the heist, complete with the discarded tags and wrapping paper.

That evening at 10 p.m., after working on the door at the Oxford Hotel, Murphy and some colleagues went to a pizza parlour on the corner of the Queen Victoria Market complex in North Melbourne. As they arrived, perhaps by sheer coincidence, Ray Chuck and another villain pulled up alongside.

"You still standing over women and little kids, you worthless piece of shit?" sneered Chuck.

"No, not today, from memory," replied Murphy.

"You threw my kid over the bed today. You think you're a big man terrorising kids like that, you dog? You'll get yours one day soon," warned Chuck as they drove away.

Murphy and his colleagues went downstairs and ordered pizzas, but Murphy was restless: the sight of this adversary had put him on edge. Sitting in the restaurant, they were a soft target. If someone lobbed a grenade down here, they would all be toast. Come on, Murph, just take it easy, his mates said. This is not Belfast, you mad Irish bastard.

"You do what you want, but I'm not staying in here," Murphy said as he got up and climbed the steps to the street. The night air was sultry and close from a summer thunderstorm. He started to light a cigarette.

With a screech of brakes, Ray Chuck's Valiant pulled up. He and his sidekick must have been sitting off watching the cops in the pizza joint. Chuck leapt from the car and strode up to Murphy, taking him by surprise. Murphy dropped his smoke and raised his fists to defend himself, but Chuck had other ideas. With both hands, he went straight for Murphy's .38 tucked into a holster at his waist. Fortunately, Murphy had just done the buckle and Chuck couldn't pull it free – otherwise he might have shot him dead right where he stood. They struggled for a moment before Chuck pulled back. His mate opened the boot of the car, pulled out a pump-action shotgun and threw it to him. He jacked a shell into the breach and, grinning at Murphy, levelled it ready to fire. He wouldn't think twice about killing a cop. Murphy was desperately kicking the front door of the restaurant with his heel to get his mates' attention, but they couldn't hear him. Just then, half a dozen Italians from the markets rolled drunkenly around the corner and walked into the line of fire. The chance to kill Murphy without witnesses had passed, so Ray Chuck and his mate jumped back in the car and roared off towards the city. The confrontation had lasted no more than fifteen seconds. Murphy's offsiders finally came barrelling up the stairs onto the street. The first cop out the door tripped on the top step and went sprawling, the car keys skittering across the pavement and into a deep puddle in the gutter. There was no chance of catching him now.

On the following Monday, they picked up Ray Chuck and his wife and took them to Russell Street. No-one believed that Chuck had pulled a shotgun on Murphy. But they left the couple in the interview room and listened in on the conversation.

"Have you still got the receipt for that shotgun?" Chuck asked his wife.

"Yeah," she said. "It's in me bra, Ray."

"Well get rid of it, love. Take it to the shithouse and flush it."

The cops got the receipt but it wasn't enough to hold him. They handed Chuck over to Murphy for further questioning.

"Hey, Murphy, just between you and me – hey! look me in the fucking eye, you crumb," said Chuck. Murphy and Chuck stood eyeball to eyeball. "One day I'm going to kill you. Don't you ever forget it. I'm going to fucking kill you," he growled.

"Don't let me see you first," said Murphy, within earshot of a dozen witnesses.

CHAPTER 26 A TOOTHLESS TIGER

A LOT OF PEOPLE, BOTH COPS AND VILLAINS, were telling Murphy that Ray Chuck was too good for him. He would be mad not to get in first and there were shooters galore who would step up. But why kill someone just for the sake of it? thought Murphy. Ray Chuck was not his enemy. He had been threatened with death numerous times – but Murphy knew Chuck was one who would have a go. He kept a weather eye on him for most of the 1970s.

The death of Collingburn had given Ray Chuck another reason to kill Murphy, but he could bide his time. There was a fortune to be made for a villain with as much dash as he had. From 1971 he had been on a spree; it began with minor stuff, pitching fire extinguishers and man-hole covers through shop windows, and moved on up to armed robbery. When things got too hot in about 1974, he took off for London, where he tagged along on a few jobs with the Kangaroo Gang, a legendary team of Aussie shoplifters led by the mercurial "King" Arthur William Delaney. But Ray Chuck was no tea leaf (thief); he was born for armed robbery. Having escaped jail on the Isle of Wight, he came home to pull off the Great Bookie Robbery on 21 April 1976. It was an audacious job executed with meticulous planning. The Consorters were furious; three detectives from the squad were to provide unofficial security for the bookmakers but on that day they had arrived late, having been sent on a last-minute

216

errand. There was talk that a corrupt senior police officer must have been involved to engineer the late arrival.

The robbery had been a textbook operation but for one vital error. They had ordered everyone at the Victoria Racing Club that day to lie face down on the floor. One bandit had said to the well-known boxing trainer Ambrose Palmer, "You too, Ambrose." Palmer recognised the voice of a man who trained at his gym. The bookie robbers' identities soon found their way to the rival Kane Gang, led by one of Melbourne's heaviest standover men, Brian Kane.

Kane had begun his career as a "fund-raiser" for Victorian Labor Party candidates, including one-time deputy prime minister Jim Cairns. Since then, Kane and his brother, Les, had become the most feared enforcers in town and important figures in the Painters and Dockers criminal network. Jealous of Ray Chuck's success with the bookies, the Kanes wanted a share of the booty. Robbing the robbers was easier than pulling off their own job.

The Consorters were following events in the underworld after the bookie robbery with great interest; some would say with an active, perhaps even proprietorial interest. After all, the job had been pulled off right under their noses and they weren't going to miss out. It's now legend that when Consorting Squad detectives found $150,000 – part-proceeds of the bookie robbery – in Dennis "Fatty" Smith's car, only 10 per cent of the money found its way into official coffers. Villains had to stay sweet with the Consorters or risk relentless persecution. The *Age* newspaper noted that "Squad members called themselves the 'Fletcher Jones boys' because, the joke went, like the clothing store of that name, they could 'fit anybody'." Certainly there was no leading gangster who didn't talk to a friendly Consorter from time to time.

Brian Kane's Consorter was Brian Murphy. As I wrote in *Big Shots*, the alliance began in unusual circumstances:

One night in a Lygon Street café in Carlton, the two Brians became acquainted as they both reached for the same short-black coffee. The proprietor had made the mistake of saying, "Here's your coffee, Brian."

A stand-off ensued over the steaming cup until the proprietor, keen to avoid a scene, sat them both at a table in order that they might get to know each other better. Kane looked at Murphy balefully and said in a low growl, "You know, Murphy, I was going to kill you [over Collingburn], and I still might …" It was nearly midnight and the café was almost deserted.

"What's stopping you then, Brian?" said Murphy.

"Don't kid yourself, copper. I could have killed you many times already. I've been watching you walking with your wife down by Station Pier. You would have been brown bread if she hadn't been with you, you know."

"Good for you, Brian. That's extremely civilised of you," said Murphy quietly as he stared into Kane's dark eyes. "So here we are. I suggest we lay our cards out. What would you say if I asked old Giuseppe here to slide back the table so we can all see what's going on here."

"Sure, Brian," said Kane. The table was eased back, and to Kane's surprise there was Murphy's .38 service revolver cocked and pointed straight at his groin.

"That's fantastic," said Kane with admiration. "You're alright for a jack. Most of the coppers are just drunken dogs and thieves. I may have misjudged you, Mr Brian Murphy." Ignoring the .38, Kane then stood up and kissed Murphy on the forehead and laughed uproariously. They went through another fourteen short blacks and finally left the café at four o'clock in the morning.

Deep in the night, Kane had confided a dark secret. "You know, as a kid I wanted to be a copper, but my old man beat me up just for mentioning it. He said if I wanted to go and get an education and make something of my life, then I'd have to go and steal the books," he said with a deep sigh. Four hours earlier he had a contract in his breast pocket to kill Murphy and now he was confessing to him like a guilty sinner. Murphy had the skill of looking into a man's heart and seeing the humanity beneath all the bad manners and bullshit.

Through this association, Murphy had obtained a ringside seat for the blood sport that played out between the Kanes and Ray Chuck from 1976 to 1982. His critics believe he was right in the thick of the action.

One afternoon, not long after the bookie robbery, Murphy and the Consorters were doing the rounds of the Richmond pubs. Murphy walked into the back bar of the Rising Sun Hotel and found Ray Chuck with eight or ten of his team. They were a motley bunch of shoplifters and robbers dressed in the latest – stolen – gangster fashions. Chuck was resplendent in a black-and-white checked frock coat with leather patches on the sleeves. Murphy told his partner to put his gun inside his pocket and if he went down to shoot as many of Chuck's men as possible.

"Raymond Patrick Chuck, how are you?" said Murphy. Chuck looked up at Murphy with seething contempt.

"Brian Francis Murphy … you're still alive. That's good, because you know I'm still going to fucking kill you," he said.

"Tsk, tsk," said Murphy. "Whatever you do, don't say anything like that in front of these dogs and rats you're mixing with," he said, pointing at Chuck's associates.

"And why would that be?" asked Ray Chuck. He felt so confident, as though he could have Murphy bashed and buried with a wave of his hand.

"Because if you kill me, it'll be one of these dirty curs that gives you up," said Murphy, pulling out his notebook. "What's your date of birth again?"

He started moving down the line of villains, taking names. One of Ray Chuck's thugs put his foot up on the chair, blocking Murphy's path.

"Where are you going?" he asked.

"I'll tell you where I'm going – I'm going right through you, you piece of shit. Get your foot off the chair, okay?"

Ray Chuck looked hard at Murphy. He could have dealt with him right there and he wanted Murphy to know that. By this time, the manager of the pub had run upstairs and locked himself inside a wardrobe.

"Let him go," said Ray Chuck.

When Murphy got outside the pub, he told the other Consorters that Ray Chuck was inside with his crew. One detective went straight to the car and pulled out two shotguns. He threw one to Murphy and suggested they storm the place and kill every last one of the gang.

"No thanks," said Murphy, tossing back the shotgun. "He kills us, there's no witnesses. We kill him, there's a million."

If it came to battle, Murphy would fight Ray Chuck on a ground of his choosing. Besides, it was more than likely that someone else would get in first. The conflict in Ray Chuck's life was rapidly coming to a head. The simmering tensions between him and the Kanes exploded into warfare in another Richmond hotel in mid-1978.

A friend of Chuck's, Vincent Mikkelsen, had refused Brian Kane's offer of a drink. The *Age* reported that "Mikkelsen committed an even graver social indiscretion by winning the fight – and biting off part of Kane's ear." Ray Chuck had interceded in the aftermath, asking that Mikkelsen be spared, and received a warning for his trouble: "If you stick your head in, it'll be blown off."

Instead, the Chuck forces got in first. On October 1978, Les Kane arrived home with his wife and kids to find assassins waiting for him. Legend has it the killers were hidden in the shower recess. When Kane came in to wash, he undressed and put his gun in the bathroom cupboard. The hit men jumped out and let fly with an automatic weapon, complete with silencer. They threw Kane's body in the boot of his own pink Ford Futura and drove away. Neither Kane nor his car was ever seen again. It's understood that the corpse was fed through a mincing machine at a meatworks plant forty minutes north of Melbourne. A story circulated that the killers had sent Kane's wedding ring back to his wife in a stick of Strasbourg salami.

Ray Chuck, Vincent Mikkelsen and Laurence Prendergast were charged with the Les Kane killing but were acquitted. Ray Chuck was still facing a committal proceeding in the Magistrates' Court over a $69,000 payroll robbery and chose to remain in custody for his own safety. The *Age* reported that Ray Chuck had taken out a hefty life-insurance policy, and asked if it covered getting "shot walking down the street". The newspaper also reported that someone had scrawled on the court's cell wall: *Ray Chuck, you will get yours in due course. You fucken dog.*

Security had been tight at the Supreme Court when Ray

Chuck faced murder charges over Les Kane in September 1979. The *Age* reported: "There were armed police, marksmen posted outside, and stringent identity and weapon checks on everyone who entered court. Even a prison chaplain, Peter Alexander, was not allowed to visit [Chuck] Bennett."

But the security at the armed-robbery committal was strangely lax by contrast. At 10.17 on the Monday morning after the 1979 Melbourne Cup, Ray Chuck was led from the cells to court by just two police officers. The original detail was to be two detectives from the Consorting Squad, Phil Glare and Paul Strang, and an Armed Robbery Squad detective, John Mugavin. For reasons only partially explained, Strang was already upstairs in court. The two cops escorted Ray Chuck across the central courtyard and into the building. They climbed the two flights of stairs to Court 10, where a killer was waiting patiently: he was in his thirties with a full head of hair and gold-rimmed glasses; dressed in a blue suit with a briefcase by his side, he looked like a lawyer waiting outside court.

As they reached the first-floor landing, the killer was descending. As they drew close, the man pulled a revolver from his coat and, with the words "Cop this, you cunt", fired three shots into Ray Chuck's torso. Blood surged from between Chuck's fingers as he crossed his arms over the wounds in his chest.

"I've been shot in the heart," he gasped. He ran down the stairs and collapsed into the arms of a uniform policeman.

He was pronounced dead an hour later. The gunman had fled through a side door, down back stairs and passageways and out of the building to a tin shed behind the police garage. The planning had been meticulous. Nails from a section of the corrugated-iron shed wall had been removed and replaced with loose-fitting screws, allowing the killer to slip through into the adjacent car park of the Royal Melbourne Institute of Technology. As the cops were frantically searching the court precinct, the killer casually walked down to the corner of Swanston and La Trobe streets, where he waited for a tram. He boarded the first tram and rode for a dozen stops south through the city and over the river. He alighted near the Shrine of Remembrance on St Kilda Road and strolled to his car, which was parked in a nearby leafy street. That night, he stayed at the house of a policeman. It's understood he was having an affair with the policeman's wife. When this arrangement became untenable a short time later (the cop found out), the killer was despatched on a chartered light aircraft from Moorabbin Airport to Adelaide, where he boarded a commercial flight to Perth.

As Ray Chuck lay dying, Murphy was driving into town in a bongo van. He had left the Consorters a year earlier and now had his own team, the Metropolitan Regional Crime Squad, based in a decommissioned police station in North Fitzroy. "Murphy's Marauders" used the bongo van, covered in stickers, dents and graffiti, for undercover work and he was taking it into Russell Street to exchange it for another car. He liked to change his profile on a regular basis.

His was a well-known face among crims but he still took pride in disguising himself. Over the years, many failed to realise they had been arrested by the infamous Brian Murphy. At this time, he had a full beard and was wearing a pair of gold-rimmed glasses, just like the killer. He drove past the crowd outside the Magistrates' Court; he thought it was part of the Builders Labourers' Federation demonstration. Good, he mused, we might get a fight out this.

When he arrived at the door of the Russell Street garage, a policeman called out: "Hey Murphy! Your mate's just been shot!"

"What bloody mate?" he inquired.

"Ray Chuck, right in the court!"

Murphy parked the van and went straight over to the court for a look. He tried to get in but was ordered to leave the scene, which was now crawling with press and onlookers. No-one would talk to him, so he went back to North Fitzroy, where he enjoyed a coffee and a game of pool at the International Café.

By lunchtime, the city was rife with speculation. Unnamed police sources told the press that Ray Chuck had been killed by a contract hit man paid $50,000 for the job. By mid-afternoon it was reported that the boss of the Consorters, Angus Ritchie, had taken a call from an anonymous informant who alleged the hit had been organised by police officers, perhaps even members of his own squad. Whoever had planned this audacious act had an insider's knowledge of the court layout and the police car park. He knew when to strike and how to get away.

That night, police raided the offices of Murphy's Metropolitan Regional Crime Squad in North Fitzroy, seizing every police diary and booking note, taking photocopies of everything and returning them by morning.

A few days later an envelope, sent anonymously by internal mail, landed on Murphy's desk. It contained the identikit picture of Ray Chuck's killer the police had put together from eyewitness accounts. WHO DOES THIS LOOK LIKE? was scrawled on it in big red letters.

That same week, the tension was so great that a sergeant led a raid on Chuck's house wearing a tin helmet. Ray Chuck's widow, Gail, had hidden her son in a wardrobe before they burst in. She told the officer that she was terrified Murphy was coming to kill them too.

CHAPTER 27   THE LIVES OF BRIAN

"I DIDN'T KILL RAY CHUCK," said Murphy in early 2009. "If I had, it would not have been in the court. It would have been me facing him head-on, either with fists or with a gun, head-on, together. He would have known it was me; that's the way I would have done the business."

For all its ferocity, the denial seems qualified and narrow. It's obvious to all that Brian Kane pulled the trigger that day, so Murphy's denial of direct involvement amounts to little. The identity of the co-conspirators is the tantalising mystery that remains. It was clear he knew the man behind the hit on Ray Chuck, but he was playing dead on me. To this day no-one has been charged with Ray Chuck's murder.

"I don't think it will ever come out. I've got my suspicions but I won't be sharing them, if Your Honour pleases," he said, hand on heart. Over months of interviews, we discussed the Ray Chuck murder from every angle and his story never wavered.

"Everyone reckoned I'd done it and I was having a laugh to meself – there's one on me belt that I've never done." He smiled at the memory. "I thought it might quieten a few more people down."

The funny thing was that he had seen Kane just a few days earlier. The Italian Festival was on in Lygon Street and Murphy had taken Margaret and his youngest daughter, Geraldine. They were walking into L'Alba Café and out came Brian Kane with a beard the same as Murphy's and gold-rimmed glasses the same as Murphy's. He even had an identical Kangol cap on. It was like catching a reflection of himself as he passed a mirror. He told Margaret, "That's Brian Kane," but before she could look, he had disappeared into the crowd.

Everyone knew of Murphy's feud with Ray Chuck. Many also knew that Brian Kane was one of Murphy's confidants. And after twenty-five years as a policeman, Murphy knew his way around the Magistrates' Court like his backyard.

There was motive and opportunity in a case for murder against Murphy, but from that point on, all was confusion and ambiguity. There were two persons of interest, Brian Kane and Brian Murphy, who looked strikingly similar. They both carried the same gun: the snub-nosed .38 that killed Ray Chuck was identical to the one Murphy carried in his ankle holster. He had switched from the long-barrelled .38 only in the past year.

Murphy turned up at Russell Street fewer than ten minutes after the shooting. It made him a possible suspect but he had an alibi. Margaret heard a radio newsflash that reported a shooting at court minutes after it had happened. She telephoned the North Fitzroy office to check Brian wasn't involved. "He's just left for town," she was told. Meanwhile, the other Brian was rolling down Swanston Street on a tram.

At least two witnesses had looked right into the killer's face but none spoke of steely blue eyes. He'd threatened a civilian witness, Raymond Aarons: "Move and I'll blow your head off." A policeman had moved towards him. "Don't make me do it," he warned. Surely a witness would remember if he had looked into Murphy's eyes.

Murphy was also a victim of his own legend. He had a reputation as a master of illusion. In January 1972, while still suspended, he had driven up to the Sunbury music festival. Putting on a limp and a grimace, he had sidled right up to a group of senior police, including Mick Miller, posing as an imbecile. No-one had recognised him until he had said to Miller: "G'day, boss!" Even then Miller had to take a second look. Everyone had a story like that about Murphy – not exactly a plus when denying involvement in a murder mystery.

But another possibility existed. At the 1981 coroner's inquest into Ray Chuck's death, counsel for the police, John Harbour Phillips, had introduced in evidence "a rumour" that Murphy and Consorting Squad Detective Paul Strang had paid a hit man $50,000 to "dispose of" Ray Chuck. Phil Glare, who had escorted Chuck to his last court appearance, confirmed he had heard the rumour, but only after the shooting.

Sergeant Noel Alfred Anderson, who had organised Ray Chuck's police escort, told the court he had also heard the rumour but only after it happened. As the *Age* reported on 25 March 1981: "He had heard rumours linking Detective Strang with an attempt to have [Chuck] Bennett killed by an English hit man, Linus Driscoll, but had heard no rumours at all before the shooting."

Ray Chuck was a security risk, Anderson said, so he had wanted at least four police escorting him. But he was short of men that day. By coincidence, the militant Builders' Labourers' Federation was holding its demo just a block away on Russell Street and 167 officers had been deployed, leaving a shortage of uniform men to escort prisoners. That was why the Consorters, Detectives Strang and Glare, were assigned to Ray Chuck with one uniform member. And Strang wasn't even on the staircase when the killer struck. He was in the courtroom with Detective Sergeant Anderson who, despite fretting about the lack of security, was prepared to allow only two men to guard Ray Chuck.

Some, more feverishly, speculated that the entire event had been choreographed – from the BLF demo, the lax security at court, the presence of the Consorters, the kill on the landing where only cops could witness it, the escape hatch in the fence. It had been set up and precisely executed by a murder squad, comprising police and criminals.

Red herrings like Murphy's arrival in the bongo van had injected enough ambiguity to distract and derail the investigation. Another Consorter, Sergeant Paul Higgins, when told Chuck was due to appear in court, had remarked: "Well, he'll be off." When asked to explain his prescient comment, Higgins said he meant to say that Chuck would "take off", but the flavour of a police conspiracy lingered on the tongue.

If this was right, then which police officers were running the show? Before this event, Murphy had made no secret of his association with Brian Kane, but now all that changed.

"By that stage, Brian Kane had given me the arse for other people. He knew I wouldn't go as far as his new chums in the force," said Murphy.

But Murphy does concede that Brian Kane had come to him asking for help in a plot to avenge the murder of his brother, Les. He wanted hit man Christopher Dale Flannery to steal a barrister's wig and gown from the law firm where his brother worked so he could get inside the court to kill Chuck, Mikkelsen and Prendergast during their murder trial. He wanted to procure explosives and guns but Murphy had refused him. By this time, Kane was knocking around with Detectives Strang and Glare, Murphy said. Strang had even come to Murphy boasting of his new informer, saying Kane now regarded Murphy as "a toothless tiger".

"That's good," Murphy said. "He won't be expecting it if I ever have to give him a sneak go and kill him."

In the end, Murphy was not even questioned by police, much less called as a witness at the coronial inquest. The *Age* reported in 1999: "The brief inquest when it finally sat raised more questions than it answered. Despite the public interest, and the time available to prepare the brief, it was a slight document."

The evidence was nothing more than a re-hash of what had appeared in the newspapers. Ray Chuck's great bookie robbers had almost pulled off the perfect heist but for one fatal slip. Ray Chuck's murderer had gone one better. He had eliminated Ray Chuck in public inside a courthouse and got away scot-free. The plot had taken investigators down baffling blind alleys and dead ends, until they were forced to concede the skill of the plotters. It was a conspiracy that anyone would be proud to own. Moreover, many said it was the kind of conspiracy that, among coppers, only Brian Murphy would dare to conceive.

*

Two days after the murder, Murphy's squad was given the special duty of guarding Ray Chuck's corpse at the undertaker's on the night before his funeral. The Kanes had boasted they would break in, cut Ray Chuck's hands and feet off and mail them to his widow as a farewell gesture. Some of the best criminals in town were filing through to pay their respects to Chuck. The police were hiding behind curtains and calling out to the heads they recognised: "There's another slab out there for you too, you dogs!"

There was no doubt the death of Ray Chuck felt like a win for police. As Murphy had told the press after winning his Valour Badge, "Criminals [were] running riot ... Certain factions in the community had been far too critical of police since 1966 … The criticism must have been very demoralising for certain members."

If the police had conspired to kill Ray Chuck, they had done society a favour – so it was felt. Some of the Consorters encouraged the rumours. A retired detective told the *Age* that squad members couldn't buy a drink in the police club for a week.

During the night, Murphy was alone with Ray Chuck's corpse for a moment. He looked down at the body, which was made up with paint, powder and lipstick for his final appearance. At thirty-one, he was still so young; what a waste of a life it had been.

"Look at this fool," Murphy murmured. "All the yahooin' and robbin' and shootin' people and this is what you end up like. You had a kid – what's he going to hear about you later? Ray Chuck, you were never any enemy of mine but I have to say I'm glad you're gone."

On the day of the funeral, Murphy's team watched proceedings from a distance, noting who turned up and who was talking to whom. One of Ray Chuck's closest mates, Brian Leslie O'Callaghan, who had been with him in Europe, had broken out of jail in Sydney. He was rumoured to be heading for Melbourne to avenge his fallen comrade.

The day had been uneventful until Murphy and a team of ten Consorters were sent to search for O'Callaghan at Ray Chuck's brother's house, where the wake was being held. Feeling confident with his back-up, Murphy and one other officer marched straight through the mourners to the backyard before anyone twigged to their identity. Ray Chuck's brother ran out of the house with a carving knife, demanding to know what the police where doing there.

"Official police business," declared Murphy, feeling the crowd closing in on him. "We could get a kicking here," he said to his partner. "The first one that comes near, you shoot fuckin' dead, 'cos we're going to get killed here," he said, looking anxiously for the other eight detectives.

Chuck's brother began shouting that he wanted to see a warrant. Without a warrant, it looked very much like Murphy had simply come to gloat. They started backing out.

"Those men over there have the warrant," Murphy said, looking around for the Consorters, who should have been close behind after searching the house. But they had left him for dead. They were standing out on the street by their vehicles, pissing themselves laughing at Murphy's predicament.

Driving away from the house, Murphy was so filled with rage he steamed up the car windows. His eyes were sticking out like crazy blue stalks. He heard over the radio the Consorters had retired to a hotel to celebrate the passing of Ray Chuck with a few beers. Murphy diverted from his route back to the office straight to the pub. The Consorters were sitting around a table, each with a jug of beer in front of him. Murphy grabbed the jugs and turned them upside down over their heads.

"Now laugh about that, you fucking dogs," he shouted as he walked out.

CHAPTER 28 STAYIN' ALIVE

Ah, ha, ha, ha,
Stayin' alive, stayin' alive.
Ah, ha, ha, ha,
Stayin' alive.

—Bee Gees, "Stayin' Alive"

MURPHY STOOD IN THE DOORWAY of Mickey's Disco, tapping his foot to the music and sipping a lemon squash. It was after midnight and he was off-duty, dressed in jeans and a polo top. In his leather man-bag, he was toting a loaded .38.

"Stayin' Alive" by the Bee Gees was the number-one hit for seven weeks in the autumn of 1978 and its hypnotic drumbeat and bass-line brought every dancing fool and his girl out onto the floor. But Murphy would keep his eyes on the crowd. Things turned ugly quickly in Mickey's, so he kept his man-bag close. If he hit you with it, it would be lights out.

Well now, I get low and I get high,
And if I can't get either, I really try.
Got the wings of heaven on my shoes,
I'm a dancin' man and I just can't lose.
You know it's alright. It's okay.
I'll live to see another day.

Mickey's Disco had been open for only a couple of months, the latest in a line of dives and discos that occupied the northern end of the old St Kilda sea baths. The baths, when they opened in 1931, had been a source of great civic pride, an architectural showpiece featuring Islamic fretwork screens, Moorish domical towers, wavy Spanish Mission parapets and decorations. It was said that the baths brought "a whiff of California to St Kilda". But they never took off with the public: the modesty that had created segregated enclosed bathing for men and women fell away in the 1930s and 1940s in favour of mixed, outdoor bathing.

By 1978, the baths were derelict. Sections of the structure had been condemned or demolished; the faded plaster facades had decayed and crumbled. There was now an unhealthy atmosphere in the precinct. The smell of sea-rotted timber and flotsam from the beach pervaded the air. Junkies used the dirty strip of sand to shoot up heroin, discarding their syringes before staggering back to the fleshpots of St Kilda's main drag, Fitzroy Street. A line of ragged palm trees along the dirty boulevard hinted at former pretensions; the whiff of the baths was more Kings Cross by the sea than southern California.

Despite its location – or perhaps because of it – Mickey's had become an overnight success. There was such a motley crew of disco desperates, villains, dealers and rogues that you could hardly move in there most nights. The club next door, the Whiskey-A-Go-Go, took the overflow. Every shithead in Melbourne seemed to be there.

Murphy had more than a passing interest in Mickey's. Some said he collected money from the co-owner, Ronald Albert Feeney, or that he was a silent partner. Murphy had certainly been closely involved in its establishment. His loyal fizz, Ivan Kane, had installed the electronics for the multi-coloured, flashing dance floor, just like the one in the 1977 disco epic *Saturday Night Fever*. His brother Pat had done the plumbing while Murphy pressed his kids into service, putting flyers in letterboxes announcing Mickey's grand opening on 13 April 1978. There had formerly been a club on the site, The Mousetrap, but it didn't have a liquor licence so it had failed by the time Feeney bought in. But Mickey's was licensed and was raking in up to $10,000 a night.

Feeney came to Murphy following a telephone call from his probation officer in New South Wales. The officer had asked Murphy to keep an eye on his charge's "general welfare" while he adjusted to life after jail. Feeney had done time for robbery and violence. He had been interviewed half-a-dozen times over murders in the past ten years, but that was in Sydney. This was a new start, Feeney said; and Murphy would see to that. Feeney soon prospered under Murphy's influence. He bought a 41 per cent share in Mickey's and owned another business outright, the Jolly Green Giant Diner in West Melbourne.

From the opening of the club, Murphy was calling in five nights a week. He would turn up at 11 p.m. during a shift and observe proceedings until closing time at 3 a.m. Or if he was off-duty, he would head out from home in Middle Park after the kids and Margaret had gone to bed.

Whether on-duty or off, he was always tooled up. Mickey's was a devil's kitchen, he liked to say: there was always something evil being cooked up in there. You could get a fight any night of the week; tough guys from all over would come looking for it. Every night, the losers would be pitched over the seawall and onto the sand.

Whether you're a brother or whether you're a mother,
You're stayin' alive, stayin' alive.
Feel the city breakin' and everybody shakin',
And we're stayin' alive, stayin' alive.

Murphy's regular attendance at Mickey's was not due solely to his love of disco dancing. The chief of Victoria's Bureau of Criminal Intelligence, Inspector Frank "The Bank" Green, was paying Murphy and another sergeant, Paul Higgins, up to $200 a week in expenses to gather information from the crowd at Mickey's. Murphy was getting excellent mail for the price of a few drinks. Some days, he would call Green a dozen times with a running commentary on the doings of the club's resident villains.

On one such night a shortish, good-looking man of about thirty approached Murphy. He stood out, even by the fashion standards of the time, in his crushed black-velvet suit, white frilly dress shirt and red bow-tie. He looked almost clean-cut with a full head of brown hair and smooth, unmarked features. He could have been mistaken for middle class were it not for the tattoos that began just past the edge of his shirt cuffs.

"Brian Murphy, is it?" he asked belligerently.

"And you would be Christopher Dale Flannery," Murphy shot back.

Flannery had been released from jail after serving time for rape and was working as a milkman down Seaford way in Melbourne's south, but the early hours didn't agree with him. He had big ambitions – to become Australia's most feared hit man – but in Melbourne in 1978 he wasn't much. Flannery's wife, Kath, was the bookkeeper for Mickey's and she had persuaded Feeney to hire him as a bouncer.

"I've heard all about you," said Flannery, pushing close to Murphy and looking for the slightest justification to king-hit him.

Murphy laughed. "Well, Chris, just about everyone has, mate, so that's not news." He smiled at Flannery disarmingly. There was no sense in showing a crim your true colours first up. Better

235

to beguile a man than rile him to win ego points. Besides, Murphy recognised in Flannery a man who could be manipulated.

Flannery was a charismatic personality and already a romantic hero to some: a former inmate, Ray Mooney, had written a play, *Everynight, Everynight*, about Flannery's early years in Pentridge Prison's notorious H Division. Everyone said he was wild and most probably a killer, but he was also someone who ingratiated himself with those he believed useful. Like so many hard heads, Flannery enjoyed talking to police. The man who would soon begin calling himself "Rent-a-Kill" wanted Murphy to like him.

Murphy came to respect Flannery's dash as a bouncer: he was fearless and ruthless. But he was also captive to his wife's wishes. One night, a patron had suggestively poked his tongue out at her. She ordered her husband to bash him; he took a rasp to the man's eyes for daring to look at her. Flannery had done as he was told but he confided to Murphy that he felt terrible afterwards. He was clearly terrified of his wife, for reasons Murphy never understood.

Murphy sealed his relationship with Flannery through a good turn. He told him that two visiting detectives from Perth wanted to see him over dinner. Flannery had form in the west, having beaten an armed-robbery charge for the hold-up of a David Jones store in 1974. Murphy promised Flannery that the West Australian cops wouldn't arrest him, question him or belt him. They just wanted to tell him something.

Flannery agreed to meet them at Marchetti's Latin Quarter in the city but only after a good deal of cajoling. After a couple of drinks over entrées and idle chit-chat, he grew increasingly agitated.

"So what's all this about?" he asked.

"Well," said one of the detectives. "We know that you're planning to break your mate Archie Butterly out of Fremantle Jail with a helicopter."

Flannery's face froze.

"You should be aware that you'll be flying in Swanbourne Army Barracks airspace, where the SAS are based." He paused. "If they spot you, they'll shoot you out of the fucking sky. So I'd think twice about it if I were you."

Flannery was thunderstruck. He jumped up as if to leave the restaurant, but then his face softened. He thrust out his hand and shook with the Perth detectives.

"Thanks very much. You've probably just saved my life," he said with genuine gratitude. Then he sat back down and the four of them enjoyed their meals, discussing their families and all manner of crim and cop psychology. Flannery was now indebted to Murphy.

But this piece of good fortune didn't slow Flannery down at all. Following a dispute, he put two rounds into another Mickey's regular on nearby Fitzroy Street. Murphy interviewed the victim, who fingered Flannery but wouldn't swear to it.

Flannery was forging a solid network in Melbourne around Mickey's Disco. He boasted that he could get inside mail from the cops courtesy of a crooked private investigator named Thomas Joseph Fabian Ericksen. Ericksen claimed a special friendship with the CIB boss, Superintendent Phil "Fat Harry" Bennett. Ericksen had been an insurance salesman before ingratiating himself with the underworld through a dodgy debt-collection agency he'd set up.

Murphy disliked Ericksen from the first day he met him in 1978 when he was still in the Consorters. That feeling only became stronger over time. Ericksen had once called the police claiming that two former cops were trying to kill him. Murphy was assigned the task of investigating. Ericksen had based his allegation on confidential police daily circulars he claimed to have read, which contained details of the ex-cops' criminal activities.

"That's a load of bullshit, Tom," said Murphy.

Ericksen, a large, well-dressed man, took exception. "You won't be in the Consorters much longer," he threatened Murphy. "You've backed the wrong horse."

Murphy was unconcerned.

"I'll be back in half an hour with a hundred men," Ericksen snorted as he stomped away.

Murphy didn't see Ericksen again for another year. Then, one night in mid-1979, he received a call from an informer: Ericksen was at Mickey's, boasting that if Murphy fronted that night, he would get him sacked. Murphy tore straight there to find him sitting with Flannery and others. Ericksen tried to ignore him but Murphy went straight up and grabbed his hand.

In response, Ericksen pulled him close and whispered, "Watch Flannery and Feeney. They're trying to set you up and get you the sack!"

Murphy pulled Ericksen even closer and replied through gritted teeth, "Who have I got to watch, Tom – you or them?"

From the beginning, the atmosphere at Mickey's had been unsavoury. Now, with the treacherous Ericksen around, it was positively toxic. Emboldened by Ericksen, Flannery began pushing for an interest in Mickey's, harassing another shareholder, Fred Labb, for a piece of the action. When Labb refused, Flannery threatened to chop off his legs and stick them up his arse. They reached an agreement soon after and Flannery became part of the enterprise.

Tom Ericksen was a weak, conniving man but he was also a politician and a manipulator. He loved setting people against one another, revelling in the conflict that ensued. And Mickey's, with its fractious cast of characters, was the perfect stage on which to play out such dramas. Ericksen hated police but coveted the kudos and influence he would gain from serving up the troublesome Murphy to his bosses. He also enjoyed the power that came with proximity to criminals such as Flannery. Thugs could make things happen for Ericksen when his sly ways could not. And introductions by Ericksen to the right people were a boon to Flannery's new business: contract killing.

One Saturday, as Murphy was coming out of the Vigil Mass, Feeney collared him to say that Flannery had been hired to kill a Melbourne solicitor. There had been a dispute over money and the solicitor's partner had turned to Flannery to solve his problem. Ericksen was mixed up in the plot somewhere too. Feeney was distraught. His plans to prosper in a legitimate business were being destroyed as Flannery and Ericksen turned Mickey's into a rat-trap of murder and intrigue. He was terrified of Flannery, and Murphy was his only hope.

Murphy rang the Homicide Squad and passed on the mail, which – remarkably – failed to spur them into action.

"Has he been killed yet?" asked the Homicide detective.

"No, of course not," replied Murphy.

"We deal with murders," said the detective.

"Then I'll tell you when it fuckin' happens!" shouted Murphy and hung up the phone.

In August 1980, Flannery and two others, Mark Alfred Clarkson and John Henry Williams, were arrested and charged with the murder of solicitor Roger Anthony Wilson. Police alleged the trio, posing as police, had forced Wilson's Porsche off the road and abducted him. They took Wilson to the bush to execute him. Flannery is said to have missed and Wilson, bleeding profusely from a head wound, to have tried to escape. Flannery was then said to have "gone mad" and emptied his gun into Wilson. They were acquitted of the murder, due largely to the absence of a body. On receiving word that the police search was closing in on the spot where he had buried Wilson, Flannery ordered a couple of young hoods from Mickey's to dig the corpse up and re-bury it in another location. A young Alphonse Gangitano, future don of the mafia-aligned Carlton Crew, later told associates that digging up Wilson's decomposing body was the worst job he had ever done. Gangitano took the exact location of Wilson's final resting place to his own grave when he was shot dead in January 1998.

On 12 May 1979, Feeney contacted Murphy once again as he was coming out of Saturday Mass. He said that Flannery had made another hit: a brothel-keeper named Raymond Francis Locksley, also known as "The Lizard". They had driven together from Melbourne to Sydney in Flannery's car the week before. Feeney said that Flannery had taken Locksley to a remote location at Menai in Sydney's south on the pretext of digging a grave. As they dug, The Lizard repeatedly asked who was going in the hole. "You wouldn't believe it," Flannery kept saying. When they finished, Flannery said "It's for you" and shot Locksley dead. On the way back to Melbourne, Flannery washed his car on three separate stops to remove any trace of soil from the murder scene and also all evidence of the trip to Sydney. The motive was pure ego. Several weeks earlier, during an argument, Locksley had accused Flannery of being as weak as piss and terrified of his own wife. It had come to blows and Flannery had come off second-best. Flannery couldn't afford such disrespect in his line of work. Around this time, he had also come to blows with Alphonse Gangitano at a barbecue at Feeney's place and copped another flogging. The tough guy was losing face and Locksley would be the one to pay the price.

From his mother's flat in Middle Park, Murphy called the Homicide Squad once more. This time, they took him more seriously. As Murphy left the flat, a car pulled up alongside. It was Flannery; he was agitated and demanded to speak to Murphy immediately. With Feeney, they drove to the Embassy Massage Parlour in St Kilda where, until his death, The Lizard had worked with his girlfriend. The Lizard's girlfriend had been inconsolable with loss, so Flannery, having caused the loss, had bought her a puppy. That's our Chris, thought Murphy, always thinking of others. During the meeting at the Embassy, Flannery repeatedly told Feeney and Murphy: "Now, whatever is asked, I've been at the club every night this week."

Later, Murphy formally questioned Flannery over the Locksley murder. Murphy used his best "slychology" on him and he was set to open up. They talked about their kids; Flannery had two. Murphy spoke of how kids looked up to their parents and the respect Flannery would lose carrying on with hoods and gangsters – when was he going to become the man his kids believed he was? Flannery burst into tears and began to talk about The Lizard's murder.

"Come on, that's the way, Chris," said Murphy, encouragingly. "It'll be a relief to get this off your chest."

Murphy reckoned later that if he'd had another five minutes with Flannery, he would have signed up, but a drunken detective sergeant let Flannery's wife into the room and the interview abruptly ceased. Murphy knew he would get nothing more out of Flannery with his wife around.

But, fake alibi or no, the police were closing in on Flannery. The Dogs were on his tail watching his movements as they tried to pin the Wilson murder on him. Flannery rang Murphy to ask why the Dogs were outside his house. Murphy told him not to worry; they were just keeping an eye out for an armed robber, Tommy "The Duck" Donald, and they thought he might drop in to see Flannery. It was a lie – the first thing that popped into Murphy's head – and Flannery was suspicious. He rang Ericksen, who in turn rang an inspector, who indiscreetly confirmed that Flannery was indeed the target of surveillance. Ericksen told Flannery that it was his mate Murphy – "the bald-headed bastard" – who had tipped off police to his involvement in both the Locksley and Wilson murders.

Flannery rang Murphy back in a rage. Why had Murphy double-crossed him? Murphy denied the betrayal, saying the inspector was feeding Ericksen a pack of lies. Flannery didn't know who to trust now, so flight was the best option. The following day, he was on a plane to Tahiti.

When Flannery returned from Tahiti, the easy familiarity between him and Murphy had disappeared.

One day, Flannery and his wife came to visit Murphy at home when he wasn't there. Margaret served them tea and cake in the front room. A friend who had the run of the place came bustling into the room and when Flannery jumped up in surprise, a gun fell from the back of his trousers. Murphy always suspected that Flannery, prompted by Ericksen, had come to kill him that day.

By now the Flannerys had run their race in Melbourne and they relocated to Sydney. In August 1980, Flannery was charged with the solicitor Roger Wilson's murder. When he beat that, he was re-arrested by New South Wales detectives upon leaving court and charged with the murder of Locksley. Murphy was summoned to Sydney to give evidence at the coronial inquest into Locksley's death. Before he left Melbourne, though, he heard that Flannery had offered New South Wales police $50,000 for his murder. The officers had also taken money to commit perjury to weaken the Crown case against Flannery.

It made for an edgy trip. Normally, when officers went inter- state, there would be detectives on hand to meet them at the airport. This was a fraternity: they would grab your bags, take you for a coffee, show you round and take you to your lodgings. But when Murphy arrived, no-one was there. He waited for three-quarters of an hour at the airport, becoming steadily more nervous. He went into the men's toilet, got his gun from his luggage and strapped it to his ankle. Finally, when two uni- formed officers showed up, Murphy thought they were drunk. His intuition told him something was amiss. Maybe they would take him somewhere to be killed on Flannery's orders. At the first set of traffic lights on the way into town, Murphy jumped out of the police car and hailed a taxi.

The taxi driver was startled. "Are you escaping, mate? I just saw you jump out of that police car."

"No, I'm a cop. But actually, yes, I am escaping. Those cops are drunk and they were taking me somewhere to fix me up."

"Fair dinkum?"

"Fair dinkum," said Murphy as the taxi roared away. Sydney- siders in the 1970s needed little convincing of corruption in their police force. It was everywhere.

They drove to the Texas Tavern Hotel, where the New South Wales cops had booked him in. It was one of the lowest estab- lishments in a city full of sleazy dives and flea-bag hotels. There were two beds in the room, so Murphy pushed one across the door and sat on the other, facing the door, gun in hand. If anyone came through, he would let fly first and ask particulars later. The flimsy particle-board walls of the room were no more than an inch thick, so he could hear everything going on around him: toilets flushing down the hall, television sets blaring, hookers arguing with their clients. He finally fell asleep in that position – his back to the wall and the gun in his lap.

At 2 a.m. he was woken by noises outside the room. He heard the sound of a key sliding into the lock and the handle being twisted. He leapt from the bed and cocked the gun. The intruders wouldn't get one foot inside the room before Murphy shot them. He contemplated putting a couple through the door but he waited, holding his breath. "I can't open the door," he heard a male voice whisper. "Out of the way, out of the way," said another. Then footsteps approached from down the hall. "Shit, someone's coming." The door to the adjacent room opened and closed. He thought he could hear breathing from next door. He sat there bolt upright, listening to every sound until morning, adrenalin coursing through his veins. The next day, Murphy had breakfast and walked to Glebe Coroner's Court, where the Sydney detectives from the airport were waiting for him.

"Hey, where have you been?" asked one. "We've been looking everywhere for you. We'd organised a barbecue and you were supposed to come, mate." They didn't mention anything about him jumping out of the police car.

Murphy was in Sydney for a whole week and the detectives repeatedly asked him out to meals with them. He would smile and refuse their offer. He had a tummy condition, he said – he was on a special diet. On the morning he was to give evidence, he walked past Chris and Kath Flannery in the courtroom. Kath looked daggers at him but Flannery was all smiles when he saw his old mate from Mickey's.

"G'day, Mr M!" he said cheerily. "How're you going, mate?"

"Don't talk to that prick," Kath snapped.

Kath noticed that Murphy was carrying a gun in a leg holster in court and made the judge order him to remove it. The proceedings were uneventful. Murphy gave his evidence before a deeply sceptical judge. His Honour found it difficult to believe that a cop could move in such nefarious circles so confidently and still retain any credibility.

The next day, when Murphy arrived at court to complete his evidence, he noticed a number of men working in the gardens across the road within the grounds of Sydney University. Too many, in fact: about a dozen, dressed in new, blue overalls. They were digging here and there, pushing wheelbarrows, throwing glances at people who came and went. Murphy walked with his suitcase straight past the court to a Lebanese café at the back of the building. He gave the owner twenty dollars.

"Search my bag and make sure there are no guns or drugs in there, okay?" The owner, somewhat taken aback, agreed.

"Here's another twenty dollars to look after it. At one o'clock I want you to call me a cab, going to the airport," Murphy said. The owner held out his hand again.

"Okay, here's another twenty bucks. That makes sixty." This was no time to be cheap.

When he had finished in court, Murphy went straight out the back door into a waiting taxi and to the airport. He was back in Melbourne before dinner. Maggie rang to speak to Margaret and was surprised when Brian answered the phone.

"Here, what are you doing home?" she asked.

"I got sick and tired of Sydney, Mum," he replied, knowing she wouldn't believe him.

"Ha, you liar!" snorted Maggie. "I see they've committed

Christopher Dale Flannery for the murder of that Lizard fellow."

"Yeah, that's good, isn't it, Mum," said Murphy, trying to conceal his unease.

"Well, it's good you're home too," she added.

No-one in Sydney seemed to miss Murphy despite his flit through the back door of the court. It was departmental protocol for Sydney detectives to escort visiting interstate policemen to the airport. Yet it wasn't until 11 p.m. the following evening that Sydney police rang D24 to notify them that Murphy was missing. They said they hadn't seen him since 1 p.m. on Friday when he left court. They feared he had been kidnapped or murdered.

The Sydney detectives had let his disappearance go for more than thirty-six hours. Of course, it wouldn't do to raise the alarm if your conspiracy was going to run smoothly. Murphy discovered there had been a plot between Flannery and his new pals in the Sydney CIB to have him killed. A gunman was going to shoot him as he left court. The killer would be unaware that the gardeners hanging around across the street were actually members of the New South Wales Special Operations Group in disguise. The SOGs would kill the gunman after he had knocked Murphy off and all would be well. Three years earlier, the idea of murdering someone at court would have seemed preposterous; but that was precisely where Ray Chuck had been hit.

Flannery was eventually acquitted of Locksley's killing, but he was happy to continue plying his murderous trade in Sydney. He formed an alliance with the corrupt New South Wales detective Roger Rogerson, and became embroiled in a vicious gang war. It's understood that his employer, Sydney crime boss George Freeman, executed Flannery in his garage with a machine-gun in May 1985. I interviewed Rogerson for a TV special in 2004 and he had this to say of Flannery: "[He] was a complete pest. The guys up here in Sydney tried to settle him down. They tried to look after him as best they could, but he was, I believe, out of control. Maybe it was the Melbourne instinct coming out of him. He didn't want to do as he was told, he was out of control, and having overstepped that line, well, I suppose they said he had to go but I can assure you I had nothing to do with it."

*

The alliances that bound the Mickey's crew soon began to unravel. In early 1980, Ericksen stepped up his campaign against Murphy, marshalling the remnants of the Mickey's crowd into making a comprehensive set of allegations. Here follows a summary.

1. Murphy held a secret financial interest in the Embassy Massage Parlour and Mickey's Disco.
2. He was behind a massive bomb that destroyed the Carlton home of criminal and prison activist Joey Hamilton in 1979.
3. While on a trip to Perth, Feeney and Murphy deposited a stolen cheque for $50,000 in a bogus account they had set up. They then withdrew the "funds" from another branch and this was how Mickey's Disco got started.
4. He deliberately caused a fire at Feeney's takeaway joint, the Jolly Green Giant, after falling out with Feeney.
5. He supplied Flannery with a chrome revolver, via Feeney.
6. He and Higgins illegally wired up Flannery with a concealed listening device to secretly record Ericksen at a meeting in a restaurant.
7. He illegally received copies of covertly recorded tapes from a source inside the Bureau of Criminal Intelligence.

8.   He always carried a second, concealed firearm in addition to his service revolver.

9.   He flew prostitutes down from Sydney for fun and profit.

10.   He was observed by a Queensland detective selling fifty caps of heroin and was a middleman for drug sales to local prostitutes.

11.   He invited Flannery to join "the team", a murder squad comprising the Kane brothers, Brian and Les.

12.   He received $12,000 to make the prior convictions of a man charged with a $150,000 break-in "go missing off the sheet" before his committal hearing.

13.   He had direct connections with the Provisional IRA in Northern Ireland. Acting as an agent, he raised money for the terrorist group in Australia.

14.   He was paid $150 a week, cash, to provide security at Mickey's. The cash book had shown payments to a "Brian" and a "Bald Eagle".

In addition to his formal statements, Ericksen also tipped off detectives that Murphy was responsible for a string of unsolved murders. Every time there was an unsolved murder, and there were plenty of them, Ericksen would nominate Murphy.

Needless to say, Murphy denied all the allegations. He had only ever been doing his duty down at Mickey's. The alliances he forged and the intelligence he gathered had led to countless arrests and were instrumental in bringing Flannery to heel. But results were not everything. After much prompting from Ericksen, investigators from B11 (Internal Affairs) were now interested in Murphy's methods and his alliances with notorious criminals. In a series of interviews in late 1980, they wanted to know which side of the line he was on. Why, for instance, did he spend so much time at Mickey's, even when he was off-duty?

"I like disco," he said. "I'd say I have about 100 disco records myself. I've taken my wife and kids to discotheques. And I'm known at Mickey's, it's close to home and I enjoy the atmosphere."

After the final, marathon interview, Murphy was given a moment to reflect on his disco days at Mickey's.

Q. 35 These are all the allegations we have to put to you. Do you have any other comment you wish to make?

A. Yes, I would like to say that I feel degraded and humiliated, no doubt just as much as you gentlemen, at having to perform the duties you have today on the flimsy remarks passed by a paranoid vindictive individual, for want of a better name, such as Ericksen, who in my opinion has purposely associated himself and aligned himself with the likes of Flannery, Clarkson, Hocking and other murder[ers] and drug pushers in an endeavour to discredit honest policemen, who he holds up to ridicule because of [their] honesty and has used [them] as a tool to frame members of the police force and the public at large for monetary and personal gain. I am convinced that these people mentioned conspired together in an endeavour to extricate Flannery and his wife, Williams and Clarkson, from the murder charges over Wilson. It is my belief that he [Ericksen] is currently selling drugs in St Kilda to prostitutes.

Q. 36 Are you prepared to read over this record of our interview with you today?

A. Yes.

Q. 37 Do you agree it is a true record of the interview we have had with you here today?

A. Yes.

Q. 38 And are you prepared to sign it as such?

A. Yes, I am.

And that was the last word on these matters. As usual, Murphy was not questioned further about any of the allegations, much less charged. Three inspectors could not frame a single offence from all of Ericksen's sensational but highly detailed claims. Once away from the tape recorder, in a room full of inspectors and superintendents, Murphy made it clear what he would do if Ericksen continued to make allegations.

"If anyone believes what Ericksen is saying about me killing people, I don't care if it is in this office or next door or in the middle of Russell Street, I'll blow his head off," he raged. "He's a low bastard and he's stitching me up. And you blokes are believing him."

The bosses didn't dare take disciplinary action. Around the same time, Murphy tape-recorded a detailed interview with one of Melbourne's top hit men, a veteran who for years had witnessed the corrupt relationships between senior police and key figures in the Painters and Dockers. This man had given explosive details of who was paying whom and what it bought them. If this information ever came out, superintendents, inspectors and even an assistant commissioner or two would be locked up. Murphy's tape had mysteriously disappeared, but even without it, he had enough dirt on certain of his bosses to bring them down. Consequently, they needed to be very careful of him; it might even have been more prudent to kill Murphy than to prosecute him. But all the bosses could do in the way of punishment for his outburst was to send him back to Russell Street CIB.

A couple of years later, Ericksen was in hospital after having a leg amputated due to complications arising from diabetes. Murphy rang the hospital and asked to speak to the nurses on Ericksen's floor.

"It's Father John Curtin from St John of God Catholic Church. I'd like to speak with Mr Ericksen, if I could," he said.

"One moment, Father, I'll put you through," replied the nurse.

"Hello?" said Ericksen in a weak, croaky voice. "Tom speaking. Is that you, Father?"

"Yes it is, you fat pig," said the bogus priest. "It won't be long until the next leg comes off and your prick along with it."

"BRIAN MURPHY! You fucking bastard!" roared Ericksen.

Murphy had given Ericksen "the best cook of all time". It felt great, as if a weight had been taken off his mind. For the past five years, Ericksen had caused him a great deal of trouble. In 1988, the National Crime Authority charged Ericksen with 195 counts of bribery and eleven counts of making threats to kill. He died in August, on the morning he was due to answer the charges.

CHAPTER 29   A WINDOW OF OPPORTUNITY

"HOW THE MIGHTY HAVE FALLEN," the Russell Street wags would say when they came to gawk at Murphy sitting behind a desk in the reserve room at Russel Street. A fortnight earlier, he had been the boss of Murphy's Marauders, a swashbuckling super cop wreaking havoc in the underworld by day and carrying on into the night at Mickey's Disco. But now the hero of a hundred hair's-breadth escapes had been brought back to earth with a shuddering thud. He was sitting in a small, windowless office with a group of misfits and lunatics. "He'll fit right in," said his critics.

His new colleagues were considered unsuitable for field policing. The reserve room was built for three but there were at least six in occupation and no telephones. There was "Tearaway Tom", an Irish detective so lazy they had to hide him in the reserve room. Three policewomen and a female clerk with spectacles like sawn-off Coke bottles completed the team. The boss, Inspector Arthur Smythe, sat in an adjoining room. He was a quirky fellow who was forever clad in a plastic raincoat, even at the height of summer. Under the raincoat he liked to team a purple coat with a green shirt. He would go through the newspapers cutting out the retail specials and coupons and rushing off in his plastic mac to the shops at lunchtime to buy them.

On the first day in this purgatory, the clerk had made some

innocent remark and chuckled to herself. Murphy had turned on her.

"What are you laughing at, you poor, stupid, ugly bastard?" he snapped. She burst in tears and ran out of the room. As soon as he said it, he realised what a terrible heel he was and his misery only deepened. He got up from his empty desk to go to the toilet.

"Where do you think you're going?" asked Inspector Smythe.

"Unless you have a milk bottle to piss into, I'm going to the bathroom." said Murphy.

*

Only a few months earlier in 1980, Murphy had been at the peak of his success. In the evenings he was busy with his "freelance" work down at Mickey's on behalf of the Bureau of Criminal Intelligence. Though Paul Higgins was officially working for the Consorters, the BCI had sanctioned their intelligence-gathering in St Kilda. In the night hours, Murphy and Higgins had *carte blanche* to get involved in every intrigue going.

But by day, Murphy was running his own squad based in a decommissioned police station in North Fitzroy. "Murphy's Marauders" had built their own legend. There were six officers in the team, all miscreants from other squads. Murphy believed that the bosses had sent these men to him on the assumption he would lead them into trouble and the force would be rid of them all. They were young officers who knew of Murphy's reputation. There was even one that Murphy had knocked out cold at Mickey's one night when he had turned up drunk and obnoxious.

He had sat them all down and told them the rules. "I'm prepared to forget what I think about you, if you forget what you've heard about me. I'm not going to do anything wrong and I'm not going to train you to do anything wrong. If you forget about me, I'll forget that if I were a senior sergeant and wanted to rid my station of thieves, bludgers, womanisers and drunks, I'd send them to work with a bloke like Murphy, knowing that at any moment the whole lot might get the sack and save a lot of paperwork and heartbreak, okay?"

Murphy never had a dud in the two years the Marauders operated. They had a brief to quell the running battles between the villains who controlled the brothels and massage parlours, but Murphy saw his remit as much wider than that. Soon, he was taking on the local Hells Angels, Italian crooks and even his old foes the Painters and Dockers.

One day in 1979, there had come a knock at the door of Murphy's North Fitzroy headquarters.

"My name is David Richards," said the caller in a clipped English accent when Murphy came to the door. "I'm a journalist and I've come to work with you on the Painters and Dockers."

"Well, you'd better come in," said Murphy.

"So when do we start?" the excited reporter asked.

Murphy's men couldn't believe it. With a reporter in their midst, they would likely end up getting the sack. What if Richards began digging around past events – such as when all the Hells Angels' motorcycles mysteriously caught fire after one of the members had exposed himself in a local pub? Or when the windows of the Hare Krishna headquarters in Middle Park were shot out? Who cares if those freaks had refused to stop chanting and ringing their bells in the dead of night? Whether Murphy had done it or not, it would look terrible in the pages of the *Bulletin* magazine, for whom Richards was writing. And what if he looked into the murky goings-on at Mickey's Disco or the mystery of Ray Chuck's murder? It didn't bear thinking about …

Sometimes the Marauders had acted like a guerrilla squad of saboteurs. One night there was a big demonstration against Prime Minister Malcolm Fraser outside the Victorian Arts Centre. The organisers had set up gas burners with big cauldrons of soup on the forecourt. Police were concerned the demonstrators were planning to throw the scalding soup on the dignitaries, so Murphy organised his team to dress like protesters to foil the plan. They travelled to town in an old furniture van accompanied by one unmarked police car. Murphy ordered his men to mingle with the protesters and, on the signal, to push the cauldrons over and belt as many as they could. Anarchy and confusion reigned when the pots went over and a huge fight ensued between them and the protesters. The Marauders ran back to the furniture van and police car, deeming the operation a huge success and a wonderful lark. Unfortunately, one of the protesters took the registration of the police car and filed a complaint for assault.

On the following Monday, Murphy got a call from a furious Superintendent Phil "Fat Harry" Bennett, boss of the CIB.

"You imbecile!" Bennett screamed, dispensing with formalities.

"Meaning?" asked Murphy innocently.

"You know what I mean. You used a police car and the number's been taken. There's hell to pay!" shouted Bennett. He had authorised Murphy to shake down the protesters and now his job was on the line.

"Now, boss, before you go off half-cocked, I suggest you check which car those plates actually belong to. Before we left Russell Street, I took the liberty of exchanging the plates with those of another superintendent's car parked in the garage."

"You bloody ripper!" said Bennett and hung up. When the

other superintendent was asked what his car was doing at the Arts Centre, he could truthfully say it hadn't left the yard all night.

But now, faced with the prospect of nursing a journalist, Murphy wasn't too keen to share the finer points of "slychology" with the readers of a national magazine.

"I'll tell you what," said Murphy to the eager young reporter. "If ever I find the trace of your tongue in anything damaging that has nothing to do with you, I'll blow your legs off – you understand?"

"Yes, yes, yes," said Richards, keen to get on with the derring-do he had been promised by Assistant Commissioner Bill Conn.

"No," said Murphy. "Go away and think about it; it might not be worth your while."

"No, no, no," said Richards, seeing a thousand scoops going down the drain.

"Go on, bugger off," said Murphy as one of his men pushed Richards out of the door. Murphy immediately rang Assistant Commissioner Conn.

"What have you done to me?" he wailed.

"Shut up, Murphy," said Conn. "Don't do anything you shouldn't do and help him where you can," he said. To his amazement, Murphy found they had even issued the bumptious little Englishman a gun. Five minutes later, Richards was back and agreeing to all conditions. Murphy had to admire him.

"That was my big break," Richards told the *Bulletin*'s Julie-Anne Davies in January 2007. "Being with Brian Murphy was the difference between getting the yarn and staying alive and ending up with concrete boots on."

The Painters and Dockers were running amok – there were regular shootings and a host of rorts down at the waterfront.

Wherever you went across Australia, there was a Painter and Docker behind the organised-crime scene. And that was while Billy Longley was still languishing in jail for Pat Shannon's murder.

It was Murphy's job to help Richards expose the Painters and Dockers. The pair set up a shipping container overlooking the pay office down at the docks. From there, they photographed men going in and out to pick up "phantom wages". Men who had never scraped a barnacle in their lives were emerging with four or five pay packets. It was dangerous work: if the Painters and Dockers had discovered they were there, they could have picked up the container with a crane and dropped it into Port Phillip Bay.

Murphy also arranged for Richards to pay a visit to Billy Longley in Pentridge. Longley had been told he would face another seven murder charges and that unless he cooperated with authorities, he would die in H Division.

The story that resulted ran off the *Bulletin*'s cover on 11 March 1980 under the headline "Australia's Toughest Criminal Talks". Longley had let fly, assuring readers that crime on the waterfront was out of control. Unbeknownst to Longley, Richards had secretly taped their jailhouse conversations over six visits.

"That was my insurance," Richards told the *Bulletin* in 2007. "He was using me because he wanted ... a retrial, and I was using him because he was the most notorious criminal in Australia and I'd got him to talk."

Richards got his scoops but Longley never got his retrial. The four-part *Bulletin* series was a landmark in Australian journalism, the standard by which investigative reporters measured themselves for a generation.

In 2007, *Bulletin* reporter Davies reflected on the aftermath of Richards' stories: "The fallout was extraordinary. Malcolm Fraser, facing an election later that year, used it to smear the ALP because of its links with the union and announced a royal commission – the infamous 'Costigan Inquiry' – which lasted four years. Back in 1980, Billy's decision to talk was the sign that the old days were over."

It was Murphy who had set the ball rolling, but he didn't care for front-page scoops and the posturing of journalists. Arrests were his measure of success. Richards had turned out to be an inventive little dynamo and had energised Murphy to resume his battles down at the waterfront. By early 1980, Murphy had gathered enough evidence to make eight key arrests among the union's leadership and criminal associates. The Marauders had marshalled at their North Fitzroy base, armed with shotguns and .38s. Murphy had spent the previous night checking and re-checking every piece of gear. This was the *coup de grâce* he had been waiting nearly ten years to deliver, ever since the Painters and Dockers had driven him out of the dry dock while he was suspended awaiting trial for Collingburn. The next morning, the adrenalin – his favourite drug – was pumping so hard he thought it might spurt from his ears. Eight warrants had been issued. There would be action, headlines, pictures of Painters and Dockers being hauled away in handcuffs. It was shaping up to be one of the greatest days of his career. The team, including David Richards, was just minutes away from rolling when an inspector from Russell Street walked into Murphy's headquarters.

"Murphy, I've been sent here from town," he said.

"Oh good," said Murphy, thankful for the extra hand.

"No, Murph, I'm taking charge of the investigation," he said. Murphy could not believe what he was hearing. "You're not to go anywhere. I'm taking possession of all the warrants and you'll take the job no further."

"Go and get fucked, would you?" Murphy laughed.

"Brian," he said. "Don't embarrass me."

The raiding party and its press corps were stood down. The crew were bitterly disappointed and urged Murphy to go ahead anyway. Surely The Skull didn't take orders like this one.

Murphy was deflated; the adrenalin rush had turned into a dull, thumping headache. Someone had pulled the pin on them. The bosses had shat themselves worrying about a national strike by the Seamen's Union and the Waterside Workers' Union, not to mention the Painters and Dockers. There wouldn't be a ship getting in or out of Australia's ports if Murphy went ahead with his raids, the ACTU had warned. The pressure was on and the bosses had blinked. Yet in spite of this, and in only a few short months, Murphy's Marauders, along with the uppity English journalist and Billy Longley, had managed to change the waterfront forever. The Costigan Royal Commission would lift the lid on the dirty days of the waterfront.

*

The hero of that hour was now sitting at a desk, staring at a brick wall and counting down the minutes of the work day for the first time in his career. The bosses were satisfied they could contain him in the reserve room. If he couldn't talk to anybody, or even see them from this tiny windowless office, his mischief-making would be limited, they thought.

It was a vain, misguided hope. On Saturday morning, Murphy awoke at 2 a.m. He lay there thinking about the brick wall and how unjust his exile was. Just as he began to feel sorry for himself, he had an idea. He leapt out of bed, got dressed, grabbed his toolbox and at 3 a.m. was walking into Russell Street head-quarters. Only the night-shift men were there and the senior sergeant's office was deserted. He set to work removing the mortar between several of the bricks – about twenty of them. He had a wooden frame and when he had removed enough of the wall, he slipped it into the gaping hole. It fit perfectly, like a boob in a bra, he thought, as he secured the architraves. He gave the frame a coat of varnish and went looking for other useful items. He came back with the sliding doors from a superintendent's book cabinet. With a little bit of re-sizing, the glass slipped nicely into the frame and rollers he had installed. He re-varnished the frame and went home extremely pleased with himself. His new window only looked onto the corridor, but the moral victory made it the most spectacular view he had ever seen.

On Monday morning, people began filing past the new window. Most didn't notice anything different but the short-sighted clerk twigged straight away. Murphy put his finger to his lips, as if to say "Let's enjoy this sport together." They became great mates from that moment on.

Later, after prayers, Superintendent "Fat Harry" Bennett came shambling down the hall past the senior sergeant's room reading a daily circular. Suddenly, a hand reached out, seemingly through the wall, and grabbed his shoulder. He jumped back in shock and dropped his papers. There was Murphy, grinning, leaning out into the corridor.

"What the fuck do you want?" Fat Harry shouted in surprise.

"Boss, I just wanted to say thanks for sending me down here. I think I was going off my head. Now I never want to leave! But guess what?" he added. "I'm still gonna shoot fucking Ericksen."

Murphy went back to his desk and spent the morning calling out to everyone in the corridor, imitating screeching birds and barking dogs and generally behaving like a lunatic. Fat Harry wanted to know who had installed the window. He rang Inspector Smythe, who called in the works manager to inspect it. He ran his hand over the varnished frame, checking the joins and sliding the window back and forth.

"That's lovely work," he said approvingly. "It's got to be ours."

The very next week, they put Murphy back on the street as a section sergeant within the CIB. Soon he was wreaking havoc in Chinatown, persecuting a gang of Vietnamese thugs who were standing over the Chinese-run gambling houses. One day, Fat Harry called him into his office; he wanted Murphy to collect a dozen bottles of red and white wine from every Chinese restaurant on the strip, a tax for operating their fantan and mahjong in the back rooms. Murphy refused, telling Fat Harry to do it himself.

CHAPTER 30 GOODBYE, MR PLATYPUS

IN LATE 1981, THE PUSS WAS DYING. He had retired little more than a year before but now he was lying in a bed at Box Hill Hospital. After recent surgery for abdominal cancer, he was going downhill fast. Murphy had slipped into the room quietly and watched Plattfuss while he slept sitting up, his massive chin resting on his chest. He had lost a lot of weight but was still a formidable figure, even in a hospital bed. Murphy thought how much he respected his old boss from the Breakers, how much he had taken from him. He would miss this big rough bastard. How many blokes in the police force could say with a clear conscience that they had done their duty like Plattfuss? Sure, he had bashed and crashed his way through life and his methods had fallen out of fashion. Right-thinking people would be appalled to know some of the cruel, brutal things he had done on their behalf, but Plattfuss knew he had always done what had to be done, nothing more or less.

When Plattfuss retired, one of the bosses gave a speech in front of all the Russell Street CIB staff.

"Keith Ludwig Plattfuss, this is your life," the boss said. "You've been quite a character, quite a character. But the police force can do without characters today. You were what you were, but we don't want blokes like you. From now on, things will be done according to Hoyle." He was addressing Plattfuss's fans as much as the man himself.

262

Murphy thought it was a terrible thing to say to a hard-working bloke. "Good on ya, Puss! You'll do me," he called out loudly from the bleachers.

The Puss turned and growled, "Shut your fucking mouth, Murphy."

Plattfuss had nothing to regret. He had served Australia with distinction from the deserts of North Africa and the jungles of Borneo to the back streets of Richmond and his legacy would live on in Murphy.

Now Murphy leant forward and kissed him on the forehead. Plattfuss opened one eye and snarled.

"Whaddya doing kissing me, you fucking poofter!" And he smiled weakly, acknowledging his protégé's love and respect.

They sat talking at length about life, death and the job. The Puss regretted he had spent so much time away from his family. He hadn't been there for his young son as much as he should have. Murphy was not to make the same mistake, he ordered.

After a while, Plattfuss began to feel a crushing weight on his chest. "Don't just sit there, Murphy, I think I'm having a fucking heart attack. Go get somebody, you imbecile," he winced.

Murphy rushed to the nurse to say Plattfuss was having a heart attack. The nurse, busy with other things, dismissed the pain as mere post-operative shock. Murphy nearly went off his head before a doctor was summoned to confirm that The Puss was indeed in cardiac arrest. They brought the resuscitation equipment in and drew the curtains around Plattfuss. Murphy was ordered to leave the hospital, as there was nothing he could do.

In December 1981, Inspector Keith Ludwig Plattfuss passed away aged sixty-one. Murphy drove to Plattfuss's house to pay his respects to his widow but when he saw her, he burst into tears. Without a word, he got back in the car and drove away. On the way to the funeral, Murphy was in a daze of grief. He lost control of his car, spinning three times across the street, miraculously avoiding both traffic and parked cars. He felt as though he were dreaming. Another motorist rushed over to see if Murphy was okay.

"I don't think so," he replied absently.

"Well, you should go home then," the motorist said.

And so he did, missing The Puss's final send-off. It would have been too emotional for him, anyway, and Plattfuss had always regarded such displays as sentimental and unmanly.

"Back to work with you, cunty! There's nothin' more to see here," Murphy could hear him saying.

CHAPTER 31   BAD LAWS AND BAD POLICEMEN

THIS WAS CERTAINLY NO TIME for complacency. B11 – as Internal Affairs was known at Russell Street, after the number on the door – were after Murphy's crew again and now they thought they had him cold.

They had been monitoring the activities of one of his protégés, Senior Sergeant Paul "Buck" Higgins, a member of the Consorting Squad. Murphy had known Higgins since the 1960s. They had officially worked together for fewer than six months at the Consorters before Murphy was given his own squad in North Fitzroy. Yet it was common knowledge that Murphy and Higgins were close, very close. Tom Ericksen had alleged that Higgins, along with Murphy, had been copping a quid to run security at Mickey's Disco.

Higgins had a reputation as a fearless and dedicated officer, holding a record eleven commendations for outstanding service. He had never wanted to be anything other than a cop and had distinguished himself from the moment he joined the force in 1963. He was everything that Murphy wanted in a protégé: tough, fearless and dogged, one of the force's best crook catchers. Now, as a senior sergeant, he outranked Murphy but it was to Murphy that he always deferred. Like many others, he would radio or telephone him to ask his advice as he prepared to do a job. If he had one flaw, Murphy told investigators, it was a lack of guile when dealing with his critics.

"With the greatest respect for Paul Higgins, and he is a close friend of mine, he tends to worry too much about people making unfounded allegations against his integrity or honesty. His indignation shows immediately on his face and unfortunately this is quite often seen, by both friend and foe, as treachery or trick."

And the Consorting Squad was no place for a guileless soul. The same cast of characters was embroiled in the mystery of Ray Chuck's murder, the Great Bookie Robbery and a vicious war in the massage-parlour industry.

The *Consorting Act* gave the police virtually unfettered access to information on the criminal classes. And information was power. What couldn't be obtained by kicking in a door might come through an illegal phone tap or a bugged hotel room. They had the power to persecute any head they chose – in the wrong hands, it was a licence to indulge cruel whims. And for a fee, that power was negotiable. A detective could uphold the law or follow the money. Either way, the day looked much the same. These bad laws made very bad cops. And the worst of them, said Murphy, was Superintendent Phil "Fat Harry" Bennett, boss of the CIB.

Higgins' problems had begun in 1979 when he fell out with Fat Harry. One night in the police club, Bennett had asked Higgins to collect protection money from illegal brothels and massage parlours on his behalf. He had bluntly refused.

Later that same year, Higgins was charged with a disciplinary offence after Fat Harry had failed to locate him on the radio one night when he was working alone. He was sent back to uniform but in 1982, Higgins successfully appealed and was reinstated as a detective.

One year later, internal investigators launched Operation

Achilles to investigate police corruption in the massage-parlour business and Higgins and his mentor, Brian Murphy, came in for close scrutiny. Operation Achilles could not gather sufficient evidence to lay any charges, but lingering suspicions led to the establishment of a new operation, Cobra, in 1986 to re-investigate Higgins and Murphy. It was an extraordinary and costly exercise. Cobra investigators reportedly interviewed 805 people, from retired police to drug dealers and murderers, in an attempt to build a case against Higgins. A list of 170 witnesses was finally compiled.

Investigators claimed that Higgins and two other Consorting Squad detectives, Paul Strang and Phil Glare, had been accepting payment from massage-parlour owner Geoffrey Francis Lamb. Lamb had been at war with another owner, Robert James Slater, and there had been a string of unexplained fires at parlours.

In a television interview in 1987, Lamb alleged that Murphy had been involved in the arson attacks. "I laughed because one of the cops sent to investigate the fires was Brian Murphy, who I knew was involved. He just came and had a talk and away he went again and then tried to load someone else with it. That … person who he did load with it apparently committed suicide leaving a note that Brian Murphy was responsible."

Lamb also said that he had paid Higgins, Glare and Strang $3000 a week to provide protection and to make life difficult for his rival, Slater. Lamb alleged that Higgins and Murphy had visited Slater to give him a beating as a warning to leave the industry. When he continued to operate, Higgins, Strang and Glare raided Slater's residence, where they "found" ten sticks of gelignite and detonators secreted around the premises. It emerged later that police had planted the explosives.

When Murphy discovered that Internal Affairs was after Higgins, he suggested they gather evidence against the police investigating his protégé but Higgins refused. Then Murphy learned the investigators were rorting their travel allowances, spending the money on dirty weekends in Bendigo. Murphy told Higgins that he was going to take out warrants against the officers for perverting the course of justice. He would do anything to help Higgins fight his accusers, but Higgins again refused. He couldn't do that to another cop, he told Murphy. And he wouldn't take the deal the Crown had offered to plead guilty. He was going to fight, no matter the cost. He would spend thirty-three months in court, lose his house, his wife and kids, his career, $300,000 in back pay, and a further million dollars in legal fees.

Higgins was finally charged in April 1987 with corruption and conspiracy to plant the explosives. In four of the six charges, the list of co-conspirators began with the name "Brian Francis Murphy".

Margaret had attended Higgins's trial and on a single day she counted that her husband's name was mentioned forty-six times. Remarkably, though he was regarded as the arch-villain behind the brothel wars, Murphy was never interviewed or charged.

Finally, after a marathon process costing the state $33 million, Paul Higgins was convicted in 1992 and sentenced to seven years' jail, with a five-year minimum. To this day, he maintains his innocence.

There were numerous anomalies in the trial. On the same evidence that got Higgins seven years, co-accused Glare and Strang were merely charged with receiving a secret commission to the value of $30. They pleaded guilty and got an eight-month suspended sentence. One of the star witnesses was Geoff Lamb's muscle, Alexander "Sandy" McRae, by all accounts a witty and engaging character. McRae was later convicted of four murders and is still a suspect in at least half-a-dozen unsolved deaths and disappearances of drug addicts and prostitutes.

Well before Higgins's trial, Glare, in a taped interview with police in 1990, confessed that he and Strang – not Higgins – had planted the explosives in Slater's house, but this tape never made it into evidence. Glare later said that prosecutors had waged "a vendetta against Higgins" and that he was told he would avoid a custodial sentence if he helped prosecutors convict Higgins. The entire racket was overseen by Fat Harry, who was paying the detectives with Lamb's money. Glare spoke of meetings he attended with Murphy and Strang where Bennett laid out the plot to get Slater, whom Fat Harry erroneously believed was an interloper from Sydney.

When Higgins was found guilty, Margaret rang Murphy to tell him the verdict. He pulled his car to the side of the road and burst into tears. He was inconsolable. They couldn't get him so they had done the next best thing and jailed his mate Paul Higgins.

One of the internal investigators said there had been "indications but not evidence" that Murphy was involved in the brothel wars. Inside the operation, a saying soon circulated: "Thank goodness Paul Higgins is not as smart as Brian Murphy."

Higgins never took the stand to give his version of events and his denial of involvement seems somewhat equivocal. Higgins hinted that there was a much deeper back-story of how the Consorters operated.

"Sometime in the future," Higgins wrote as he sought to appeal to the High Court, "I intend to tell all about how it really was at the time. As it stands to date, because of the treatment the Crown has subjected me to, I owe only my family an explanation of my so-called corruption payments. Where is my money, new cars and businesses comparable to Strang and Glare? The Crown looked for and obtained a scapegoat and went to the jury with one. Fortunately for some, the writing was on the wall, so many took the opportunity to opt out and cover what had been a past of deceit [and] greed."

Murphy visited Higgins every month for the five years he was in jail. Some said Higgins was doing Murphy's time.

CHAPTER 32 THE GREENGROCER'S MAIL

WHILE VICTORIA POLICE SPENT MILLIONS trying to nail Higgins, he and Murphy continued catching crooks and cultivating informers. In the early 1980s, Alan David Williams was one of Australia's biggest heroin dealers but he forgot the cardinal rule of the business: never get high on your own supply. His raging addiction made him paranoid and vulnerable – malleable to a master player like Murphy. Murphy had known Williams since the 1960s when he was a stick-up man in the Painters and Dockers, and he had become one of The Skull's best informers. They had a simple code: when Williams had important information, he would telephone Murphy at home. If he was out, Williams would leave a message: "The greengrocer rang."

Informers, Murphy used to say, were like manure: they gave you good results but they were stinky and unpleasant to handle. Williams's mail was good but he was most definitely a piece of shit, a smack-dealing dog. They don't get much lower in the underworld.

Murphy had always been prepared to overlook minor sins in order to focus on the big picture. Only he and the informer knew which deeds went unpunished. But eventually Williams went way too far – right off the map. On 6 June 1984, Christopher Dale Flannery, on Williams's orders, attempted to murder a New South Wales undercover Drug Squad detective, Michael Drury, in his Sydney home. Drury was washing dishes at the kitchen sink when he was hit in the stomach and chest. He survived, despite losing a huge amount of blood. He thought he was dying when he gave a statement saying that the New South Wales detective Roger Rogerson had offered him a bribe on behalf of Alan Williams.

Drury had narrowly missed nailing Williams on heroin trafficking after a sting in Melbourne went awry. The detective had been working on a Sydney–Melbourne heroin ring and set up a buy and bust at a North Melbourne motel to snare Williams. Drury was to pay $110,000 for a suitcase of heroin, whereupon Victorian cops were to make the bust. However, the Victorian cops botched the arrest and Williams fled with the heroin, throwing it away as he escaped through Melbourne University. He was later apprehended in Adelaide and charged with trafficking. An accomplice, another ex-footballer, Jack Richardson, had earlier been charged. Williams knew prosecutors would rely heavily on Drury's evidence and arranged for Rogerson to offer Drury the bribe to back off. He refused the bribe but did not report Rogerson. Meanwhile, it was said that Williams's co-accused, Richardson, was preparing to fizz to the cops on the heroin deal. Paranoia overcame Williams. First Richardson disappeared on 4 March 1984. Then Williams commissioned Christopher Flannery to kill Drury for $100,000: $50,000 beforehand and the balance on completion.

It was a diabolically stupid act that set off a deadly chain of events. Another of Murphy's fizzes, Richmond drug dealer Dennis Bruce Allen, or "Doctor Death" as he called himself, was outraged at Williams's actions and swore he would kill him. Williams had jeopardised everyone's business. There were untold riches to be made from the heroin trade under the protection of crooked cops in Victoria and New South Wales; to kill a cop like Drury would only bring retribution down on everyone. In the month after Drury's shooting, Allen tried unsuccessfully to position Williams for assassination on two occasions. Allen also had links with Roger Rogerson. Williams was the only one who could link Rogerson to the bribery of Drury and Flannery to his attempted murder.

These goings-on disturbed Murphy greatly and he decided to act. It wouldn't do to have informers murdering each other. Even more troublesome was the idea that Williams would plot the murder of a cop. The consequences would be far-reaching. As John Silvester and Andrew Rule wrote in *Underbelly: A Tale of Two Cities*: "The Drury shooting would prove to be the tipping point. The fallout would result in the destruction of many of the established criminal fiefdoms and the cosy police–gangland franchises that controlled organised crime in Sydney for decades."

In Victoria, Murphy and Higgins might even be held responsible for the actions of their informer, Williams. Murphy had already been linked with Flannery through Mickey's Disco. Perhaps, some speculated, he was part and parcel of the whole fiasco.

One evening, Murphy and Higgins organised to meet Williams, who was out on bail for the heroin charges, at Katani Gardens overlooking St Kilda beach. It was 7.30 p.m. when they met and the three men strolled around the gardens in the twilight for more than an hour. Williams was using heroin heavily at the time and Murphy found it difficult to keep the conversation on track. His informer was going off on tangents, raving about this villain and that cop, the myriad plots and intrigues swirling around him. But Murphy wanted to gain Williams's confidence, so he let him waffle on.

Then Murphy told Williams how friendly he had been with Flannery, how he had tipped him off when the plan to break Archie Butterly out of Fremantle Jail in Western Australia had been discovered. Williams desperately needed a friend. He wanted to trust Murphy so he dropped his guard. He confessed to Murphy that he had paid Flannery to hit Mick Drury. Flannery had taken the first $50,000 instalment but graciously waived the balance because Drury had survived. Williams said he had even supplied the gun and a flak jacket. He told how Flannery had fired two shots at Drury in rapid succession – a hallmark of New South Wales police weapons training – to make it look like a police hit.

Unbeknownst to Williams, Higgins and Murphy made statements based on the conversation to Homicide detectives and Williams was later charged with conspiracy to murder Drury. But Dennis Allen was not finished with Williams. He organised a jail escapee, Roy "Red Rat" Pollitt, to shoot Williams as he arrived at his Lower Plenty home in Melbourne. On the day of the hit, what can only be called an extraordinary coincidence took place. Murphy and Higgins met Williams in a café in the city and warned him that New South Wales police had sent a death squad to Melbourne to kill him that night. Murphy later said it was only a ruse; he had no idea Allen had organised the hit. Williams went straight to a phone on the wall of the café and rang his wife, telling her to get out of the house immediately. In his panic over the news, Williams forgot that his brother-in-law, Lindsay Simpson, was coming to visit that night.

When Simpson pulled up in Williams's driveway, Pollitt thought he had his man. With gun drawn, he ordered Simpson to kneel down and, despite his protests that he was not Williams, Pollitt shot him dead in cold blood.

That night, Williams, in a state of abject panic, rang Murphy to tell him the news. He wanted Murphy to come over to his house immediately.

Murphy refused, saying Williams should call the police.

"They're already here but they're drunk."

"Well, call your solicitor then," Murphy suggested.

"He's here and he's drunk too," he wailed.

Williams was on his own. These consequences were of his own making and Murphy would not protect him now. He was soon arrested and faced court in Sydney over the bribery charges. Murphy and Higgins went to Sydney to give evidence in the committal hearing against Williams. They were booked into a Coogee motel but walked straight out again after checking in. They spent the few days in a secret location, concerned their former fizz might seek revenge for their betrayal.

During the cross-examination, Williams's counsel suggested that his client's previous statements were made under threat and duress. Williams claimed that Murphy and Higgins had threatened to kill him as they walked around the Katani Gardens that night in March 1984. Murphy replied that if he was going to murder Williams, Katani Gardens would be the last place he would do it. The magistrate interrupted.

"And why would that be?" he asked, falling under the spell of Murphy's storytelling.

"Because it's full of poofs and they'd call the police in a second if anything happened."

Murphy felt he had given superb evidence. Williams glowered at him as he resumed his seat behind the prosecutor; he was eyeballing every witness, trying to intimidate them. It made Murphy's blood boil. Through sheer stupidity and paranoia, Williams had caused all this trouble and still he seemed arrogant and unrepentant. Suddenly Murphy felt a hand on his knee. He reacted instinctively – "Get your hands off me" – before looking to see whose hand it was. A young man with warm, friendly eyes was sitting next to him.

"Brian, I'm Michael Drury. I just wanted to say that you two are the only policemen in Australia that have stuck by me. Thanks."

Williams was duly committed for trial and the magistrate rose, leaving the players of the drama to face each other. Williams' bail had been extended and he was free to go for the moment. From a safe distance, he was mouthing threats and curses at Murphy. Even then, Murphy could still play with his mind.

"There's something you don't know, Alan. There's something you don't know. Come over here and I'll tell you," he said, smiling.

Williams couldn't help himself. He came over and craned his head down to listen. Murphy grabbed the much bigger Williams by both ears and tried to bite his nose off. For all his cool "slychology", there were moments when the beast bared its teeth, literally, and this was one of them.

"What's going on here?" cried the horrified magistrate.

"I was just whispering something to him, Your Honour," said Murphy, releasing Williams's head and patting him on the shoulder.

Faced with his own confessions, Williams pleaded guilty to the bribery charges and received a twelve-month suspended sentence. He moved to the Northern Territory to start a new life, kicking his smack habit and working for almost a year. But the New South Wales Police were not prepared to let the Drury shooting go unpunished. Officers from Taskforce Omega soon arrested Williams. In 1992, he told authors Silvester and Rule: "When I was arrested in the Territory, I was told: 'The deal is this. You can either do life lagging over a crooked copper or you can tell us what happened and jump the box [give evidence] against him.'"

Eventually Williams pleaded guilty to conspiring to murder Mick Drury and received a fourteen-year sentence. He gave crucial evidence against his alleged co-conspirator, Roger Rogerson, but the jury acquitted the once-distinguished New South Wales detective. Rogerson has always denied any involvement.

Williams served four and a half years. Upon release, he tried to get his life back on track, but the lure of heroin was too great and he was soon introduced to the misery his own drug dealing had wrought. In the depths of his decline into suspected HIV-related hepatitis and madness, he became obsessed with Murphy, blaming him for ruining his life.

In mid-2001, Murphy took his grandchildren to the movies and stopped at a North Melbourne café to buy the kids some lunch. When the owner saw Murphy, he warned that Williams had been there just minutes earlier looking for him. He had declared loudly that he had a gun and had come back to murder Murphy. A few days later, Williams was dead. The cause was natural, his story anything but.

CHAPTER 33 MAD BULL LOST ITS WAY

Oh, see the fire is sweepin'
Our very street today
Burns like a red coal carpet
Mad bull lost its way
War, children, it's just a shot away
It's just a shot away
                —The Rolling Stones, "Gimme Shelter"

EVERY DOG HAS ITS DAY and a bitch two Sundays, the saying goes. When Murphy caught up with "Mad Max", he was going to shoot him dead. And woe betide anyone who got in his way.

Pavel Marinof had been a factory worker with a sideline in burglary until one night in June 1985, when police pulled him over for questioning in a Cheltenham industrial park. They made a cursory search of Marinof's car and found items used for burglary. They began a body search but he broke away and ran, turning to fire a shot and wounding Sergeant Brian Stooke in the arm. Next he shot his partner, Senior Constable Peter Steele. Then Marinof calmly walked back and put two more rounds into Stooke, paralysing him for the rest of his life. The legend of Mad Max was born.

Later that night, Marinof burst through a police blockade, firing shots from a .357 Magnum and trying to run officers down. A high-speed chase ensued through Melbourne's south-eastern suburbs. Marinof led the cops to Noble Park train station where, according the *Herald Sun*, he waited for the police "in a double-handed combat stance". He wounded Constable Graeme Sayce and Sergeant Ray Kirkwood before running into a nearby school. He then shot a Canine Unit officer, Sergeant Gary Morell, who had tracked him to the school. The gunman then reportedly hid in the roof cavity of a nearby home for the next three days before catching a taxi out of the area.

When the city awoke to news of a crazed gunman on the loose, the Major Crime Squad had been at headquarters since 4 a.m. planning a strategy to catch Marinof. Murphy was loudly condemning the officers who had let Mad Max slip through their fingers. Steele and Stooke, the officers who had first pulled him up, only had themselves to blame. They had failed to search Marinof adequately; it was their own fault he had shot them. "Failure to search is failure to find," he pontificated. The other three wounded officers had also failed to observe basic protocols.

This was the last thing the department needed. At fifty-three, Murphy was a dinosaur compared with his colleagues at the Major Crime Squad. He had applied to go to Major Crime after a period of general CIB duties as section sergeant in the early 1980s. At Major Crime Squad, he would be allotted a crew. His remit was not as wide as it had been in the days of Murphy's Marauders, but at least with his own crew, he had reclaimed some control over his destiny. He was a throwback to an era that had ended many years ago, an oddity in a force now striving for conformity. He didn't care; he had taken to wearing a furry Cossack hat during the winter months. He was giving his eccentricities full rein.

It was decided at a meeting of the bosses that Murphy's crew would chase Marinof, alongside a full-scale man-hunt and a $50,000 reward, and would work on it until he was caught. There was an added bonus to this: Murphy and his partners, Kevin Hicks and Bernie Elliott, would either kill Marinof or make such a mess that they would get the sack, a win-win for their critics.

Murphy and his crew hunted Marinof day and night for more than two months. They were putting in 22-hour days, clocking up at least two or three raids a day, kicking in doors and searching houses from top to bottom. Though Rumanian by birth, Marinof had plenty of friends in the Yugoslav community and it was thought he was being harboured. It was also a chance for people in the Yugoslav community to get square with those they didn't like. There was a torrent of mail coming in, most of it contradictory or just wrong, but the police had few sources in the community and they were forced to eliminate every potential lead or suspect.

For Murphy's team it was like tracking a ghost. At first, Murphy relished the job, craving the daily fix of adrenalin that came with kicking in doors and questioning suspects. But soon, doubts began to creep into his mind. Approaching a house, he would be thinking: "Is this the house? Is Marinof waiting behind this door ready to blow our heads off?" Throughout his career, he had never hesitated; there was never any doubt at such moments. Instinct had always guided him. Now he imagined what lay beyond the threshold – a gunman running on instinct. He thought back to what his first chief commissioner, Alexander Duncan, had said after swearing in Murphy and the others back in 1954: "We have trained you to the best of our skill and ability for the past three months. And we now put you on the streets. The problems you face there, you will ne'er find the answers in a book."

Murphy thought he would have the answers when the questions were posed, but he was going in cold. His mind was also full of premonitions and omens. A few times he felt he had missed Marinof by seconds or perhaps by the thickness of a sheet of masonite. Several times he actually felt Marinof's presence or the sensation of being watched. He concealed his doubts by driving the crew ever harder, attacking their task with maniacal ferocity. And they were making a mess all over town. One family sued Murphy and his crew for causing $500,000 damage to their home. A woman had jumped out of a window, breaking an arm and a leg in the fall to avoid facing Murphy. The press got onto the story, photographing the search warrant bearing Murphy's name. Concerned, Margaret asked what was going on.

"Nothing," he replied.

"I know what your 'nothing' means."

The man-hunt was taking its toll on him. He was losing weight, going from ninety-six kilograms to just seventy in a month. He was ravenous all the time but could never satisfy his hunger. It was like shovelling food into a furnace. And he was irritable like never before. If he got into a minor disagreement with Margaret, he had to leave the room for fear he would go off his head. The kids crept around on the rare moments Dad was home that winter. The slightest thing, a cheeky answer back, even a sudden noise, could ignite a poisonous rage. It was frightening even to Murphy, because he had no control at all over his moods. He felt like a clock spring being wound ever tighter and tighter. It was only a matter of time before the mechanism exploded.

It was Bernardine, his eldest daughter, who turned the key to its point of release. Wilful and self-possessed, Bernardine had always known how to push her father's buttons. They had an argument in the kitchen and Bernardine, always one for the dramatic, stormed off and slammed the door. A piece of coloured leadlight that Murphy had made fell from the door and shattered on the floor. The temperature in his head rose beyond boiling point. Everything that was swirling in his mind – the man-hunt for Mad Max, the pursuit of Paul Higgins, the campaign by the bosses to sack him – built up to an unbearable whine in his ears. A surge of white-hot anger took hold and he watched himself draw his .38 from his ankle holster and set off in pursuit of his daughter. Murphy stalked her to the back lane. He crept along, looking under parked cars, pointing his gun menacingly. In those first few seconds, he might have shot Bernardine had she not escaped; he was sure of that. But then his conscious mind regained control and he stood there shaking, looking down at his gun, wondering what he had become. At that moment he knew the job was nearly finished for him.

He sought medical help. A doctor diagnosed hyperthyroidism, an overactive thyroid gland. His body had been producing three-and-a-half times more thyroxine, a hormone that controls the metabolism, than normal. The doctor ran through the symptoms: weight loss accompanied by increased appetite, anxiety, fatigue, weakness, hyperactivity, irritability, apathy, delirium and hair loss. But for the hair loss – it's hard to get beyond bald – he ticked every box. Before Christmas 1985, he took sick leave and recovered swiftly after taking the right medication.

On 24 February 1986, two detectives acting on a tip-off pulled Marinof over on the Hume Highway, forty-five kilometres north of Melbourne. Marinof shot and wounded both, but one detective, despite a gaping wound in his chest, fired his pump-action shotgun as Marinof tried to escape, killing him. Murphy was out fishing on the bay when he heard the news. He was two days off coming back to work.

He resumed catching crooks at a cracking pace on his return. In 1986–87, he and Paul Higgins ran Dennis Bruce Allen, the drug-dealing, murdering fiend who called himself "Doctor Death", as a key informant. They passed on information that led to the conviction of thirty-two armed robbers in one year on Allen's mail; but again Murphy was accused of crossing the line. He had been photographed going in and out of Allen's house in Richmond by the Dog Squad as they investigated Allen for murder. He was prepared to give evidence for Allen at his bail hearings to keep his star informer out of jail.

Internal Affairs cops were now watching his every move. Allen's house, where they met, was bugged so that the Dogs could listen to every conversation they had.

The last twelve months on the job was the only time Murphy hadn't looked forward to going to work. That deep rumble of excitement in his guts was gone. The bosses were looking for any chance to rid themselves of him. He was a problem to them, a reminder of a discredited past, a talisman for the rogues and crooks in the ranks. He had fallen out with a number of men in the squad and they were biding their time. One afternoon in early 1987, Murphy left the St Kilda police complex to visit a highly trusted informer, telling the senior sergeant where he was going. He spent about an hour with the informer, picking up some valuable intelligence before going home. At two o'clock the next morning, the telephone rang at home. It was the informer's wife; she was distraught. The police had just been there and pistol-whipped her husband. They had stolen $112 from her purse, six dozen cans of beer from the garage and hauled her husband away for possession of a firearm. They had brought the gun with them, she said.

Murphy raced to work early to find out what had happened

but there was no record of any arrest on the previous night and the senior sergeant knew nothing about it. Later in the morning, the senior sergeant came back to Murphy and said he had found a handwritten note saying there had been a raid and arrest that night. The note had been slid into the small space between the senior sergeant's desktop and the drawers below. Murphy related the call from the informer's wife. The senior sergeant didn't want to know; he had to wait until the informer complained before he could do anything about it. Then the crew who had bashed his informer turned up. One had a plastic evidence bag containing the gun in question. He pranced past Murphy's desk, dangling the bag in his face.

"I wonder whose fingerprints we'll find on this gun, eh?"

The bent cop knew what he was doing. The informer knew better than to complain about his treatment. He couldn't back Murphy up if it came to court, for fear of being exposed as a dog. The informer would cop it sweet and pay up to make the mess go away. Everyone in the room expected Murphy to blow up in a final firestorm of anger, but he sat there, silent, waves of fury radiating from him. He slid open the drawer where he kept his gun but he found it was gone. One of his crew had seen the storm about to break and had taken it when Murphy's back was turned. He feared Murphy was going to kill someone and that it would be the epitaph on his career: a wild cop who finished up in jail for the murder of one of his own.

Two months later, the informer came before court but the police produced no evidence and the case was dismissed. Another month later, two detectives came to Murphy's house asking whether he had picked up $20,000 cash from the informer. They said the money was due to them for making the gun disappear from evidence but they hadn't been paid. It turned out another cop had double-crossed them, picked up the money himself and pocketed it.

Thirty years had passed since Murphy had taken on the sugar bags of South Melbourne who stood over the SP bookies, and nothing had changed. Of course, there were times when Murphy himself had crossed the line, but he had never lost sight of justice, or at least his version of it. But he was powerless before the laziest, most corrupt elements of the force, men who would load a suspect, take money from a woman's purse, commit perjury and then cop a quid to back off. Murphy's mates would not always be there to hide his gun.

So in February 1987, when a colleague suggested it was time to chuck it in, Murphy agreed without emotion. Members who had reached the age of fifty-five or had thirty years of service could now take an early retirement. The colleague typed the papers and Murphy signed them without a second thought. He finished on 26 April 1987, thirty-three years to the day after he had signed on. He went on one last raid in Richmond at 3.30 that morning but the suspect was out. He returned to the office and was told that an inspector had a brief to charge him with conspiracy to pervert the course of justice. He rang the inspector to say that if he intended to lock him up, would he mind organising bail so he could attend his own send-off that night? He would meet him at the city watch-house to surrender. The startled inspector replied that there was nothing in the brief to justify charging Murphy. It would go no further.

Murphy sat at his desk until 4 p.m. waiting for the traditional call from the bosses to congratulate him on thirty-three years of service. The phone never rang. Mick Miller, now chief commissioner, later wrote him a kind letter of congratulations, but that was the only acknowledgment he received from a commissioned officer. He hopped a ride home with a colleague, who promised to meet him that night for the send-off. The colleague never showed.

One newspaper carried a report of Murphy's retirement under the headline "CRIMS BREATHE A SIGH OF RELIEF".

"Some heavy crims have been breathing much easier since the early retirement of super cop Brian Murphy," the article said. Some of the best crims are wearing uniforms, thought Murphy as he read the story.

That Sunday, Murphy went to church with Margaret just as he had without fail every week for the past thirty-three years. He had joined the church choir. The adrenalin of the street was replaced with the soaring majesty of his favourite hymn:

And He will raise you up on eagles' wings,
Bear you on the breath of dawn,
Make you to shine like the sun,
And hold you in the palm of His hand.
You need not fear the terror of the night,
Nor the arrow that flies by day,
Though thousands fall about you,
Near you it shall not come.

CHAPTER 34 SO BE IT

BILLY LONGLEY SAID THAT if you nursed a mug, he would die in your arms. Most of the mugs he had nursed had gone that way, but he had got it right with Murphy. Longley had been home a year after spending thirteen in jail for the murder of Pat Shannon. There was a knock at the door. A team of detectives from the Major Crime Squad had come to search his house. He was suspected of gun running, they said. They turned the house upside down. Longley's heart was sinking. He still owed the system a number of years on parole; if they caught him with anything, he would go back to jail and probably die there. The cathedral-like silence of Pentridge H Division would kill him this time. One of the detectives was flipping through Longley's teledex when he came upon Murphy's name.

"You know this bloke, do you?" asked the young detective.

"He's a very dear friend of mine," replied Longley.

The detectives went out to the car and contacted Murphy to verify the friendship. When they came back, the senior man spoke to Longley.

"Jeez, you're a lucky man!" He held up a haversack, opened it and pulled out a pistol. "This was going to be yours."

*

It occurs to me that Murphy could well have stepped straight into darkness when he left the police force. There were times when he did stray there. He maintained his old informers until one by one they started dying. Still invincible (in his own mind) at seventy-six, he expected to outlive them all. He and Billy Longley ran their mediation business until, in his eighties, Longley could no longer get about. Murphy talked Longley through his black depressions, which probably saved his life. He made him believe that even an old knockabout could hope for a proper funeral in a church where they played "Amazing Grace". Murphy fit back into family life easily, but he now had time to minister to the errant of the underworld and to guide and encourage a new generation of police while plotting the demise of the bosses.

To live on both sides of the thin blue line was to taste a little of the rush he still occasionally craved. After he retired, Murphy would visit his mother's house and ask her if there was any mail. Later in the day he would ask again, and perhaps a third time.

"Here, you clod, there's no mail. You're not in the police station now."

Maggie lived into her nineties and the anger in the blue eyes she passed on to her son never dimmed. He made her breakfast every morning for the last ten years of her life. They would discuss the latest scandals, enjoying the simple pleasure of sharing old hatreds.

When we first met in 2004, Murphy was covering Melbourne like some kind of vigilante, gathering intelligence on a gang war, tipping off cops to the latest rort, advising and counselling some of the heaviest men in town. Part of him never left the cops, while part of him always sided with ordinary people against them. Another part wouldn't hesitate to take action when no-one else would. A few years before, some drug dealers had been selling in his back lane. One day, he opened the roller door and challenged them. They told him to fuck off, so he smashed them both in the face with a shovel. They never came back.

He was terrifying for the uninitiated; truly the enigma everyone said he was. It was like looking at the sun through binoculars. I asked him to help me understand the Melbourne underworld and he drew me into it. A reference from Murphy opened doors all over Melbourne. We moved from café to café across the city in Murphy's maroon Ford as he covered his beat. Whatever the crims couldn't tell him, the cops could. A few hours with Murphy and you could make a citizen's arrest or rob a bank. Just like another *Bulletin* journalist, David Richards, a quarter-century earlier, my success as a reporter was down to Murphy. There were times when I glimpsed his dark arts, the subtle dissembling, the forensic problem-solving and the fearless ability to intervene.

I came to understand him; he was no enigma but a product of times all but forgotten. He grew up when people were still intimately connected. On Morris Street, South Melbourne, the iceman came to the door, the rent collector went house to house every Monday. The bread, the milk and the firewood were all hand-delivered. The priest would bring salvation while the garbo took the rubbish. People knew what was happening in their neighbours' homes. They knew who was in jail, who was a drunk, a thief or a fence. They knew whose kids went to school without breakfast, whose wife got a belting when her man was drunk. They realised what they had when next door they had nothing and the value of help when no-one else would step in. And Maggie never let them forget it. They owned their house and lived in relative abundance, so there was always something they could do. His father, Reg, taught him that the law was not everything. The law kept poor people hungry when there was food in the stores; the law protected thugs who terrorised their families. Beyond the law, there was what was right in the circumstances. And you defended that turf with all the means necessary. To survive you needed love and hate in equal measure.

Lately, I have noticed a change in him. Perhaps it is advancing myopia or a touch of cataract, but Maggie's fire is cooling in his eye. He has become more accepting. His attitudes are changing. Once he believed Nelson Mandela was a communist but not anymore. He knows it's no longer appropriate to handle suspects and informers the way they did back in the 1960s. But he never shied away from the truth in this story, even when it might damage him. It was fact, it happened and I was there, he would say. *End of discussion.* Some things he will take to the grave. It's just like in a police interview: you don't get locked up for the answers to questions you were never asked. I tried my very best to trip him up, but how could I succeed where the best investigators in the state had failed?

Most importantly, he did not seek or need my approval for these stories. There is a moral certainty in Brian Francis Murphy. Before God, he knew whatever he did was right. You may not agree. Even He may have trouble with some of it. But so be it.

ACKNOWLEDGEMENTS

I would like to thank Brian Murphy for his endless enthusiasm for this project and his willingness to confront the truth no matter the cost.

The Murphy family deserves special thanks for helping with this book and for putting up with The Skull all these years too. I understand that the family will learn much about their patriarch for the first time in this book. It's my privilege to bring his story home to them.

Brian's wife, Margaret, was a kind and gracious host to me and members of my family on many occasions during the two years of writing this book.

Thanks also to former colleagues Harry Kramme and Jimmy Keegan, the late Paul "The Tooth Fairy" Egan and Ivan Kane's partner, Gail. Billy "The Texan" Longley contributed an enormous amount to this book too. His strength of character in taking Murphy as he found him should be commended.

Former Victoria Police Chief Commissioner Sinclair "Mick" Miller is still one of the finest men in the state and I owe him my thanks.

The widow of the late Corporal James Gardiner helped me, even though the memories were painful. The human cost of Australia's involvement in the Vietnam War continues to accumulate.

Jon Lelleton, one of Melbourne's finest legal minds not at the Bar, filled in many gaps and helped me trip up his friend Murphy when it was required. His friendship and counsel has been a delight.

Masanita Binti Abdullah lived this story with me through its research and writing and never flagged in her support. She never complained even when she had to type words a proper Malaysian lady never should.

A huge thanks must go to the team at Black Inc., including Morry Schwartz, Chris Feik and Adam Shaw for sharing my vision when others couldn't.

And special thanks to my children Noliwe, Jack and their mother, Sekai Nzenza-Shand, for putting up with my absences from duty and for listening to the endless Murphy anecdotes.

Thanks also to the staff at the Eastern & Oriental Hotel in Penang, Malaysia, where much of the manuscript was written.

Lastly, thank you to my parents, Dr John and Robin Shand. They always encouraged the storyteller in me. At least these days, the tales are true.